This collection of clearly written chapters by a range of scholars is a valuable contribution to the growing corpus of literature on Gukurahundi. It represents an important new resource on the atrocities; and on transitional justice and peacebuilding for policy makers, students and academics alike.
- *Dr Khanyisela Moyo, Transitional Justice Institute, University of Ulster.*

This eloquently constructed critique is a bold attempt at assessing the various dimensions surrounding the lack of progress in addressing the darkest period of post-colonial Zimbabwe – the Gukurahundi atrocities. The authors exhibit both intellectual courage and sober inquiry into the barriers standing in the way of uncovering truth, securing memory, delivering justice, ensuring healing and accountability for victims. The chapters have laid bare the leadership vacuum that haunts Zimbabwe on the evidence of the national failure to urgently address this outstanding national question.
- *Deprose Muchena, Senior Director, Regional Human Rights Impact, Amnesty International.*

This book is not only an ode to the victims of the Gukurahundi massacres in Matabeleland, but also a recognition of the continued pain of the survivors. It delves deep into the struggle to achieve true justice in the face of historical distortion of the narrative and attempts to deflect responsibility for these mass crimes by a government composed of some of the alleged perpetrators. It challenges attempts to erase what took place, including the heinous sexual attacks on women, and touches on disinformation in reporting by some in the media at the time. The book also represents hope. Hope that through writing, remembering, retelling and memoralisation, truth, justice and accountability will eventually prevail.
- *Tiseke Kasambala, Director, Africa Programs, Freedom House.*

MEMORY AND ERASURE

Memory and Erasure:

Gukurahundi and the Culture of Violence in Zimbabwe

edited by

Mandlenkosi Mpofu

and

Percy F. Makombe

Published by the Centre for Innovation and Technology (CITE),
45 Moffat Avenue, Hillside, Bulawayo, Zimbabwe. 2022
<www.https://cite.org.zw/>

with

Weaver Press, Box 1922, Avondale, Harare, Zimbabwe. 2022
<www.weaverpresszimbabwe.com>

Second edition, 2023.

© This second collection (CITE)
Each individual chapter the authors.
© Cover image: Owen Maseko
Cover Design: Danes Design, Zimbabwe
Typeset: Weaver Press, Harare
Printed by: DP printmedia, Bulawayo

All rights reserved. No part of the publication may be reproduced, stored in a retrieval system or transmitted in any form by any means – electronic, mechanical, photocopying, recording, or otherwise – without the express written permission of the publishers.

CITE ISBN: 978-1-77931-630-1 (p/b)
Weaver Press: 978-1-77922-427-9 (p/b)
Weaver Press: 978-1-77922-428-6 (ePub)

Contents

	Contributors biographies	ix
	Acknowledgements	xii
	'Ode to the Nameless' – Gugulethu Siziba	xv
	Note to the Second Edition	xvii
	Foreword – Shari Eppel	xxi
	Introduction: Fighting for the Right to Remember: the Plight of Zimbabwe's Gukurahundi Victims – Mandlenkosi Mpofu and Percy F. Makombe	xxix
1.	*Criminalising the Subaltern: Gukurahundi, Reconciliation and Transitional Justice in Zimbabwe* – Mandlenkosi Mpofu and Percy F. Makombe	1
2.	*'Bandwagoning or Intended Action?': Examining Zimbabwe's Legal Framework on Peacebuilding* - Cynthia Chigwenya	16
3.	*The Gukurahundi Transitional Justice Deadlock in Zimbabwe* – Pedzisai Ruhanya and Bekezela Gumbo	37
4.	*Sexual violence: Gukurahundi's Public Secret* – Sibonginkosi Moyo-Mpofu	49
5.	*Dismembering Memory of a Genocide: Contestations over Bhalagwe Mass Graves Memorial Site* – Mbuso Fuzwayo, Samukele Hadebe and Dion Nkomo	63
6.	*The Linguistic Dimensions of Gukurahundi in Zimbabwe* – Busani Maseko and Dion Nkomo	81
7.	*Public Media and Genocide: The Role of* The Chronicle *during the Gukurahundi Genocide in Zimbabwe* – Bhekinkosi J. Ncube	96
8.	*Making sense of that 'moment of madness': Virtual discussion of Gukurahundi on social media in Zimbabwe* – Gibson Ncube and Yemurai Chikwangura-Gwatirisa	110
9.	*Gukurahundi Atrocities and Accountability Challenges in Zimbabwe: A Case For International Justice –* – Siphosami Malunga	126
10.	*Unforgettable Memories: A Survivor's Story* – Jameson Moyo	145
11.	*Mehlomakhulu Dox*	171
	Bibliography	179

Contributors biographies

Cynthia Chigwenya is a political researcher and pracademic who has conducted extensive studies on reconstruction in post-genocide Rwanda, conflict mediation in South Sudan, and traditional justice mechanisms and reparation grants in post-conflict societies. Her academic background is Criminal Justice; she holds an MA in Development Studies and an MPhil in Social Policy and Development. Cynthia delivered a TEDx talk titled, 'Post-Conflict Identity' in which she spoke about Gukurahundi and her lived experience while working for the Rwanda National Commission for the Fight Against Genocide. She currently serves as the African Union's Youth Ambassador for Peace for Southern Africa and has engaged various national and international organisations, including holding a research position in the South African Parliament.

Yemurai Chikwangura-Gwatirisa holds a Double Masters from the Universities of Bremen (Germany) and Porto (Portugal) as well as a PhD from Nairobi University. She lectures at Botho University (Botswana). She was a postdoctoral fellow at Rheinisch-Westfälische Technische Hochschule-Aachen University (Germany). Her current research work is focusing on a comparative study of cultures of trauma, memory and remembering. Her broad areas of research are in literary and intercultural studies, gender and memory studies.

Shari Eppel is a Zimbabwean who lives and works in Bulawayo. A forensic anthropologist, she has been involved off and on for more than twenty years with the exhumation and reburial of those who died in the 1980s in Matabeleland. A clinical psychologist by training, Shari has also tracked the socio-cultural and political impact of exhumations and reburials on families and communities over more than two decades. In recent years, this has increasingly become work with the next generation of survivors, as transgenerational memory and trauma is now a reality.

Mbuso Fuzwayo is the secretary general of Ibhetshu Likazulu, a grassroots human rights organisation that fights for the dignity and justice for victims of the Gukurahundi genocide, an initiative based on truth-telling. He is a peasant farmer who was born in Midlands and witnessed the excesses of the Fifth Brigade on the poor and elderly in his village.

Bekezela Gumbo is a PhD Candidate at the University of the Free State and a principal researcher with the Zimbabwe Democracy Institute. His research interests include transition politics, socio-economic development and sustainable peace building.

Samukele Hadebe is a senior researcher at Chris Hani Institute, COSATU, Johannesburg and a research associate at the Sociology Department, Rhodes University. As a researcher and writer on Ndebele language, literature, culture and history, Dr Hadebe has paid particular attention to the effects of the Gukurahundi genocide on the affected communities in Matabeleland and Midlands. He has been instrumental in the efforts to memorialise the Gukurahundi genocide.

Percy Fungayi Makombe is a former team leader for the Democracy and Governance cluster at the Open Society Initiative for Southern Africa. He has also worked in journalism with *Moto* magazine, the *Zimbabwe Independent, Africa Film & TV,* and as a correspondent for *Mundo Negro, Nigrizia* and *Africa News Bulletin*. His research interests lie in understanding how societies and the world deal with issues of power, leadership, equality, freedom, representation, and change. Makombe holds an MPhil in Policy Development and Practice, as well as an MA in Globalisation and Communications.

Siphosami Malunga is the Director of Programs at Open Society–Africa. He is a human rights lawyer with extensive experience in justice and governance. Malunga previously led Open Society's work in Southern Africa as executive director of the Open Society Initiative for Southern Africa. He has held UN posts focused on democracy, governance, development, peacekeeping, post conflict recovery, and transitional justice around the world. Malunga is a regular contributor on political and economic governance as well as human rights and accountability issues in national, regional, and international publications. He holds an LLB (Zimbabwe) and an LLM (Oslo) and is a doctoral candidate at the University of Witwatersrand.

Busani Maseko is a Post-Doctoral Research Fellow in the School of Language at North-West University in South Africa. He holds a PhD in Languages, Linguistics and Literature, an MA in Applied Linguistics and an Honours Degree in Linguistics. His research interests broadly straddle the areas of language planning and policy, multilingualism, language and social justice and sociolinguistics. He has published articles in accredited journals such as *Language Matters, Southern African Linguistics and Applied Language Studies* and *the South African Journal of African Languages*.

Sibonginkosi Moyo-Mpofu is a Canon Collins Scholar and a PhD candidate at the Critical Studies in Sexualities and Reproduction Research Programme at Rhodes University, where her research focuses on sexual violence during the Gukurahundi genocide. She is also a programme officer at a Bulawayo-based non-governmental organisation, whose focus is deepening democracy, and promoting social and transitional justice in Matabeleland communities still living with the legacy of Gukurahundi.

Mandlenkosi Mpofu is a Senior Lecturer in the Department of Journalism and Mass Communication, University of Eswatini where he teaches media economics, entrepreneurship, and research methods. He has conducted research in popular culture, alternative media, media and corruption, and in civil society and the state. Mpofu worked for more than ten years in CSOs and in international development in Zimbabwe and Malawi, in areas of freedom of expression, and governance and effective participation. He also worked as an online editor in Zimbabwe's largest independent newspaper group. He is currently engaged in programmes creating platforms for citizen participation and transitional justice in Zimbabwe.

Bhekinkosi Jakobe Ncube is a Global Excellence Stature Postdoctoral Fellow in the Department of Communication and Media Studies at the University of Johannesburg, South Africa. He has interdisciplinary research interests which include politics and the media, community media, ethnic minority media, the implications of computational journalism and social media and journalism. His recent research focused on the online constructions and contestations of ethnic identities. Ncube is also a senior lecturer at the National University of Science and Technology, Zimbabwe.

Dion Nkomo (Professor) is an NRF SARChI Chair for Intellectualisation of African Languages, Multilingualism and Education at Rhodes University. His areas of academic interests include language planning and policy, multilingualism, language teaching, lexicography, translation, terminology, and higher education studies. He is an NRF-rated scholar, a postgraduate supervisor, an editor of Lexikos, the journal of the African Association for Lexicography (AFRILEX), and a member of various academic, professional bodies and research projects working on language and educational matters.

Gibson Ncube lectures at Stellenbosch University. He has held fellowships supported by the Stellenbosch Institute for Advanced Study, the National Humanities Center (USA) and Leeds University Centre for African Studies (UK). He has published widely in the fields of comparative literature, gender and queer studies as well as cultural studies. He co-convened the Queer African Studies Association (2020-2022) and was the 2021 Mary Kingsley Zochonis Distinguished Lecturer (African Studies Association UK).

Pedzisai Ruhanya is a lecturer in the Department of Creative Media and Communication a the University of Zimbabwe, and a postdoctoral research fellow at the University of Johannesburg.

Acknowledgements

Memory and Erasure has taken almost two years to develop. Sincere gratitude is owed to the authors, who have been patient, and have attended to endless comments and edits. So too the anonymous peer reviewers who have been candid and, in some cases, brutal with their reviews; they got us here.

The publishers – Irene Staunton and Murray McCartney at Weaver Press – have also kept us on our toes. Irene has nurtured many writers, of both fiction and non-fiction. We thank her for having the patience to work with, and listen to, editors whose combined experience is just half of hers. No writer could ask for a better publisher.

We are also grateful to Zenzele Ndebele and the Centre for Innovation and Technology (CITE) for raising the resources for this publication. The seminar organised by CITE during the film festival in October 2021 provided a critical space for the authors to present their reviewed drafts and to receive further feedback from participants and fellow authors. Zenzele and CITE have also continued to shine the light and tell the story of Gukurahundi, so that this tragic chapter of our history is not buried under some cowering narrative of 'moving on' and 'letting bygones be bygones'. We must also thank The Royal Netherlands Embassy for providing the financial support which made it possible to publish this book, as they have provided support for CITE's annual film festival. We extend our gratitude to CITE's development partners, who make a lot of the organisation's work possible. We also with to thank the Open Society Initiative of Southern Africa for partnering with CITE on some of the work on Gukurahundi.

It is impossible to discuss Gukurahundi without making reference to that ground breaking human rights report - Breaking the Silence. We therefore feel honoured that Shari Eppel, who was the primary researcher and author of that report, agreed without hesitation to write the foreword to our book.

Finally, a big thank you to our families for the many hours that they allowed us to be unreachable.

Mandlenkosi Mpofu and Percy F. Makombe
October 2022

Ode to the nameless

Gugulethu Siziba (1979-2017)

To disappear is not to be
It is to be unseen and not to see
Bodies that fade into nothingness
Footprints that vanish without a trace
Grasps that slip through fingers and plunge into the darkness
Into the abyss called nowhere
To disappear
It is to be unheard
To speak silent words
It is to be invisible
Not to speak or write
Except in a code that is illegible
It is to be intangible
It is to not exist
Or to exist only in memories that persist
Figments of the mind
The sight of the blind
And secrets of the divine
They seek yet they cannot find
Invisible men and women
The grim reaper's harvesting season
Swallowed whole by the earth
And hidden in its dark folds and embrace
To be unknown and not to know
To be denied names
To be denied rest
Even in death
They were
Yet they never were
How do we mourn or shed tears?
When we know not where they lie
This is the epitome
Of deaths undefined and unknown
Mass graves are the abodes
Of figures condemned to die

Unknown and unmourned
Without names
Without tombstones to mark their resting place
Without days to commemorate their departure
Like guests who just upped and left
No goodbyes or handshakes
Blowing restless winds
To disappear is not to be
It is to be unseen and not to see
It is to be unheard
To speak silent words
Yet in the blind sight that does not see
In the deaf ears that do not hear
And the silent mouths that do not speak
You can hear the names
The nameless and unknown have many names
One of the names is Gukurahundi

Note to the Second Edition

Mandlenkosi Mpofu and Percy F. Makombe

Memory and Erasure is part of a growing body of academic literature to properly document and narrate the Gukurahundi genocide which, hopefully, may contribute to survivors and victims' families' quest for justice and closure. Deployed in January 1983, the Fifth Brigade's legacy has continued to cast a dark shadow not just over Matabeleland and Midlands, but over the entire country. As the title of the book – and also the chapters – forcefully underline, a culture of violence led by the state and those who control its levers pervades the whole of Zimbabwe and continues to do so partly because of the failure to address the Gukurahundi genocide and its aftermaths, which marked the height of Zimbabwean authorities' tendency to use violence to crush dissent and opposition.

Collectively, these essays explore different aspects of the Gukurahundi in order (1) to challenge the silencing of the genocide as a mainstream public issue in Zimbabwe, (2) to demonstrate how, deliberately and systematically, Zimbabwe's rulers have refused to allow this issue to be resolved and have, in the process, completely disregarded the views, demands, feelings and sensitivities of affected individuals and communities, (3) to explore and critique the institutional, legal/constitutional and political frameworks that have sustained the failure to find a solution, (4) to demonstrate how Zimbabwe, as a state, bears collective responsibility for Gukurahundi crimes and should therefore hold itself accountable and institute a clear and honest programme to provide a lasting solution that does not lead to further division, and (5) this collection emphasises, in various ways, that the solution to the political culture that has engulfed Zimbabwe and prevented it from attaining its independence goals lies in resolving the aftermath of Gukurahundi and addressing the culture of violence, repression and impunity in Zimbabwean politics.

In this second edition, three chapters have been added (8, 9 and 11). As the collection demonstrates, various jurisdictions within Africa and beyond have with good open leadership been able to address past injustices and crimes against humanity.

None of these models have appealed to Zimbabwe's rulers, because revealing the truth would force perpetrators to explain their own role in the genocide, and accept whatever form of retributive justice is meted out.

While the state's spokesmen may publicly proclaim sympathy with Gukurahundi victims and arrange high profile meetings intended to showcase their initiative, the leaders of Zimbabwe's Second Republic like their predecessor, Robert Mugabe, have so far outrightly refused to offer a clear apology to Gukurahundi victims, accept the state's responsibility, and acknowledge their own role within it.

However, attempts to erase Gukurahundi from public memory have failed. This is because details of the genocide and what individuals, families and communities experienced have been passed down from generation to generation; now third generations, who did not directly experience the atrocities, have become more vocal in expressing their frustrations and anger. In so doing the divide between the (generalised) victims, the Ndebele and the (generalised) perpetrators, the Shona, grows wider and more intransigent creating a great rift in the idea of nation. We should note here that the ruling party has consistently used the metaphors of war, of fighting an 'enemy' against any individual, party, NGO or medium that challenges it.[1] The future of the country depends on the holistic sense of nation, of a people moving forward together, not on perpetuating these reductionist, damaging tropes.

In Chapter 9, Gibson Ncube and Yemurai Chikwangura-Gwatirisa respond to the issue of silencing of discussions, debates and discourses on Gukurahundi in Zimbabwe's official platforms by exploring how this is being challenged in a connected world where many young people, even in a poor country like Zimbabwe, are spending much of their lives on social media platforms. The two authors illustrate that, through such interaction, on platforms over which the Zimbabwean state cannot exercise effective control, younger generations of Matabele citizens are more daring in their discussion of Gukurahundi than their predecessors, thereby ensuring that the debate is kept alive and questions continue to be raised.

Using novelist Novuyo Rosa Tshuma's characterisation, Ncube and Chikwangura-Gwatirisa emphasise the point of Gukurahundi as the 'original sin' in terms of all that has gone wrong since Zimbabwe became independent. This emphasises the point, made in many of the essays, that a culture of violence by the state against its citizens has dominated Zimbabwean politics from election to election because of the failure to effectively deal with Gukurahundi crimes.

Chapter 10 by Siphosami Malunga explores the Gukurahundi legacy from a legal angle, picking up from Cynthia Chigwenya in Chapter 4. Malunga interrogates the challenges in achieving justice and accountability. He discusses the gravity and scale of the crimes, the level of perpetrators, and the opportunities and constraints

---

1   See, for example, *The Language of Hate* (2008), Media Monitoring Project, Zimbabwe.

to universal and other forms of extra-territorial justice mechanisms. Malunga also explains/explores the limitations of the Zimbabwe criminal justice system and concludes that international justice fora should assume responsibility and address the atrocities.

In Chapter 11, we have a personal story from Mehlomakhulu, a woman who experienced Gukurahundi as a school child in the Matabeleland South district of Gwanda. Like Jameson Moyo's testimony (Chapter 10 in this edition), this story reminds us that Gukurahundi was about real lives, many of whom survived and have to navigate life through the nightmare of dealing with their horrific experiences, without any professional help. Both these stories were narrated on different occasions to our publisher, Irene Staunton. We are very indebted to Irene for helping us accommodate these personal narratives, as well as for her role in the whole project.

Many of the men at the helm of the current administration were at the centre of the government's policies and actions during the Gukurahundi, as senior government, army or security officials. It is therefore unsurprising that these leaders have used their current positions to suppress any meaningful discourse on the Gukurahundi, or to try and hijack the narrative in order to deflect from their own actions. It is our hope that *Memory and Erasure* will deepen information and comprehension of the Gukurahundi atrocities, the hurdles to establishing responsibility at the national and international levels, and the prospects and options for seeking and gaining international justice against perpetrators.

March, 2023

Foreword

Shari Eppel

The struggle of man against power is the struggle of memory against forgetting

(Milan Kundera)

This is a very important volume, for many reasons. January 2023 will mark 40 years since the first deployment of the Fifth (5) Brigade, which was named by then Zimbabwean Prime Minister Robert Mugabe as the 'Gukurahundi' brigade.[1] Tragically, four decades after 5 Brigade was responsible for mass rape, mass beatings, mass property loss – and the extra-judicial killings of thousands – that occurred in the Matabeleland and Midlands provinces of Zimbabwe between 1983 and 1987, very little has been done by the state to address the destruction of social fabric that resulted, or to formally recognise the terrible scale and impact of what happened. Contesting versions of the history remain, with differing understandings of this past becoming more, rather than less, entrenched. The state contests that by 1982, there were bands of ZAPU-sponsored dissidents actively undermining the newly post-colonial ZANU-PF government, and that these bands had to be brought under control in order to ensure the stability of Zimbabwe as a nation.[2] In 2022, many who remained dominant in Zimbabwe's ZANU-PF government still maintained that what happened in Matabeleland was some kind of civil war, with armed combatants on each side clashing as equal forces.[3] There has been some vague acceptance by government, never very formally expressed, that civilians died,

---

[1] 'Gukurahundi: Ten Years Later', *Zimbabwe Defence Forces Magazine*, 7.1 (1990).

[2] The new state inherited complex legacies from the war for independence that have been covered very well in other volumes. To mention a few: Ndlovu-Gatsheni 2012b; Mazarire 2017; Auret 1992; Martin and Johnson 1981; Bhebe and Ranger 1995; Raftopoulos and Mlambo 2009.

[3] 'Gukurahundi: Govt adopts victim-centred approach', *Sunday Mail*, 7 September 2022. This is one recent example of the state's version of these years. Minister of Justice Ziyambi Ziyambi emphasises that both Mugabe and Nkomo had to 'come to their senses' to end the 'hostilities' and says nothing about the excesses against civilians.

but that this was unavoidable, or even what they deserved, on the grounds that they might – or might not – be supporting dissidents.[4] At the time, the international community was quickly aware of civilian atrocities, as this cable to Washington from a US diplomat in March 1983, makes clear:

> The mailed fist policy of the Government of Zimbabwe is directed not only against dissidents themselves but against the entire Ndebele populace which is deemed to be the sea in which the enemy fish swim (Cameron 2018: 6).

The British High Commissioner noted in a diplomatic cable that, 'Men, women, and children have been victims, often simply because they could not prove they had not assisted dissidents' (Cameron 2018: 12). In March 1983, the Zimbabwean Minister for State (Security) made this policy of generalised punishment crystal clear when addressing rallies of already-brutalised and terrified rural villagers in Matabeleland North. He claimed that the government reserved the right to 'burn down all the villages infested with dissidents', adding that 'the campaigns against dissidents can only succeed if the infrastructure that nurtures them is destroyed'.[5]

Whatever the intention of the state was in facilitating thousands of arbitrary extra-judicial killings and punishments of entire villages and provinces – and it has yet to truly acknowledge, never mind explain, its intention – the understanding of countless victims on the ground has remained that they were targeted because they were from the minority Ndebele ethnic group, and because they supported the opposition ZAPU political party headed by Joshua Nkomo. The soldiers, as they beat and killed people, repeatedly indicated that 'all you Ndebeles are dissidents', because they were considered to all support ZAPU (Alexander et al. 2000). Being Ndebele was conflated with being a ZAPU supporter, and this justified the terrible punishments that followed for everyone. Werbner (1991: 159) observes that the catastrophe of quasi-nationalism is that

> it can capture the might of the nation state and bring authorised violence down ruthlessly against the people who seem to stand in the way of the nation being united and pure as one body… It is as if quasi-nationalism's victims, by being of an opposed quasi-nation, put themselves outside of the nation, indeed beyond the pale of humanity.

It must be noted that by the government's own reckoning, the dissidents

---

4 Robert Mugabe's famous 'moment of madness' reference to Gukurahundi is one such grudging recognition, made at Joshua Nkomo's funeral in 1999. This can be set against Mugabe's comment in 1983 that, 'Where men and women provide food for dissidents, when we get there, we eradicate them. We don't differentiate when we fight, because we can't tell who is a dissident and who is not' (Berkeley and Schrage 1986).

5 *The Chronicle* 5 March 1983.

numbered 'never much over 300' (Berkeley and Schrage 1986: 16). How, then, should we reconcile the state-acknowledged existence of fewer than 400 dissidents, with the murders of an estimated 10,000 to 20,000 civilians, including women, the mass beatings of tens of thousands, and systematic rape on a mass scale, including of school girls?[6] Thousands of rural villagers in Matabeleland are still asking this question, and are waiting for the formal, state-sanctioned chance to be heard, to narrate what happened to them.

A second reason that this volume is significant, is that this is the first time an entire volume of edited essays primarily on the topic of Gukurahundi has been published.[7] Furthermore, all the authors are Zimbabwean, and most are from Matabeleland. One chapter offers a direct victim's horrifying account of his arbitrary and repeated exposure to torture and the murder of others. A second recalls her frightening experience of being a schoolgirl subject to the commands of the Fifth Briagade. What should also be noted, is that several of the current authors are from what might be classified as the one-and-a-half generation: they were primary school children when Gukurahundi happened, as opposed to being adolescent or adult, meaning that they were not personally physically tortured. However, this generation of small children nonetheless witnessed and heard many atrocities, and have grown up with these often confusing and always terrifying memories. To have seen your parents come home weeping, and tortured, or for your parent not to come home because they were now in a mass grave, or to have witnessed the adults you respect being humiliated at urban road blocks, meant that you were also a first-hand victim of Gukurahundi, someone whose life from then onwards was knowingly or unknowingly shaped by these events. Now in their forties and fifties, this generation has taken on the task of making Gukurahundi the subject of careful analysis and scholarship, of dealing retrospectively with much of what they and the adults in their homes experienced during those years. Other authors in this volume are second generation Gukurahundi descendants, born after 1987. They have brought a current focus to past events; their young eyes and minds highlight the continuity of some aspects of Gukurahundi into the present.

What this means is that if the state and those implicated by Gukurahundi were hoping to outwait victims with the assumption that the issue and the memories

---

6 Estimates of the dead from this era range from, most conservatively, 7,500 (CCJPZ and LRF 1997: 157) to the higher figure of 40,000 in the CITE *Gukurahundi Genocide* documentary. Joshua Nkomo (1984) refers to 20,000 dead. The exact figure will most likely never be known, but 20,000 is the most commonly used figure in academic sources, such as Doran (2017) and Coltart (2016).

7 There have been individual memoirs published, and CCJPZ and LRF (1997) remains the most comprehensive Zimbabwean record of the massacres. There have been many edited multi-author collections dealing more broadly with the political violence of the ZANU-PF state since the advent of 'the Zimbabwe Crisis' post 2000, but this is the first volume looking primarily at Gukurahundi and its legacies.

will die with them, they need to pay attention and see that this is a misguided assumption. If anything, the voices are gaining momentum and courage as the decades and generations pass, as the outspoken chapters in this book illustrate. As George Orwell wrote in '1984': 'Who controls the past controls the future: who controls the present controls the past.' But transfer of historical memory has already occurred in relation to Gukurahundi. In a world with an avalanche of ways of digitally sharing the past and the present, controlling aspects of Zimbabwe's media, as well as taking draconian measures to limit freedoms of movement, association and expression within the nation, is no longer a powerful enough tool to control memory and enforce forgetting. Nor is intimidating rural villagers with threats: this may well have silenced the villagers concerned, but not their children and grandchildren in the diaspora. Controlling what is said within the borders of Zimbabwe is no longer a sure way of controlling the present and therefore the past. Werbner's (1998) comment on memory comes to mind:

> Subjected to buried memory, people do not so much forget as recognise – and often ever more forcefully – that they have not been allowed to remember.

The title of this book – *Memory and Erasure* – can therefore be seen almost as ironic; state attempts at erasure, although consistent, have at least partially failed. This volume itself is proof of that. But this is not to underplay the risks that many citizens of Zimbabwe have run, and continue to run, in trying to speak out on this issue and to make demands for acknowledgement and truth-telling, never mind demanding solutions to the much harder issues of restorative justice, reparations, memorialisation, exhumations and reburials. Simple truth telling and formal remembrance remain tough tasks. The repeated destruction of memorials to the Gukurahundi dead in Bhalagwe Camp speak to these dangers and the courage it takes to dare to remember. This intolerance of memorialising Gukurahundi was internationally acknowledged in September 2022 by the UN Committee on the International Convention on the Elimination of All Forms of Racial Discrimination, which noted in its periodic review of Zimbabwe:

> The Committee was disturbed by reports that the Gukurahundi atrocities, which resulted in the killing of around 20,000 Ndebele speakers in the 1980s, continue to be a source of ethnic tension, with many victims remaining traumatized and barred from participating in mourning and commemorative activities by State agents.[8]

Nobody should underestimate the levels of fear that persist among Gukurahundi survivors. While the silence has been broken in places, most notably among the

---

8 'UN Committee flags Zimbabwe over ban on Gukurahundi memorials', *ZimLive*, 1 September 2022.

younger generations of activists, many victims still live with deep-seated misgivings at speaking out. There have been multiple statements in the media since 2018 quoting President Mnangagwa and other government officials announcing that talking about Gukurahundi was allowed – which in itself is an acknowledgement that it may not previously have been allowed.[9] Yet, the reality on the ground is that fear is still often overriding, and no formal forums have been provided for hearings, despite multiple announcements in the media over the last three years that hearings are about to take place.[10]

In 2018, the launching of the National Peace and Reconciliation Commission (NPRC) through the passing of its associated legislation, offered hope to those in Matabeleland and the Midlands. With the constitutional mandate to 'ensure post conflict justice, healing and reconciliation', the initial willingness of the NPRC to place Gukurahundi at the top of its five-year action plan was promising.[11] However, from June 2019 onwards, there was a move by President Mnangagwa to give the Council of Chiefs the mandate to oversee and resolve the Gukurahundi issue, which appeared to solidify by August 2019.[12] This placed the NPRC in an awkward position: Chairperson Nare felt the commission was being side-stepped, as meetings occurred between the chiefs and the presidium that excluded the NPRC.[13] Sadly, the NPRC had by then only made promises to deal with Gukurahundi but had not yet done anything material. In December 2019, most disappointingly, exhumations and reburials that our team had been asked to carry out by families and the NPRC were suddenly cancelled at less than a week's notice.[14] The five families, who had been planning for months for their reburials, were devastated. In spite of promises that this had been a postponement, by the end of 2022, the families had not been allowed to have these exhumations, nor had they (or we) received adequate explanation for their sudden halt. This caused heartbreak on top of heartbreak and served to underline why affected regions have little faith in the state to deliver on any issues related to Gukurahundi. The marginalising and disempowering of the NPRC from dealing with any aspect of Gukurahundi was seemingly cemented in 2021, when most of the original NPRC commissioners were replaced, and the focus of the

---

9 'Talk openly about Gukurahundi, says Vice President Mohadi', *The Chronicle,* 22 July 2019.

10 'Gukurahundi fear persists... Communities still afraid to open up on atrocities', *The Chronicle,* 18 December 2019; 'Special Gukurahundi Committee established', *The Chronicle,* 13 March 2020; 'Gukurahundi hearings to start early next year', *The Chronicle,* 4 December 2020; 'President makes bold moves to resolve Gukurahundi', *The Chronicle,* 15 September 2021.

11 I was among many in civics who worked with the NPRC and UNDP to concretise their five-year action plan, only to see it binned when the new commissioners came into office.

12 'ED tackles Gukurahundi with chiefs', *The Chronicle,* 29 June 2019.

13 'Peace Commission shocked after Mnangagwa snub in Gukurahundi reburials', *NewZimbabwe,* 6 December 2020.

14 'NPRC prepares for Gukurahundi victims exhumations, reburials', *The Chronicle,* 10 October 2019.

commission was immediately and firmly shifted to other issues, in spite of only two years of their five-year plan having elapsed. The current NPRC commissioners have refused to be drawn into discussions about Gukurahundi since 2021, simply 'noting' any attempts to get them involved.[15]

On the other hand, since 2019 there have been multiple meetings between the Council of Chiefs, the President and various civic organisations. The initiative to put traditional leadership in charge of Gukurahundi seemed to have opened a promising avenue to provide spaces for victims to be heard, and to be offered reparations and reburials.[16] If one was to follow the press reports in the state-run The Chronicle newspaper in Bulawayo, one could be forgiven for believing that there is a vibrant chiefs' initiative involving hearings and trainings running full-tilt in Matabeleland.[17] However, those of us who have worked weekly on the ground in Gukurahundi-affected areas for many years observed that by the end of 2022 this initiative remained more a matter of talk than action. The chiefs have remained without resources to reach out, and without any formal training in how to take up this formidable task of hearing from and healing their people. In my observation, the chiefs are more than willing to pick up this task and are fully aware of its importance. However, they are also aware that they need skills and support, especially training of local villagers to offer psychosocial support for victims, and in how to handle documentation, before launching into hearings. Moreover, individual chiefs are waiting for guidance from chiefs in the council, which has not been forthcoming. And the chiefs are constantly reminded that they owe their position to the state and can be displaced if they do not toe the state line. They therefore feel that they must wait for clear direction and state resources to take up this role in any meaningful way. In the meantime, many victims, already elderly and in frail health, have continued to die unheard and un-helped. At the end of 2022, it was really not obvious that the state had either a clear idea of what was needed to open the space to victims of Gukurahundi, or a clear intention to really move in this direction. Nor did the state instil confidence in anyone, when the Speaker of the House, Jacob Mudenda, called on the NPRC to 'speed up the process of addressing Gukurahundi and bringing closure before the 2023 elections'.[18] One wonders what kind of process anyone could possibly envision, in which a genocide that has been silenced for forty years could be 'closed'

---

15 Personal experience, reinforced by discussions with other civic actors.
16 'Gukurahundi: chiefs to engage key stakeholders', The Chronicle, 23 December 2020; 'Gukurahundi tops agenda as President meets chiefs', The Chronicle, 19 August 2021; 'Gukurahundi resolution: chiefs to map way forward', The Chronicle, 11 December 2021; 'Conflict Resolution training for chiefs ahead of Gukurahundi hearings', The Chronicle, 5 January 2022.
17 A quick 'Gukurahundi Chiefs' search on the *The Chronicle* website, https://www.chronicle.co.zw/?s=chiefs+gukurahundi, turned up more than twenty links to articles over the last few years.
18 'Mudenda tells NPRC to address Gukurahundi before 2023 election', *NewZimbabwe*, 19 May 2022.

in the space of a few months.

The concern is that before the chiefs' initiative has had a chance to become active on the ground, the state will arbitrarily shift the goalposts as they did with the NPRC: overnight, this elusive task of dealing with Gukurahundi could be reallocated from the chiefs to some other body, or there could simply be an announcement the issue has been 'dealt with' and that the nation must stop looking back. The struggles for truth, for the right to know, for the right to mourn, remain uphill ones.

The third reason that this book matters, is found in the subtitle: 'Gukurahundi and the Culture of Violence in Zimbabwe'. Most chapters draw a direct link between the violence of the 1980s, through to the state violence since 2000 and up to the present. This is why what happened in the west of Zimbabwe should be understood by the whole nation, and not only those directly affected by Gukurahundi. Just as Gukurahundi was driven by extreme political intolerance of ZAPU and its perceived threat to a one-party ZANU-PF state, so in 2000 the rise of the first meaningful political opposition since the disappearance of ZAPU resulted once more in massive political repression. This opposition was the Movement for Democratic Change (MDC), which almost won the parliamentary elections in June 2000, in spite of widespread state repression and violence by ZANU-PF and the state in the months ahead of this election. The ensuing massive state backlash, with politically motivated beatings, rape, property destruction, arrests and general abuse of the law to undermine and incapacitate the MDC, was a recognised strategy to those in Matabeleland. What became known as the Zimbabwe Crisis, post 2000, had its roots back in Gukurahundi, and before that, back into colonialism (Raftopoulos and Mlambo 2009). Tragically, it has always been the case in this land, once Rhodesia, Zimbabwe since 1980, that whoever unleashes violence in the name of the government of the day, has always had de facto impunity. If we are to understand the present dilemmas that Zimbabwe faces, and if we are truly to protect our future from further eras of human rights abuses, we need to fully address all our pasts – colonial, Gukurahundi, and the outbreaks of political violence since 2000. Of all these eras, Gukurahundi still remains the least well documented, which is why this volume is so important.

This is a book of courage, one that speaks to academic excellence in the upcoming generations of Zimbabwe. I note with sadness that so many of the brilliant minds that have contributed to this volume are no longer among us here, but have been pushed into the diaspora, along with hundreds of thousands of their fellow Zimbabweans. This is the inevitable consequence of decades of violence and economic collapse. Zimbabweans may never have been as sorely in need of hope as they are as 2022 draws to a close. This book is a step towards that hope. It is evidence that memory of Gukurahundi is not erased, nor will it be, regardless of the passing of time.

Introduction:
Fighting for the Right to Remember: the Plight of Zimbabwe's Gukurahundi Victims

Mandlenkosi Mpofu and Percy F. Makombe

He asked her, 'How do people start to recover after experiences of tremendous violence?' She thought about it, and answered, 'with truth, which comes from memory'.

Emily Jastromb (2011), narrating how she came to write the paper 'Facing History – Memory and Recovery in the Aftermath of Atrocity'.

ZANU-PF has dominated Zimbabwean post-independence politics for more than four decades, first under Robert Mugabe and then under Emmerson Mnangagwa, who was always an influential figure and lieutenant throughout Mugabe's long rule. Under their leadership, egregious human rights violations have occurred, and heinous acts of violence have been committed against perceived opponents and dissenting voices. The chapters in this book have one theme in common, which is that the victims of the Gukurahundi genocide, which took place between 1983 and 1987, have been subjected to further injustice because of the authorities' refusal to address this cruel past. This ugly history has given rise to contestations about whose story should be told and who should be believed regarding the Gukurahundi atrocities.

According to Jastromb (2011) ignoring atrocities impedes healing and sows the seeds of more bloodshed. She argues that the first significant step towards healing and lasting peace is taken when a nation acknowledges the brutalities by honouring and giving space to individual and collective memory. This also suggests that the pursuit of truth cannot be limited to official accounts of what happened and why. In the same way that doctored official records are about erasure and conquest, remembering as a component of memory becomes an act of resistance and fighting back. Alexander characterises this tension between official accounts that somehow seek to justify Gukurahundi and the repressed memories of the victims/survivors as a 'noisy silence', in which 'those subjected to state violence and its lingering legacies struggle both to make themselves heard and to imagine new political possibilities and terms of belonging' (Alexander 2021: 763). This loud silence has been raised by many authors from various challenging perspectives.

The brutality suffered by the victims has been well documented. Werbner (1995), observed that for many victims of Gukurahundi violence 'the Fifth Brigade was felt to be an evil even greater than the Rhodesian army' (p.196). Writing not long after the end of the Gukurahundi operation, Werbner (1995) noted that the anger and frustration of victims was even worse because they had fought (as communities and individuals) in the liberation struggle to end colonial subjugation only to suffer brutality from the state in a 'free' Zimbabwe.

Despite this deep feeling of injustice, victims have had to contend with a state which quite literally denies the Gukurahundi and in the absence of 'an official truth-telling forum or process of accountability that might have created and legitimated a shared story, however problematic' (Alexander 2021: 763). Instead, as Alexander writes, the state seeks to impose 'justificatory' accounts of events on the victims. A critical question is how should people remember and deal with such extreme acts of iniquity committed at the behest of senior ruling party and government leaders?

The Gukurahundi genocide has been characterised by official refusal to acknowledge or recognise the violent past and more importantly the state's responsibility for that violence. The current Minister of Justice, Ziyambi Ziyambi, has even reiterated – on more than one occasion – that Gukurahundi was resolved with the signing of the controversial Unity Accord in 1987; a position that even contradicts his administration's policy.[1] What this betrays, to paraphrase Werbner (1995), is that the Zimbabwean state under former president Mugabe and now under President Mnangagwa does not seem to understand why Gukurahundi victims are unwilling or unable to forget the violent injustices perpetrated against them. Survivors have also had to contend with a political culture in which national unity, in whatever form, is prioritised over their needs.

The question that runs throughout the volume, therefore, is whether it is possible to achieve justice for victims of Gukurahundi when most of the people in power today were perpetrators. This is the context in which the question of transitional justice (TJ) is raised in this collection. Most of the authors suggest that TJ mechanisms which could have helped resolve the Gukurahundi were not adopted in Zimbabwe because the authorities have been more concerned with controlling the memory of events or at the very least hoped that with time those events will be forgotten. This builds onto Eppel's (2013) argument that it may be impossible to implement effective

---

1 'Ziyambi digs in on Gukurahundi', *The Standard,* 25 September 2022 [https://www.thestandard.co.zw/local-news/article/200000015/ziyambi-digs-in-on-gukurahundi] accessed 26 September 2022.

mechanisms of TJ unless a country achieves a moment of real transition. Such a transition should, inter alia, lead to the establishment of credible and professional state institutions that can deal with critical aspects of the genocide to give closure to individuals and communities who desperately need it. Currently, the National Peace and Reconciliation Commission (NPRC), which is constitutionally mandated to deal with resolution of conflicts including the Gukurahundi, has not managed to execute its duties effectively mainly because it lacks the political independence and autonomy to do so.

The term 'transitional justice' is itself contentious, but as argued by Sriram (2007), it generally refers to a combination of legal, political, and moral measures for dealing with past violence in nations undergoing political transition. TJ has its roots in the wave of upheavals that followed the end of the Cold War, particularly in Eastern Europe and Latin America. It was assumed that the transition was from autocratic systems of government to liberal style democracy (Arthur 2009). With this understanding it could be argued that it is a misnomer to talk about TJ in Zimbabwe, where the party that orchestrated the genocide is still in power and continues to defend its actions and to explain the Gukurahundi in a justificatory manner. However, TJ is expanding to include promoting accountability, healing, conflict resolution, national dialogue, memorialisation and in some instances, bringing perpetrators of horrific crimes before tribunals (Leebaw 2008). Some authors have insisted on intentionally carrying women's voices and understanding their experiences and the violence visited on them (Rubio-Marin 2006) as part of an effective mechanism of TJ.

The title of this volume emphasises the concerted efforts by the government using state institutions and even quasi-state groups aimed at erasure of the memories of Gukurahundi victims. Victims and subsequent generations have further continued to endure state sanctioned marginalisation and the denial of the right to remember this past without interference. This failure, indeed reluctance, to find redress for victims has burdened Zimbabwe with tension and distrust, which sometimes runs along ethnic lines.

Official denial of the Gukurahundi is linked to the criminalisation of ethnicity and the refusal to engage with the genocide's ethnic dimensions (Mhlanga 2013). As an establishment, Zimbabwe is uncomfortable with any discussions of ethnicity or ethnic relations in the post-colonial state. Gukurahundi therefore has to be dealt with in a context where 'any attempt to discuss ethnicity risks being labelled as "tribalism" and, therefore, divisive to a supposedly "united nation"' (Mhlanga 2013: 47). In concurrence, Ndlovu and Dube (2013) observe the subtle nature of the denial of Gukurahundi, in which attention is shifted to claims that 'the Zimbabwean genocide had no ethnic dimension whatsoever' (p. 361) and was not targeted at a specific ethnic group (see Vambe 2012).

Worryingly, the divide in collective memory over the Gukurahundi cuts across Zimbabwe's political divisions, to the extent that even in the political opposition and in broader civil society there is no appetite to empathise with victims of Gukurahundi, except as a way of using the genocide to condemn ZANU-PF in order to elicit international support (see Alexander 2021). Alexander calls this engagement a form of 'retrospective empathy' which is self-serving; Gukurahundi is given attention not for the sake of the victims, but in order to show the world the kind of people that opposition activists are dealing with.

One of the most vivid demonstrations of the collective failure to include Gukurahundi in understanding some local struggles in the country was the Zimbabwe Lawyers for Human Rights' (ZLHR) much publicised refusal to defend members of the Mthwakazi Liberation Front (MLF) against charges of treason in 2012, on the grounds that the MLF practised separatist politics and were therefore tribalists (see Mpofu and Moyo 2017). The respected ZLHR, which went on to offer free legal services to leaders of the dreaded Zimbabwe Liberation War Veterans Association, refused to recognise the persecution of activists on grounds that would resound more with ZANU-PF propaganda in the 1980s.

Alexander explains how, as Gukurahundi unfolded, ZANU-PF propaganda diffused through the rest of the country (outside Matebeleland and parts of the Midlands that were experiencing Gukurahundi), in a manner that is to an extent still enduring today:

> ZANU (PF)'s Gukurahundi narrative powerfully shaped the views of Zimbabweans who lived beyond the reach of state violence, creating a shared view. Many knew little of the extent of repression. Where news of violence trickled out from beyond the curfews, media clamp-downs and official denials, it was dismissed by people who wanted to believe in the good intentions of the new government and its model of black majority rule ... (Alexander 2021: 769).

Verheul's observation that the Harare-based ZLHR's failure to understand the plight of the MLF activists was because of a legal consciousness 'shaped by a history of repression that did not include Gukurahundi' (Verheul 2017 in Alexander 2021: 777) underlines the point that it is not just the perpetrators of Gukurahundi that victims have to contend with, but also many sections of the Zimbabwean population that did not experience the genocide. This also means, sadly, that justificatory official narratives of events have had an impact on the nation's memory, if not its psyche.

Despite the denial of space by the state and the challenge of gaining sympathy from Zimbabwean society in general, there has been so much 'telling' about Gukurahundi by victims' groups and by various organisations such as Ibhetshu likaZulu and CITE, as well as by academics who have challenged official accounts. While these efforts (of 'telling') may not amount to the redress of the injustices that victims wish to achieve, the state is aware of the power of telling as a potential arena of political productivity (see Alexander 2021) and mobilisation. As Alexander argues, persistent demand for injustice to be recognised by the very authority that perpetrated it can translate into concrete formulation of demands for action. This may explain the official determination to prevent or control any dialogue on the subject.

Two events in September 2022 underlined the importance of the major themes in most of the chapters in this volume. First, the United Nations condemned the failure by the Zimbabwean state to facilitate the memorialisation of the Gukurahundi genocide by the victims. Second, on 7 September 2022 Zimbabwean President Emmerson Mnangagwa toured the Kigali Memorial, which was erected in commemoration of the victims of the genocide against the Tutsi in Rwanda.[2] Mnangagwa's words at the memorial are worth reproducing:

> This day is the most sad and dark experience of my entire life where I have been exposed to the most cruel practice carried out by our own people against another section of the community. I pray that this sad and dark period of the history of this country should never be allowed to happen again, not only in this country but on our continent Africa and the human race. I congratulate my dear brother president Paul Kagame for fostering peace and harmony. May his legacy be carried forward by the next generation. Sad history. Never to happen again.

That many stories on independent Zimbabwean online news websites saw the president's visit to the memorial in Kigali as hypocritical is not surprising, since back home there have been concerted efforts led by the government to prevent any form of memorialisation of the Gukurahundi.

When he first ascended to power, Mnangagwa hinted that Gukurahundi would be resolved once and for all, and that survivors and victims' families would be listened to, in terms of their demands. His 'Second Republic', Zimbabweans were told almost ad infinitum, was ushering in a 'new dispensation' where there would be more openness in society in general and Gukurahundi survivors in particular would be allowed to speak freely about their promises, and where the contentious issues of exhumations and reburials would also be openly addressed. The government has, however, directly and indirectly, prevented communities and activists from carrying

---

2   'Two-faced Mnangagwa honours Rwanda genocide victims', *Zimlive*, 8 September 2022 [https://www.zimlive.com/2022/09/two-faced-mnangagwa-honours-rwanda-genocide-victims/] accessed 12 September 2022.
'Mnangagwa Rwanda genocide honour riles Gukurahundi activists', *CITE*, 8 September 2022 https://cite.org.zw/mnangagwa-rwanda-genocide-honour-riles-gukurahundi-activists/] accessed 12 September 2022.

out any activities in memory of the genocide freely. Shari Eppel explains in the foreword to this volume that exhumations and reburials requested by families of victims have been frustrated in ways which underline authorities' insensitive attitude and strengthen affected communities' lack of faith in the state.

The subject of the Gukurahundi has drawn irritation, disdain and at times anger from the government. Minister Ziyambi Ziyambi, for instance, has even suggested those clamouring about justice for victims of Gukurahundi are 'parroting European thinking' and seeking to stoke ethnic tensions.3 The collective conclusion from these chapters, therefore, is that Mnangagwa has effectively continued the attitude of former president Mugabe on Gukurahundi. This means that 1) the government begrudgingly acknowledges Gukurahundi but does not accept responsibility; this acknowledgement is sometimes couched in language that actually blames the victims for the actions of the state. 2) the government prevents open discussions on Gukurahundi and makes every effort to take control of and convolute narratives. 3) the government does not come up with any clear programme of addressing the genocide according to the wishes of the affected population and communities.

The chapters are arranged as follows; in the first chapter, Mpofu and Makombe explore the government's ineffective response to the Gukurahundi genocide. They analyse the complexities of Zimbabweanness and identity and demonstrate how the failure to address Gukurahundi issues has impacted on Zimbabwe's potential to be a state in which diversity is embraced and celebrated. Like other authors in the volume, they raise the issue of reconciliation and TJ and reach the same conclusion as Eppel (2013) that it is impossible to implement effective mechanisms of TJ unless a country achieves a moment of real transition.

Chigwenya picks up the issue of TJ in Chapter 2 and discusses it in the context of peace building. In an illustrative contrast with TJ programmes in Rwanda, Chigwenya characterises the Zimbabwean TJ approach as lacking authenticity and being nothing more than 'bandwagoning', which means playing to the gallery to give the impression of concern to the watching public so as to enhance democratic credentials. In Chapter 3, Ruhanya and Gumbo argue that much of the challenges of TJ in Zimbabwe stem from having perpetrators in office, being expected to lead the process. Securocrats, with the military at the centre, have maintained a stranglehold on key state institutions in Zimbabwe and are responsible for defining the terms of engagement on how to deal with TJ questions.

In Chapter 4, Moyo-Mpofu gives a harrowing account on sexual violence as a

---

3 'Ziyambi digs in on Gukurahundi', *The Standard*, 25 September 2022 [https://www.thestandard.co.zw/local-news/article/200001015/ziyambi-digs-in-on-gukurahundi] accessed 26 September 2022.

weapon of war used by the Fifth Brigade. She raises critical questions about the lack of sustained research and documentation of the crimes of sexual violence perpetrated during Gukurahundi and is exasperated that this subject remains cloaked in silence as a 'public secret'. In Chapter 5 Fuzwayo, Hadebe and Nkomo deal with the struggles of activists, communities, victims and survivors seeking to memorialise the genocide through erecting plaques in honour of those who perished. They narrate the insensitive destruction of these memorial plaques followed by an equally purblind reaction of the government, whose spokesmen have even mocked the powerlessness of the survivors, thereby revictimising them.

An important aspect of this volume is the emphasis that Gukurahundi is not an episode that is fixed in the five years over which it occurred. This point is also emphasised in Maseko and Nkomo in Chapter 6. The two authors argue that the insincerity of the government in dealing with healing and reconciliation fuelled a perpetuation of Gukurahundi which is now manifested in the state's linguistic practices and policies, among other things. They further explain how government officials have consistently used reckless language to describe victims of the Gukurahundi, with Mnangagwa featuring as one of the main culprits. In Chapter 7, Ncube explores the role of the state-controlled media during the genocide, and meticulously explains how it suppressed news on state atrocities and actively helped the government to cover up Gukurahundi crimes. In the last chapter of the book, Moyo gives a moving personal testimony of the horrors of Gukurahundi, which offers a glimpse into the nightmares that survivors live with on a daily basis. Such testimonies, like the collective work in this volume, remind us again of the importance of using our memories to counter the narratives of the perpetrators.

1

Criminalising the Subaltern: Gukurahundi, Reconciliation and Transitional Justice in Zimbabwe

Mandlenkosi Mpofu and Percy F. Makombe

Zimbabwe in transition and the Gukurahundi genocide

This chapter seeks to examine the failure of the Zimbabwean state to deal with the Gukurahundi genocide. Focusing on the current government under President Emmerson Mnangagwa, we place the questions of identity and 'Zimbabweanness' in relation to the failure to resolve Gukurahundi. We argue that the history of Gukurahundi has impacted on Zimbabwe's ability to be an inclusive state where diversity is accepted and celebrated. We then move onto Zimbabwe's approach to resolving the Gukurahundi genocide. Here, we hope to shed light on how Mugabe's handling of the aftermath of the genocide has continued under Mnangagwa. Throughout the chapter, Alex Boraine's (2006) analytical framework for transitional justice (TJ) is employed to critically analyse Zimbabwe's approach to the resolution of the Gukurahundi genocide. We contrast the acts of the government with Boraine's five-step analytic framework, which focuses on accountability, truth recovery, reconciliation, institutional reforms, and reparations, to explain why efforts to resolve the contentious issue of Gukurahundi have failed. In conclusion, we concur with Eppel's (2013) premise that a country cannot implement effective mechanisms of TJ and peace building unless it achieves a moment of real transition. In the context of Gukurahundi, the unity accord of December 1987, the government of national unity of 2009, and the November 2017 coup did not result into such a transition.

The Gukurahundi genocide has hung like a huge shadow over Zimbabwe's transition because of failure by successive ZANU-PF governments to find a lasting solution. The genocide has received much academic attention over the past decade (see Eppel 2008; Maedza 2019; Ndlovu-Gatsheni 2012a; Alexander 1998; Mpofu 2019; Ncube and Siziba 2017a), so here we do not wish to offer an extensive narration, besides what may assist in our discussion. The argument in this chapter is that the government needs to acknowledge the role and responsibility of the Zimbabwean state, the scale of violence and the damage to communities. Further to that, there is need to set up a clear, functional TJ mechanism to quickly address the grievances of survivors and families of victims. We argue that the lack of such a mechanism in the Unity Accord in 1987 led to the first failure to deal with the genocide.

The Zimbabwean government bears full responsibility for Gukurahundi; claims that it was a mere operation conducted to combat a dissident insurgency in Matabeleland and the Midlands (Maedza 2019) are not credible. It is an established fact, for instance, that then PM Robert Mugabe's government entered an agreement with North Korea soon after independence in 1980, to train a crack army (the Fifth Brigade) that would report directly to Mugabe, long before any perceived dissident threat (Eppel 2008). The Fifth Brigade was officially established in August of the same year and pursued a violent, sinister agenda that targeted people in Matabeleland and parts of the Midlands. As other chapters in this volume also point out, the Gukurahundi operation essentially equated being Ndebele with supporting Joshua Nkomo's PF-ZAPU, which had fought for independence alongside Mugabe's ZANU-PF. Being Ndebele was also by extension equated to sympathising with dissidents (CCJPZ 1997), as ZANU-PF targeted PF-ZAPU's base in order to secure political hegemony (Eppel 2013: 213) through the establishment of a one-party state. The scale and level of violence and the fatalities experienced during the Gukurahundi genocide surpassed what many communities endured during the 15-year-long war for liberation (Eppel 2008). In that war, over 25,000 civilians died across the whole of Zimbabwe (Mills and Wilson 2007), which illustrates the grim kill rate of the Gukurahundi genocide affecting around 15% of the population.

Between 1983 and 1987, the provinces of Matabeleland South and Matabeleland North, and large parts of the Midlands province suffered heavily as the Fifth Brigade and other state organs such as the Central Intelligence Organisation, police and other army units, ravaged through communities. Thousands more suffered through torture, rape and other forms of state-sanctioned violence and intimidation, including mass starvation and the burning of property (Cameron 2018). Cameron (2018: 2) observes that 'the atmosphere of fear and mistrust' that the Gukurahundi created between Matabeleland and the Zimbabwean government has persisted beyond that period, thus hindering full reconciliation. Eppel (2013) echoes these sentiments, and further makes the important observation that since Gukurahundi, Zimbabwe has habitually followed episodes of state violence with the granting of amnesty to the accused, thereby encouraging impunity.

Whereas physical violence in the form of the Gukurahundi genocide was the most visible manifestation of ZANU-PF's campaign to establish its dominance, imaginations of the new nation as expressed through various forms and platforms provided the ideological context and justification for the violence. The Unity Accord signed between Nkomo and Mugabe in December 1987 was a missed opportunity to address some of these issues. While helpful in ending the atrocities, it unfortunately failed to establish a TJ mechanism to address the genocide itself, as was the case for instance with South Africa's Truth and Reconciliation Commission (TRC) a few years later. Furthermore, serious concerns about national identity, belonging and inclusivity that were central to the genocide were left completely untouched. The Gukurahundi genocide itself was completely disregarded in the accord and received no mention.

The absence of adequate recognition and acknowledgement has resulted in no compensation for individual victims, survivors and communities, further compounding the general lack of development in the region. It has also meant that the state has not assisted in many efforts by families of victims to find closure, such as through exhumations and reburials of victims, and through memorialisation activities. As a result, many families still do not know what happened to their relatives. Despite official commitments, many victims of the Gukurahundi have struggled to access important national documents such as death certificates (of parents or relatives), birth certificates and identity cards, which are critical for all aspects of life for citizens of Zimbabwe.[1] The blanket amnesty in 1988, which was meant to end banditry and to integrate dissidents back into society, primarily benefited state perpetrators including the Fifth Brigade, whom it shielded from prosecution and scrutiny and senior leaders of both parties, who secured positions in the resultant administration. The accord was therefore seen as a betrayal by many victims, for whom it represented political emasculation (Eppel 2008).

It is against this background that President Mnangagwa's attempts to resolve the Gukurahundi since assuming power following the November 2017 coup is analysed in this chapter. Dealing decisively with the Gukurahundi genocide and listening to victims and survivors' concerns was one of the most prominent of the promises the post-coup administration made.

---

1 'Destruction of Gukurahundi memorials prolongs torture of victims and their descendants', *Daily Maverick*, 26 January 2022 [https://www.dailymaverick.co.za/article/2022-01-26-destruction-of-gukurahundi-memorials-prolongs-torture-of-victims-and-their-descendants/]
'Documentation of Gukurahundi victims remains a pipe dream', *CITE*, 30 December 2021 [https://cite.org.zw/documentation-of-gukurahundi-victims-remains-a-pipe-dream/] both accessed 17 July 2022

Under Mugabe's rule, Zimbabwe was, through many national projects and platforms, imagined as a Shona nation. The disproportionate promotion and celebration of Shona heroes from the pre-colonial past and the liberation struggle is a well-documented example of that. In the context of Gukurahundi, the genocide itself as well as experiences of victims, survivors and their communities need to be incorporated into the memoralisation of the Zimbabwe nation. But as Fuzwayo, Hadebe and Nkomo write in this volume, the state itself has interfered with such memorialisation through systematic vandalism of plaques erected in memory of Gukurahundi genocide victims at Bhalagwe, south of Bulawayo, and other sites. Using Boraine's analytical framework for transitional justice, we argue that official reluctance to take full responsibility for the past is behind Zimbabwe's failure to resolve the genocide.

ZANU-PF and national identity

Since the first decade of independence, whenever ZANU-PF feels threatened, its default mode is to lash out and label its opponents 'enemies of the state'. Central to this is the collapse of national identity into something defined in line with ZANU-PF values and – as we illustrate – being Shona as well. For ZANU-PF, a national identity should be something simple and monolithic, defined by the party and what it stands for. Anything else is unacceptable and seen as a challenge to national values, particularly if there is also a challenge to ZANU-PF's political dominance and hegemony.

In Anderson's (2006) imagined communities, people of the same nation feel that they are the same even though they might never meet each other. This feeling brings people together as it gives them a kind of comfort zone. It is this same feeling of togetherness that has been exploited by authoritarian regimes to mobilise loyalty. In the Zimbabwean situation for example, the official understanding of national identity in the first instance seems to be one that is based on supporting the ruling party. The construction of a 'Zimbabwean' is largely based on a process of differentiation – the 'them' and 'us' distinction. Mugabe, who kick-started his rule with what appeared to be a statesman's speech where he defined Zimbabwe as being for all people who lived in it regardless of whether they were black or white, quickly turned back on this statement as PF-ZAPU and Ndebele people had their 'Zimbabweanness' questioned.[2]

Later, Mugabe and ZANU-PF would also deploy the language of identity when their grip on power was threatened by Morgan Tsvangirai's Movement for Democratic Change (MDC). Tsvangirai's loyalty to Zimbabwe was questioned

---

2 Mugabe's speech as the flag of the newly independent Zimbabwe was raised, summed up in the words, 'If yesterday I fought you as an enemy, today you have become a friend and an ally with the same national interest, loyalty, rights and duties as myself' (Meredith, 2002).

and the MDC was constantly portrayed as not homegrown and therefore a foreign stooge created to undermine the gains of Zimbabwe's liberation struggle. During the same period (2000-08), segments of the Zimbabwean population in particular white commercial farmers, were portrayed as invaders and enemies to justify the deployment of violence against them. The Zimbabwe National Army also ruled out saluting Tsvangirai (if he won elections) on the basis that his lack of liberation war credentials made him unsuitable to lead the country.

Part of the method of defining national values in Zimbabwe seems to be to make other contesting definitions invisible. Just as was done with PF-ZAPU and the people of Matabeleland in the early 1980s, the thought was cultivated and encouraged that the MDC did not have national interests and by implication those who supported the MDC could not be regarded as Zimbabweans, if they were Zimbabweans, then they were not right-thinking Zimbabweans. By continuously harping on 'colonialism', 'exploitation' and 'liberation' ZANU-PF and the public media try to invoke an emotional attachment to the 'imagined nation' which mirrors only their selective memories. As Smith (1991:21), has argued, it is mythical ties of tradition, history and ancestry that help build the concept of the nation as a family and hence present a basis for exclusion and divisions. This entails an element of dichotomising, which leads to the construction of 'them' and 'us' (Fowler 1991). People who do not agree 'are branded as 'subversive', 'perverts', 'deviants', 'dissidents'...' (Fowler 1991: 51). One has to be in ZANU-PF to be accepted as one with national interests at heart. This has resulted in a selective tradition in which liberation history is retold in ways that cement the ruling party's edifice, while excluding and demonising 'others' inside and outside the ruling party, reflecting ZANU-PF's intolerance of diversity.

It is within this framework that ZANU-PF appropriated the liberation struggle to portray itself as the authentic liberator, while PF-ZAPU was disparaged and portrayed as a party of dissidents (Muzondidya 2009), to further justify the use of violence against its supporters. The narrative about who liberated Zimbabwe was dominated by 'the use of Shona pre-colonial heroes and historical moments while marginalising those of the Ndebele' (Muzondidya 2009:184). Phimister cynically notes that 'Zimbabwean history is reduced to a succession of *chimurengas*! never (...) *umvukelas*' (2012: 28).[3]

Throughout Zimbabwe's historical transitions, state media political discourse has been one where the country is repeatedly cast as being under siege from dissidents if not foreign forces. Challenging ZANU-PF is therefore understood to mean challenging Zimbabwe's values and threatening national identity. The small coterie of expert opinion that dominated the news during the Mugabe-Tsvangirai electoral

---

3 'Umvukela' is the siNdebele word for Zimbabwe's war for independence; Chimurenga is the Shona equivalent, which is used officially.

tussles give a glimpse into how Mugabe's ZANU-PF ruling party framed those that challenged its hegemonic dominance. Save for their different names, they all seemed to be reading from the same script – MDC equals sell-outs, equals foreign, equals puppet and equals white. ZANU-PF on the other hand equals national interests, equals home grown, equals black and equals Zimbabwe. They all sought to promote what Ranger (2004) has called 'patriotic history', under which ZANU-PF further manipulated historical memory in ways favourable to itself.

The theme of a country whose national interests and values are under siege provides a useful opportunity for the ruling elite to market itself as a defender of national values and identity. The ruling ZANU-PF's liberation credentials and its control of the public media provides it with a perfect opportunity to consolidate its political legitimacy. Zimbabwe is shown as a victim of external aggression and ZANU-PF as the party that is supposed to defend the country against aggressors. By providing the first line of defence, ZANU-PF wants to be seen as a repository for national values.

Gukurahundi: Mugabe's approach

The Gukurahundi atrocities left a lasting emotional scar, and the Mugabe regime did little to alleviate the suffering of the survivors and victims. As discussed in the preceding section, the suppression of information regarding Gukurahundi has been exacerbated by the rhetoric of ZANU-PF officials who are obsessed with controlling the narrative of what happened during the genocide, thus aggravating the sense of injustice by affected families. Both former president Robert Mugabe and current president Emmerson Mnangagwa failed to create the necessary frameworks and conditions to address the Gukurahundi genocide in a manner that would meet victims' expectations and achieve some closure for individuals, communities and the entire country. Instead, there has been a systematic suppression and a rampant criminalisation of the discussion or evocation of Gukurahundi (Ncube and Siziba 2017: 233) in whatever form. Arrests and intimidation of citizens who evoke Gukurahundi outside the government's acceptable frames betray the desire by both leaders' regimes to control the narrative and all actions pertaining to the Gukurahundi. There has been, evidently, an unwillingness to allow a thoughtful and trusted process to deal with the past, if the government cannot control such a process.

The Unity Accord signed on 22 December 1987 by ZANU-PF and PF-ZAPU was the first missed opportunity as the Gukurahundi massacres were not made part of the final settlement between the two parties. Pertinent questions such as the exhumation and reburial of victims by their families, reparations and other remedies which could have been part of the discussions, were also not addressed. If anything, part of the legacy of the unity accord was to stop completely any public discourse on Gukurahundi.

While several CSOs pursued the subject through various projects in communities and sometimes through civil-society led discussions, this was done outside any framework by the state to tackle the subject. If anything, the state did all it could to thwart such efforts, while doing nothing to help communities deal with the past. This is why even within Zimbabwe's public sphere Gukurahundi was a suppressed subject until the publication of CCJPZ's *Breaking the Silence* in 1997, which ruffled the ZANU-PF establishment's feathers. Gukurahundi was a 'closed chapter' finalised by the Unity Accord between ZANU-PF and PF-ZAPU. Or, as Mugabe put it at Nkomo's funeral in 1999, a regrettable 'moment of madness' from which Zimbabwe had moved on and should not return. Therefore, 'any dialogue on or discussion of Gukurahundi was not only erroneous and ill-advised, but in essence went against the spirit of national unity and reconciliation' (Ncube and Siziba 2017: 232).

Two incidents under Mugabe's rule illustrate this point. The banning of sculptor Owen Maseko's Gukurahundi exhibition in 2010 (Mpofu 2019; Ncube and Siziba 2017) and the arrest of cabinet minister Moses Mzila-Ndlovu and Catholic priest Marko Mnkandla for holding a prayer service for Gukurahundi victims in Lupane, Matabeleland North in 2011. The two cases and many others illustrate official attitudes towards the Gukurahundi. Mzila-Ndlovu was, ironically, one of the ministers appointed to the Organ on National Healing, Reconciliation and Integration in the Government of National Unity (GNU) when he was arrested for the crime of attending a prayer service in memory of victims of the Gukurahundi genocide.[4] Even that position and the framework of the GNU could not provide a safe window for survivors and victims' families to hold the event without offending the system. For successive terms therefore, Mugabe's regime portrayed any attempt to discuss Gukurahundi as a rejection of the unity accord. Suppression of open debate on Gukurahundi and of calls for a resolution was presented as central to preserving the unity accord to ensure peace and stability.

Gukurahundi policy under Mnangagwa: a change of strategy but more of the same

Under Mnangagwa's short reign there has been a realisation that it is not possible to shut down discussions or even protests over Gukurahundi. There has also been an attempt to give the impression that demands are being attended to, or at least have been taken seriously. There are a number of reasons behind this seemingly

---

4   The coalition government made up of ZANU-PF and two factions of the MDC, which ran Zimbabwe between 2009 and 2013, under a Global Political Agreement which was brokered by former South African president Thabo Mbeki. It is a sign of the level of hostility towards any memorialisation of Gukurahundi that the prayer meeting could be broken up during this period.

empathetic shift. First, in a social media age it is impossible to control all spaces of public communication, which is also complicated by a world in which local struggles are quickly taken up by international organisations and global media. Second, upon assuming power, Mnangagwa and his administration needed to project an image of a government that was keen to right the wrongs of the past in order to satisfy some of the constituents that supported the coup (Raftopoulos 2019; Moore 2018; Helliker and Murisa, 2020); the desire to create the image of a new, progressive regime is captured in the terms 'Second Republic' and 'New Dispensation' and the slogan 'Zimbabwe is Open for Business', which became nomenclature in the post-coup period. But that is the extent of the differences between Mnangagwa's rule and that of Mugabe concerning Gukurahundi. For the Mnangagwa regime as well, Gukurahundi is a subject that should not occupy public attention. But failure to prevent that eventuality means that the government must take the initiative in order to control both the pace and the extent of any efforts.

Effectively, the Second Republic has dangled the hope of resolving Gukurahundi to desperate communities, but its actions on the ground, together with its leaders' rhetoric, indicate no change from Mugabe's attitude. Many examples support these observations. The first example relates to how the Mnangagwa regime has treated the institutions that could play an effective role in the resolution of the Gukurahundi; that is, the National Peace and Reconciliation Commission (NPRC) (which we discuss later), traditional leaders and CSOs. The regime has vacillated between empowering the NPRC to deal with Gukurahundi, and offering the same role to Matabeleland chiefs, to the extent that many communities may not be clear now about whom to approach. Following a meeting between President Mnangagwa and traditional leaders in October 2020, the government announced that chiefs would take the lead on the sensitive issue of exhumations and reburials.[5] Apart from undermining the role of the NPRC and apparently duplicating roles, entrusting chiefs with that responsibility is problematic. Generally, chiefs are seen as an extension of the Zimbabwean party-state, there are few instances where they openly contradict the government or the ruling party, mainly because chiefs rely on the ruling government for resources.

Secondly, the Mnangagwa administration's strategy of managing Gukurahundi has constituted the co-optation of regional CSOs, which led to the formation of the Matabeleland Collective (MC) as an umbrella CSO purporting to speak on behalf of the whole of Matebeleland on the Gukurahundi genocide and other pressing issues such as development. In essence, however, the MC initiative became an impediment to communities' efforts to have their grievances addressed in an

---

5 'Chiefs take over Gukurahundi exhumations', *Sunday Mail*, 25 October 2020 [https://www.sundaynews.co.zw/chiefs-take-over-gukurahundi-exhumations/], accessed 30 May 2022.

honest and participatory manner[6] and translated into weakening and incapacitation of CSOs and community-based organisations that could advocate on behalf of survivors and victims' families.

The third example is the rhetoric of the government, which consistently contradicts public commitments to resolve Gukurahundi. A few illustrations will suffice. In 2019, while commenting on xenophobic attacks on Zimbabweans in South African, then deputy Minister of Information and Publicity Energy Mutodi, called Ndebele people refugees living in Zimbabwe because of the magnanimity of their Shona counterparts.[7] If the failure to censure Mutodi was surprising, what is even more disappointing is that ZANU-PF leaders have not relented from such insensitive utterances. The rhetoric played out in full motion at the burial of a chief in Lupane District in May 2022, when ZANU-PF's secretary for administration, Obert Mpofu, reacted to a pastor's call for the need for honesty over Gukurahundi by warning that such talk was intended to cause divisions and to 'destroy'.[8] This insensitive rhetoric is even exhibited by the president himself. In a disturbing video first circulated on social media networks in March 2021, President Mnangagwa is heard warning rural Zimbabweans to rid themselves of 'mapete' (which is Shona for cockroaches). Maseko and Nkomo observe (in this volume) that in 1985 Mnangagwa, who was then Minister of State Security, used similar imagery of cockroaches to describe Ndebele supporters of PF-ZAPU as the Gukurahundi raged. The president's repeat of such language more than two decades later is an indication that no lessons have been learnt from the Gukurahundi. The words were also shocking because such imagery was used by Hutu supremacists to describe their victims in the genocide against the Tutsi in Rwanda; their continued use by the president therefore displays entrenched insensitivity towards victims of Gukurahundi.[9]

We argue, therefore, that Mnangagwa's administration has raised hopes of being serious about resolving Gukurahundi only as a posture. In reality, it has sought to frame and control both the process and the narrative to its advantage, and not in the interest of survivors and victims' families. A consistent factor in this approach is that activities that are to be carried out whether as part of healing processes or establishing the truth must be done under the leadership or guidance of the government and

---

6 'Matabeleland Collective collapses, new coalition formed', *CITE*, 7 February 2020 [https://cite.org.zw/matabeleland-collective-collapses-new-coalition-formed/], accessed 30 May 2022.

7 'Mutodi blasted for labelling Ndebeles refugees', *CITE*, 4 September 2019 [https://cite.org.zw/mutodi-blasted-for-labelling-ndebeles-refugees/], accessed 30 May 2022.

8 'Obert Mpofu offside on Gukurahundi', *CITE*, 30 May 2022 [https://cite.org.zw/obert-mpofu-offside-on-gukurahundi/], accessed 30 May 2022.

9 Mnangagwa was reported by *The Chronicle* as having chillingly said that the supporters of PF-ZAPU deserved to be exterminated using DDT. As they rightly point, the language captured both the disdain for those targeted by the Gukurahundi campaign and also captured the level of dehumanisation and brutality.

institutions that the government controls.

Boraine's framework of transitional justice and the Gukurahundi genocide

In this section, we employ Alex Boraine's (2006) analytical framework for transitional justice (TJ), which explains how countries emerging from a past characterised by an undemocratic, oppressive and violent order may deal with that past. In his seminal article, 'Transitional justice: A holistic interpretation', Boraine outlines an analytical framework built on five pillars of transitional justice: accountability; truth recovery; reconciliation; institutional reform; and reparations. We discuss them in that order to explore whether they can offer useful insights in relation to Gukurahundi and current efforts to address it. Boraine's discussion on accountability, the first pillar in his framework of TJ, lays bare the insurmountable task that Zimbabweans face in trying to resolve the Gukurahundi genocide.

Accountability is not just important in order to correct the wrongs of the past, but especially to make sure they will never be repeated again in future. It must begin with taking stock of what happened and having those responsible account for their actions. This is an important step in establishing the truth through both forensic work and documentation, and through an open, credible system in which victims in particular have confidence. In order to achieve that, a framework must be created to punish those responsible for violations. Such punishment could take the form of legal prosecutions, which would have three advantages: to prevent high-ranking perpetrators from returning to positions of authority; to break the cycle of violence and collective reprisals by punishing those who bore the greatest responsibility; and third, to avoid summary justice. Comparing the NPRC Act (2018) to Rwanda's Articles of Organic Laws (2001), Chigwenya (in this volume) observes that whereas Rwanda's law provides for the prosecution of persons accused of genocidal crimes, in Zimbabwe post-conflict justice is stripped of retributive measures. Eppel (2013) concludes that granting amnesty instead of bringing perpetrators of state violence to justice has resulted in impunity and repeated cycles of politically motivated violence in Zimbabwe. Making those responsible for the Gukurahundi genocide account for their crimes remains an insurmountable task in Zimbabwe, not least because of the issue of incumbency.

Boraine's second pillar, truth recovery, therefore faces daunting obstacles in this scenario, as official reaction to calls for honesty about Gukurahundi injustices have shown in Zimbabwe. As Eppel (2013) further points out, ZANU-PF's approach is that in Matebeleland, 'healing' must take place without 'revealing'. Obert Mpofu's passionate pushback against calls for truth-telling at the chief's funeral must be placed in this context. Sadly, many such utterances such as then Vice-

President Report Phelekezela Mphoko's speech at the funeral of the first chairman of the NPRC, Cyril Ndebele (which we explain in the last section), indicate that Mpofu's outburst is currency in ZANU-PF as far as resolution of Gukurahundi is concerned. Boraine's call for a mechanism to facilitate truth-telling as part of dealing with the past poses one of the biggest challenges standing in the way of resolving the Gukurahundi genocide. ZANU-PF has, over the years, successfully presented a scenario in which reconciliation and justice are mutually exclusive in as far as Gukurahundi is concerned (Eppel 2013). Within that, the idea that revealing the truth or calling for the truth serves no other purpose than to open old wounds, threaten the unity accord, and undermine peace, has become a hegemonic position.

To put this in perspective, let us revisit the legacy of the commander of the Fifth Brigade, Perence Shiri, who died in July 2020. Shiri was a top ZANU-PF official and also held the influential portfolio of Minister of Lands and Agriculture in Mnangagwa's government at the time of his death, having been one of the most senior army leaders at the time of the coup against Mugabe. Although his starring role in the Gukurahundi genocide was well-known, Shiri managed to rise to the rank of Air Marshall, the overall in command of Zimbabwe's Air Force. When he died, several of Shiri's allies implored people to stop associating the former commander's name with Gukurahundi and to focus on forgiveness instead of opening old wounds.[10] Forgiveness and reconciliation were, in this narrative, not possible if people insisted on what Boraine calls 'truth recovery'.

Boraine argues that true reconciliation, the third of his five pillars, can only be achieved if it is victim-centred. Victims should be confident that their grievances occupy centre stage in the process and are addressed not swept aside. We may go further and posit that even if they completely reject all the solutions that are suggested, they should still be listened to, if not indulged. In her review of the mechanisms for TJ under Zimbabwe's Global Political Agreement, Eppel (2013) demonstrates that a major challenge was the failure to make victims' demands central to official processes. Using as an example the famous Mothers of the Plaza de Mayo in Argentina's capital Buenos Aires, who have marched every week since 1977 demanding to know the truth about their children who were disappeared during the period of military repression in that country, Eppel emphasises that it is also the legitimate choice of victims to remain un-reconciled and to refuse to forgive their perpetrators even when they accept resolutions. In the case of the Gukurahundi, victims' cries about exhumations and reburials, compensation, and justice are given less priority than, seemingly, the perpetrators' calls for reconciliation and cohesion.

---

10 'Mliswa says Mnangagwa not to blame for Gukurahundi massacres', *Nehanda Radio*, 18 January 2017 [https://nehandaradio.com/2017/01/17/mliswa-says-mnangagwa-not-blame-gukurahundi-massacres/] accessed 30 May 2022

There is no attempt under the current scenario to seek true reconciliation based on the needs of those who were victims of the genocide, which Boraine argues is necessary to achieve transitional justice.

Boraine's fourth pillar, institutional reform, is important in meeting the mechanisms of the other pillars in his framework. Zimbabwe's current attempt to address the Gukurahundi genocide is faltering largely as a result of its weak institutions. As we argue below, while the NPRC has a constitutional mandate, its failure to act independently of the ruling government undermines its ability to deliver on that mandate. Using the South African TRC as a benchmark, Boraine argues that although individual hearings are an important step in establishing the truth, truth commissions must also hold institutional hearings. In the South African case, the TRC called heads of institutions particularly the army and the police to explain their actions and the role those institutions played in committing injustices. This is important for two reasons; to hold institutions that were responsible for the repression of citizens to account and make them explain the role they played in the painful past, and second, to make them explain how they see their role in the future. In Zimbabwe, such an approach is necessary because outside the Fifth Brigade itself, the role of other state security organs such as the police and central intelligence remains opaque at best.

Perhaps one of the thorniest issues in resolving the Gukurahundi under both Mugabe and Mnangagwa is the issue of compensation of victims and survivors. Boraine's fifth pillar, reparations, should be viewed as the most tangible manifestation of the state's efforts to remedy the harm suffered by victims. In Zimbabwe, the harm includes loss of homes and livelihoods, rape, physical harm including loss of limbs and loss of life, and irreparable damage to families and also to communities. One of the most emotional losses is captured in CCJPZ's ground breaking report:

> The … Fifth Brigade soldiers arrived and ordered my husband to carry all the chairs, a table, bed, blankets, clothes and put them in one room. They also took our cash – we had $1500 saved, to buy a scotch cart. They then set fire to the hut and burnt all our property … They accused my husband of having a gun, which he did not have. They shot at him. The first two times, they missed, but the third time they shot him in the stomach and killed him. They then beat me very hard, even though I was pregnant. I told them I was pregnant, and they told me I should not have children for the whole of Zimbabwe… they hit me on the stomach with the butt of the gun. The unborn child broke into pieces in my stomach. The baby boy died inside. It was God's desire that I did not die too. The child was born afterwards, piece by piece. A head alone, then a leg, an arm, the body – piece by piece (CCJPZ 1997: 52).

Subsequently, many development failures in regions that suffered the Gukurahundi can be traced to that experience (Ndlovu-Gatsheni 2012), meaning that the losses have been passed down to other generations. Furthermore, nothing tangible in the form of compensation or reparation is offered as such talk is shot down by authorities, who emphasise the preservation of the unity accord and peace.

There are several challenges to meeting the pillars of Boraine's framework for TJ, not least because of the time that has lapsed, as Eppel (2013) meticulously explains. The attitude of the current government has already been explained and is unlikely to change. However, even where there could be some will it may be difficult, for instance, to provide reparations at individual level because many victims may not be in a position to prove, let alone quantify their losses now. Furthermore, while perpetrators may be known at the top level, individual perpetrators – the soldiers and other security details who terrorised villagers – may be difficult to identify. In terms of reparations, however, Eppel (2013) has suggested that in many meetings with CSOs, victims have raised the issue of reparations at a community level, such as meeting development expectations, providing infrastructure and opportunities, and meeting other societal demands.

The National Peace and Reconciliation Commission

The National Peace and Reconciliation Commission (NPRC) should be in a position to address some of the issues that we have raised so far. The commission is one of the five independent commissions established in terms of Chapter 12 of the Constitution which was adopted in 2013. The objectives of the NPRC commission are stated in section 252a-j. Among these objectives, a), b), and c) relate closely to the work of the commission in promoting justice, healing and reconciliation. The NPRC is meant 'to bring about national reconciliation by encouraging people to tell the truth about the past and facilitating the making of amends and the provision of justice.' Notably, there is no mention of Gukurahundi in the stated objectives of the NPRC, it is merely referred to as 'the past' or in some cases 'the conflict' (Part 6, section 252a & c). We see this as a weakness that is tantamount to repeating the mistake that was made in the unity accord. As Ruhanya and Gumbo also argue in this volume, the magnitude of the Gukurahundi genocide is such that it requires a commission to exclusively deal with it and call it for what it is. The failure to provide for that means that the Gukurahundi genocide is generalised and dealt with as one of many issues generally covered in the objectives of the NPRC. In June 2021, the NPRC's new self-appointed spokesman, Obert Gutu, caused anger when he dismissed the Gukurahundi genocide as 'a small, tiny fraction of the commission's mandate'.[11]

---

11 'Fury as Obert Gutu calls Gukurahundi massacres 'a small tiny fraction'', *ZimLive*, 23 June 2021, https://www.zimlive.com/2021/06/fury-as-obert-gutu-calls-gukurahundi-massacres-a-small-tiny-fraction/ [accessed 15 May 2022]

Besides failure to outline a clear programme for dealing with Gukurahundi, the calibre of commissioners is therefore also questionable, and highlights further the commission's complicated relationship with the ruling government, which constantly dictates the boundaries within which the commission should operate. While our focus is the current government, it is worth noting that under Mugabe's leadership, the NPRC faced similar challenges. As highlighted above, at the funeral of former NPRC chairman Cyril Ndebele, then Vice-President Mphoko painstakingly explained how he (as Vice-President) had dictated to Commissioner Ndebele the issues to focus on, among which he said was the need 'to tackle the Gukurahundi issue in a manner that did not emphasise finger-pointing'. Among other thorny issues, Mphoko explained that he had directed the NPRC not to address what he called 'other scars'. These scars included demands for an apology from President Mugabe, which Mphoko declared would never happen. Becoming more condescending, Mphoko further revealed that President Mugabe had previously appointed a three-man team headed by former Matabeleland North Governor Welshman Mabhena, but that team was forced to stop working after people began raising the issue of compensation to victims of Gukurahundi.[12] Mphoko's speech was revealing in terms of the control that the government sought to exert and actually exerts on the NPRC.[13] Under President Mnangagwa, the NPRC has been fairly visible but not much has been achieved despite numerous outreach meetings and pronouncements on issues to be done.

For instance, in October 2019, the NPRC announced that it was preparing for exhumations and reburials of victims of the Gukurahundi. NPRC chairman Sello Nare revealed in an address to chiefs from Matabeleland the decision to begin this work followed a meeting with the president, in which it was agreed that exhumations should start as soon as possible. Nare's emphasis that, 'The involvement of the president gives us a positive indication that the process should kick off as soon as possible' should be seen as worrying.[14] On the surface, it was meant to reassure chiefs and other stakeholders that there were no stumbling blocks anymore to this critical issue. The underlying discourse, however, was that exhumations and reburials could not proceed without the consent and direction of

---

12 'Gukurahundi dominates Ndebele funeral' *Newsday*, 13 October 2016 [https://www.newsday.co.zw/2016/10/gukurahundi-dominates-ndebele-funeral/] accessed 30 May 2022

13 Alexander (2021) narrates that the composition of the NPRC was met with hostility in Matebeleland over the lack of representation from the region. The first public meetings were disrupted by activists who lamented that only one out of eight commissioners was Ndebele. To some, this suggested that perpetrators or 'their siblings' (Alexander 2021: 779) had been appointed to deal with the genocide. Against this background, retaining Gutu was therefore insensitive.

14 'NPRC prepares for Gukurahundi victims' exhumations, reburials' *Chronicle*, 10 October 2019 [https://www.chronicle.co.zw/nprc-prepares-for-gukurahundi-victims-exhumations-reburials/] accessed 30 May 2022.

the president or his government.

Another major shortcoming of the NPRC is inherent in section 251(1) of the constitution where a time span of 10 years is set for existence of the Commission. Considering that the NPRC started in August 2013, it means that in the absence of an amendment, the lifespan of the NPRC is about to come to an end. This would be unfortunate as there are no discernible achievements on national healing by the Commission, never mind the specific Gukurahundi thorny justice issues which remain unresolved.

Conclusion

The shadow cast by the Gukurahundi genocide on Zimbabwe is unlikely to be vanquished outside a sincere process in which the interests of survivors and victims or their families are placed ahead of those of the ruling elite, as is the case with current endeavours. Despite its many problems, Mnangagwa's new dispensation promised a new chapter in which such an approach could be adopted. But Mnangagwa's republic suffers from the same insecurities that characterised Mugabe's rule and is sadly run by most of the people who were in senior positions during the Gukurahundi and in much of Mugabe's rule. This makes any chances of a fair and satisfying resolution of the Gukurahundi genocide quite grim. None of the efforts thus far meet any of Boraine's framework and this is unlikely to change as long as the perpetrators of the genocide remain in power. But more exposure of the crimes of the Gukurahundi, including academic research and documentary films have meant that attempts to suppress it have been futile. This could yet force the government into a more sincere effort to find finality, if only to remove this yoke from its neck.

2

'Bandwagoning or Intended Action?': Examining Zimbabwe's Legal Framework on Peacebuilding

Cynthia Chigwenya

Introduction

Since independence, Zimbabwe has recorded destabilising incidents of violent conflicts, with scholars such as Benyera (2014) dubbing the nation 'a chronically violent state.' These conflicts include the killing of about 20,000 civilians between 1983 and 1987 during an operation known as Gukurahundi; the food riots in 1998; fast-tracked land reform since 2000, which resulted in violence against white farmers; and continuous electoral violence against opposition parties and civilians dating back to the early 2000s. While land expropriation is primarily viewed as violence against white farmers, there were displacements of farmworkers, some of whom moved to informal settlements and later became victims again of Murambatsvina.

The 2005 Operation Murambatsvina[1] was characterised by the forceful removal of inhabitants of places the state demarcated as slum areas across the country in an alleged bid to restore order in urban cities. However, Human Rights Watch hints at a politicised Operation Murambatsvina, with a targeted population and expected political outcome by the executioners. Although violations against farmworkers, and victims of Murambatsvina, are not the foci of the chapter, they substantiate Benyera's claim and underscore a continued loss of lives, homes, and livelihoods through monopolised violence. Further, the post-March 2008 contested election period was defined by widespread state-orchestrated violence, and the same *modus*

---

1 Murambatsvina, loosely translated, means clear the filth or drive out the rubbish. (Potts, 2006)

operandi was employed in the following electoral periods.

The mass human rights violations that occurred during these varied phases remain unaccounted for, and much of the work to address the past has predominantly been driven by community leaders and civil society organisations (CSOs), with little support from the government. In January 2018, however, Zimbabwe witnessed a shift in domestic policy as the parliament and the incumbent president enacted the National Peace and Reconciliation Bill into law, which is the National Peace and Reconciliation Commission Act (NPRC Act). Nhengu and Murairwa (2020) comment that the ratification of the Bill had stalled since 2008 as it was part of the post-conflict reconstruction system proposed under Zimbabwe's Global Political Agreement (GPA).

Despite ratification challenges, the NPRC Act was eventually enacted, and it stands as the only legal framework on peacebuilding and reconciliation. This chapter seeks to explore this Act against the enormous task of redressing various conflicts and reconciling the Zimbabwean society. Applying the provisions of the NPRA in real-life situations to produce practical and real remedies and results for people helps to move the NPRA from being a theoretical policy framework into a real and practical tool to resolve problems associated with Zimbabwe's violent past.

The rationale for centering this chapter mainly on the NPRC Act's provisions is that the terms have indisputable implications on how this Act is applied. In reference to the title, the concept of bandwagoning is borrowed from the psychological phenomenon of adopting certain behaviours, styles, or attitudes because others are doing so. In this context, bandwagoning connotes the pursuit of deficient peacebuilding initiatives for reasons including calculated political moves, aimed at boosting democratic credentials rather than victim-oriented ones. This study will use examples from other post-conflict contexts in Africa to establish any norms between the NPRC Act, laws adopted in Rwanda and practices in neighbouring South Africa. Lastly, the chapter offers recommendations on prerequisites for enhanced efficacy of the NPRC Act.

Understanding post-conflict peacebuilding

This section aims to place this research within international normative processes of resolving conflicts; therefore, the existing literature on post-conflict peacebuilding will be explored. Given the cyclical nature of Zimbabwe's history of violence (Dzimiri, Runhare & Mazorodze, 2014), post-conflict herein is based on the conclusion of singular events rather than a complete end of violence followed by durable peace. The normative peacebuilding processes are associated with the end of the Cold War, which brought a shift of focus from peacekeeping to peacebuilding in international conflict management. The move towards global governance is also noted by scholars such as Bellamy (2010), who remarks that 'there is broad agreement nowadays that the international community has a responsibility to help states and societies to rebuild after war'. Although the post-modern paradigm and scholars such as Rita Abrahamsen challenge the orthodoxy that powerful states should intervene, one cannot dismiss the advantages of global effort towards peacebuilding.

Scholarly debates aside, Uvin (2002) notes that the differences between peacekeeping and peacebuilding are that the former prevents the resumption of fighting following a conflict, whereas the latter is centred on creating societal change to address its root causes. Peacebuilding is of particular interest to this publication. For Murambadoro (2015), peacebuilding is an activity of fostering non-violence, justice, and stability in a conflict-stricken community. The existing literature on peacebuilding presents two categories of peace, namely, positive peace and negative peace. The latter exists when there is no direct violence and is secured by putting an end to the immediate source of violence. Therefore, negative peace offers immediate relief to conflict by using external actors to stop the conflicting parties from physically fighting. However, it is limited in establishing durable solutions to prevent further conflicts.

In contrast, positive peace involves processes that enable conflicting parties to develop a desirable relationship that allows them to resolve their disputes through peaceful means. Brounéus (2008) argues that positive peace offers long-term relief to conflict because it instils practices and processes that transform negative attitudes, behaviours, and perceptions, which harbour conflict. Positive peace includes psychosocial attributes such as fostering relations so that the offenders and survivors can reconcile and live harmoniously over time. An example of positive peace in practice is the case of Rwanda in 2003, where the National Prison Fellowship brought together former perpetrators and survivors of the 1994 genocide to live together in reconciliation villages, known as *imidugudu* as part of reintegration, as stated by Mafeza (2013).

In Zimbabwe's case, however, one can argue that neither amnesties including the Indemnity and Compensation Act of 1975, the Amnesty Ordinance of 1979, and the General Pardon Act of 1980 nor accords such as the Lancaster House Agreement of 1979, provided durable solutions to prevent further conflict. This assertion is substantiated by the clashing of former combatants of the Zimbabwe African National Liberation Army (ZANLA) and the Zimbabwe People's Revolutionary Army (ZIPRA) in 1981 (Doran, 2017), the occurrence of Gukurahundi massacres and the war for land reclamation from the white minority, also known as the third *chimurenga*. In sum, treaties such as the Lancaster House Agreement of 1979 and the Unity Accord of 1987 provided short-term solutions. Thus, they are classified herein as negative peace.

Against this backdrop, this chapter explores the provisions of the NPRA in tandem with facilitating the establishment of positive peace within the Zimbabwean society. Peacebuilding in this chapter shall refer to a range of diverse efforts by the government and civil society to redress the impacts and underlying causes of altercations before, during, and after violent conflicts. Peacebuilding mechanisms after singular conflicts will be assessed in line with establishing positive peace, and the state's role is of primary interest.

International frameworks: the Genocide Convention

In relation to normative processes that ensue series of violent and protracted conflicts, the United Nations General Assembly's adoption of the Convention on the Prevention and Punishment of the Crime of Genocide (UNCPPCG) in 1948 – an accord that was approved out of the intention to redress the aftermath of the Holocaust is one of the cornerstone frameworks on redressing violence, particularly mass killings. The UNCPPCG stipulates that genocide is a crime under international law,[2] meaning that the act is categorised under the most heinous of human rights and humanitarian law violations.

Although Article II of the UNCPPCG (1948) stipulates that genocide refers to any of the following acts committed with intent to destroy, in whole or in part, a national, ethnic, racial, or religious group, the question of whether the Gukurahundi massacres can be defined as such remains highly contested. Further, Zimbabwe's NPRC Act of 2018 does not criminalise the Gukurahundi massacres, suggesting that retributive justice (punitive) is not one of the methods through which this legal framework aims to deliver peace. In contrast, Rwanda's Organic Law no. 40 of 2001, which followed the Constitutional Court ruling N° 47/11.02/00, declares that the purpose of the Organic Law (2001) is to organise the trial of persons prosecuted for having, between 1 October 1990, and 31 December 1994, committed acts qualified and punished by the penal code, which constitute:

(a) either crimes of genocide or crimes against humanity as defined by the Convention of December 9, 1948, preventing and punishing the crime of genocide, by the Geneva Convention of August 12, 1949, relating to protecting civil persons in wartime and the additional protocols, as well as in the Convention of November 26, 1968, on imprescriptibly of war crimes and crimes against humanity;

or

(b) offences aimed at in the penal code, which according to the charges by the Public prosecution or the evidences for the prosecution or even what admits

---

2 Lemkin (1947) 'Genocide as a Crime under International Law.'

the defendant, were committed with the intention of perpetrating genocide or crimes against humanity (Organic Law, 2001: Article I).

Rwanda's Organic Law delineates the specific crimes it is aimed to resolve. Also, the Organic Law declares that the definition of genocide in Rwanda will be in accordance with the Convention of 9 December 1948, which is the UNCPPCG. This shows that post-conflict peacebuilding in Rwanda, at least on paper, is in line with the international provisions and norms of conflict resolution. By defining the mass killings of 1994 as crimes, there is a legal basis to initiate retributive justice, which is concerned with crime as a violation of the law and relies on punishment and correctional action for wrongdoing.

The National Peace and Reconciliation Commission (NPRC) Act

In contrast to the Organic Law, Zimbabwe's National Peace and Reconciliation Commission (NPRC) Act was enacted in 2018, in line with Sections 251 and 253 of its Constitution (as amended in 2013), which provide for the establishment of a National Peace and Reconciliation Commission. This constitutional amendment was adopted as part of the terms of the Global Political Agreement signed by the three main political parties in the Government of National Unity in 2008. Part I of the NPRC Act (2018) states that its purpose is to put the Commission – NPRC – into operation, 'to confer additional jurisdiction on the Commission, including its investigative powers; and to provide for the terms of office.'

Part II of the NPRC Act details its functions, which are to ensure post-conflict justice, healing and reconciliation, to develop and implement programmes to promote national unity, and to bring about national reconciliation by encouraging people to tell the truth. The differences between the opening Articles of the Organic Laws (2001) and the NPRC Act (2018) are the main functions of these legal frameworks. The Organic Law, on the one hand, mandates organising the trial of persons prosecuted for having committed genocidal crimes, thereby accentuating the foremost response to the crime of genocide, which is retributive and punitive. The NPRC Act, on the other hand, aims to ensure post-conflict justice without incorporating retributive measures against perpetrators. This non-judicial approach ill-aligns the NPRC Act with the UNCPPCG as an international framework.

The NPRC Act juxtaposed with Rwanda's Organic Law

There are several themes which this study can explore to assess the differences between post-conflict resolution in Rwanda and Zimbabwe through the Organic Laws and the NPRC Act, respectively. Harris and Fiske (2009) define dehumanisation as perceiving a person as non-human in ways such as reducing them to an animal, or a sub-human and erasure of empathy; it is one of the methods that are common to the Rwandese and Zimbabwean cases. The warfare tactics employed during Gukurahundi such as torture, rape, and extreme humiliation were meant to debase the victims, their families, and their communities; in some cases, victims were forced to commit bestiality, witnessed by their family and community members (Doran, 2017). Moreover, the term *gukurahundi* itself refers to 'the first rain that washes away the chaff before the spring,' connoting worthlessness hence the need to be discarded or washed away.

Similarly, Raisov and Simsek (2018) observe that in the years leading to and during the Rwandan genocide, Tutsis were referred to on media platforms as *inyezi*, meaning cockroaches or derogatorily called snakes whose heads had to be cut off or tall trees; which needed to be 'trimmed.' Against this backdrop, the Organic Laws and the NPRC Act ought to address, in theory, and practice, the emotional damages of conflict such as dehumanisation. According to Article 72 of the Organic Law (2001), persons found guilty of dehumanisation are liable to the loss of civil rights such as the right to vote. This measure can be classified under retributive justice and initiatives aimed at deterring the recurrence of similar offences. In the NPRC Act's case, however, dehumanisation is not legislated. The homogenisation of peacebuilding without dissecting the impacts of dehumanising acts and language presents a deficiency in achieving positive peace.

Another perceptible difference between the NPRC Act and the Organic Law are the implementing agencies, making institutional reforms an important theme in analysing the provisions and applications of these legal frameworks. Berkeley and Schrage (1986) argue that the perpetrators of the Gukurahundi massacres were the Fifth Brigade, a special unit of the military, whose chain of command bypassed the intermediate levels observed by the rest of the army. The Fifth Brigade answered to then Prime Minister, Robert Mugabe, who later became the president for over 35 years. The lack of institutional reform in Zimbabwe's political leadership, which has been dominated by the ZANU-PF party, has implications on peacebuilding. In relation to retributive justice, which views the state as the custodian of the rights of its citizens, and the administer of punishment where the criminal code is flouted (Corey & Joireman, 2004), the delay in legislative processes such as enacting the NPR Bill into law meant that peacebuilding initiatives lacked legal grounding.

In Rwanda's case, the end of the genocide marked a complete shift in political affairs; Mamdani (2001) notes that the Rwandan Patriotic Front's (RPF) victory set off a massive exodus of Hutus from Rwanda.' By July 1994, RPF had eventually defeated the Rwandan government forces, thereby forcing the interim government to flee into Zaire, and ending the genocide. One can note a total change in Rwanda's political governance, which has been dominated by the 'liberating' RPF party since

1994. As a result, the ruling RPF could adopt an assertive and retributive justice system, as provided by the amended Constitution and the Organic Law, whose main purpose, as articulated in Article I, is to prosecute.

Adding to the challenge of limited institutional reforms, Zimbabwe's NPRC Act has its own shortcomings. Section 242(1), (2) of Zimbabwe's Constitution (2013) states that the Chairperson of the NPRC and at least eight of the twelve committee members must be appointed by the president. Coltart (2018) discloses that the current President, Emmerson Mnangagwa and his Deputy, the retired army general Constantino Chiwenga were directly involved in Gukurahundi. This argument does not only implicate the current leadership; it presents the environment in which the NPRC Act is implemented as inconducive for achieving positive peace. Section 242(1), (2) of Zimbabwe's Constitution puts the NPR Commission's autonomy at risk of political interference, while the concept of punitive justice might remain elusive as the NPRC Act does not stipulate any punishable crimes.

Further, there are challenges relating to memorialisation, which Amadiume and An-Na'im (2000) define as the organisation of collective events in a manner that is not only remembered but influential. Memorialisation activities include commemorative gatherings, church services, funerals, exhumations, and reburials, and the building of places of remembrance such as museums and monuments. These activities have the potential to aid reconciliation; places of remembrance can be understood in tandem with acknowledgement of atrocities and honouring the dead. Throughout Zimbabwe, several places where significant historical events occurred have been recognised. However, the memory of Gukurahundi was not preserved at the national level, whereas there are numerous memorial centres in Rwanda with six major ones comprising of *inter alia*, Nyamata, Murambi, Ntarama, and the Kigali Genocide Centre.

Transitional Justice: a conceptual framework

Although the previous section, which juxtaposed the NPRC Act with Rwanda's Organic Law, found the former wanting in retributive justice, which limits its alignment with the UNCPPCG. Zimbabwe's NPRC Act (2018) possesses aspects of the concept of transitional justice. The United Nations (2010) states that 'transitional justice consists of both judicial and non-judicial mechanisms, including prosecution initiatives, facilitating initiatives in respect of the right to truth, delivering reparations, institutional reform and national consultations. Mainstream literature identifies criminal prosecutions, truth commissions, reparations and institutional reform as measures that can be used to deliver transitional justice. The definition of transitional justice in this study is based on both the needs and expectations of victims to whom justice is owed, albeit with a focus on restoring peace in the Zimbabwean society.

The judicial mechanisms referenced from the UN's Transitional Justice Framework (2010) include using the criminal justice system with the intent to: facilitate the rehabilitation of offenders; prevent recidivism; provide moral support for victims; and ensure that criminal proceedings are fair. It follows that judicial transitional justice mechanisms comprise both restorative measures, concerned with crime as a violation of the law and relies on punishment and correctional action for wrongdoing, and retributive mechanisms, administered as a corrective measure that is due to the state, in its capacity as the custodian of the rights of its citizens (Corey & Joireman, 2004). Since the NPRC Act does not criminalise the incidents of violence it is mandated to redress; this conceptual framework will assess the extent to which it aligns with the normative non-judicial measures such as reconciliation, reparations and amnesty.

1.   *Reconciliation*

There are complexities associated with reconciliation as a concept; however, the existing literature shows a consensus that reconciliation involves the restoration of fractured relationships. A renowned example is South Africa's Truth and Reconciliation Commission (TRC), which was set up to address the legacies of the racially segregating apartheid regime through truth-telling (Graybill, 1999). According to the chairperson of the TRC, Archbishop Desmond Tutu (1998), reconciliation is both an ongoing process and an end result, which can be achieved through methods such as truth-telling, reparations, acknowledgement of the other, forgiveness, testimonies, and dialogues. The extent to which these measures are integrated into the NPRC Act's provisions will be explored in the following sections.

2.   *Reparations*

Another concept of restorative transitional justice is reparations i.e. monetary or material compensation offered to victims to acknowledge injustices, permeate the imbalances created by the effects of violence and foster social solidarity (Benyera, 2014). In the African context, reparative initiatives have been established in countries such as South Africa, Sierra Leone, and Morocco after mass human rights violations or conflicts. In South Africa, the President's Fund that was established in 1995 in line with recommendations of the TRC, in Sierra Leone, a Special War Fund for Victims (SWFV) started operations in 2009 and gave medical support to victims of war and sexual violence; while Morocco's reparation programme paid collective reparations to approximately 16,000 individuals and/or families (Fernandez, 1999; Hayner, 2011; Slyomovics). Further, Reyntjens (2013) states that victims of the Rwandan genocide receive a reparative grant known as FARG. The incorporation of this concept in the NPRC Act will be used to evaluate this legal framework against its mandate.

3. *Amnesty*

Finally, on non-judicial methods is the use of amnesty in transitional justice. Amnesty generally refers to an official pardon granted by the state to individuals or groups convicted of offences; however, Kayitana (2017) argues that they are a preferred political technique for enabling transitions from authoritarian rule. The purpose of this political compromise is to create conditions for truth-telling and reconciliation; thus, these concepts interrelate. Mashingaidze (2021) recounts that in Zimbabwe, the Amnesty Ordinance of 1979, the General Pardon Act of 1980 and the in April 1988 amnesty without trial were granted. Despite the assumed advantages of amnesties, such as encouraging truth-telling, they will be measured herein in line with ensuring positive peace.

An overview of state-led peacebuilding initiatives

An overview of existing and previous state-led peacebuilding initiatives is relevant in assessing the context in which the NPRC Act was enacted and will be implemented. Previous initiatives provide a basis for juxtaposing the strength and shortfalls of this NPC Act.

1. *The Unity Accord of 1987*

The Unity Accord is a legal agreement, which is associated with the 'ending' of the Gukurahundi massacres that resulted in the death of approximately 20,000 civilians between 1983 and 1987 (Murambadoro, 2015). The signing of the Unity Accord by ZAPU and ZANU-PF political actors, including Joshua Nkomo and Robert Mugabe, respectively, was followed by amnesty ordinances of 1988 under which amnesty without trial was granted to perpetrators, including those of the Gukurahundi atrocities. Therefore, amnesty as a transitional justice method laid the foundation for peacebuilding in newly independent Zimbabwe. However, this initiative did not address the root causes of the Gukurahundi conflict; more specifically, ethnic tensions amongst the black community remained unresolved hence the exploration of the NPRC Acts' potential to resolve the Gukurahundi massacres.

In reference to the main categories, namely positive and negative peace, the Unity Accord provided an ephemeral solution to violence in post-independence Zimbabwe; thus, it is classified herein as a negative peace initiative. However, the annual Unity Day celebrations on 22 December are the only state-led ceremony associated with Gukurahundi. In relation, Doran (2017) comments that the media plays an ambiguous role in appreciating the conflictual nature of Gukurahundi, which led to the need to sign the unity accord. Based on an experiential perspective, during the Unity Day festivities, it is difficult to distinguish the victims from the offenders since commemorations are politicised, with the ruling party taking the spotlight.

2. Organ for National Healing, Reconciliation, and Integration (ONHRI)

Zimbabwe's Organ for National Healing, Reconciliation, and Integration (ONHRI) was established under Article 7.1 (c) of the Global Political Agreement (GPA) and annexed in the amended Constitution of Zimbabwe (2013). The structure of ONHRI mirrored the composition of the signatories of the GPA, namely, ZANU-PF, Movement for Democratic Change-Tsvangirai (MDC-T) and Movement for Democratic Change (MDC-M).[3] At its inception, it was composed of three government representatives from these political parties, namely, John Landa Nkomo (ZANU-PF), who was the chairperson; and two co-ministers, Sekai Holland (MDC-T) and Gibson Sibanda (MDC-M) (ONHRI, 2014). The following projects were implemented under ONHRI.

(a) The History of Conflict in Zimbabwe Research Project

Under the History of Conflict in Zimbabwe Research Project, co-ordinated in collaboration with the Midlands State University (MSU), ONHRI called to attention the need to develop a database of empirical studies on the history, trends, extent, and status of conflicts in Zimbabwe. Additionally, this project sought to examine how Zimbabwe has historically dealt with its conflicts and ultimately draw lessons in conflict prevention, resolution, and reconstruction (ONHRI, 2014). These resolutions suggest a long-term relief to conflict; thus, they qualify as positive peacebuilding initiatives, dependant on effective implementation.

(b) Zimbabwe National Policy Framework for Peace and Reconciliation (ZNPFPR)

In 2012, ONHRI launched the Zimbabwe National Policy Framework for Peace and Reconciliation (ZNPFPR), which called for the establishment of the independent National Peace and Reconciliation Commission (NPRC) that is mandated by the Act that this study explores. The provisions of the ZNPFPR that the NPRC ought to have supportive structures at national, provincial, district, and village levels to ensure the establishment of an enabling environment in which peacebuilding dialogues can be facilitated among civilians. Following the enactment of the NPRC Bill into law in 2018, the Commission was institutionalised, and investigations into periods of conflict have been initiated despite criticisms of inefficiency and unrepresentativeness of the victims' needs and scepticism of the

---

3 MDC-M was an acronym coined by the media to distinguish it from the wing of the party led by Tsvangirai, Mutambara insisted, however, that his faction was the MDC.

NPRC's real intentions.

(c) Traditional Mechanisms, Approaches and Systems for Peacebuilding, Conflict Resolution and Reconciliation (TMASCRR)

Complementing the establishment of ZNPFPR in 2012, ONHRI set up the Traditional Mechanisms, Approaches and Systems for Peacebuilding, Conflict Resolution and Reconciliation (TMASCRR). The TMASCRR aligns with the growing debate that is advanced by scholars including Murambadoro (2015) and Benyera (2014) on the need to explore traditional-based mechanisms to redress injustices and ensure reconciliation. These scholars suggest the incorporation of practices such as *nyaradzo*, traditional memorial ceremonies, *ngozi* (an avenging spirit) and *gwava* (bringing the deceased's spirit back to the realm of the living).

Overall, traditional justice practises, particularly reburials, relate to the restoration of dignity and redressing dehumanisation or inhumane treatment. However, these mechanisms are not stipulated in the NPRC Act's provisions; they are not institutionalised in Zimbabwe's legal framework, the NPRC Act. ONHRI's TMASCRR project dating to 2012 highlights cognisance, yet the NPRC Act of 2018 makes no provisions for incorporating traditional methods of peacebuilding. ONHRI's initiatives evince that Zimbabwe's peacebuilding process is not limited by a lack of policies and frameworks but ineffective implementation.

Despite the potential of traditional mechanisms in enhancing restorative justice, Benyera (2014) criticises ONHRI for inefficiency due to factors such as a 'too general and ambitious mandate', limited commitment and lumping together (too many) conflict-related issues. These challenges short circuit the possibility of establishing positive peace in Zimbabwe. Apart from structural challenges, the United Nations Development Programme (UNDP) report (2014) noted that during planning, implementation and reporting on ONHRI's programmes, a lot of time was spent balancing the interests of either ZANU-PF, MDC-M, or MDC-T (the political parties that negotiated its establishment). This suggests that from the onset, political interests interfered, causing issues of transitional justice to be sensitised within the organ that laid the foundation for the NPRC and its governing Act, the NPRA of 2018.

The NPRC Act and its mammoth task

Given that this study has explored the NPRC Act juxtaposed with Rwanda's Organic Law and the UNCPPCG and presented non-judicial measures of transitional justice as more applicable to Zimbabwe since its legal framework is not punitive, this section will assess the Act in line with reconciliation, reparation, amnesty, and positive peace. Further, reference will be made to identified themes, including dehumanisation, institutional reforms, and memorialisation. The concepts and themes aim to show the practicality of the NPRC Act in realising restorative justice, which is its primary mandate in the absence of retribution.

The main purpose of the NPRC Act (2018) is 'to put the National Peace and Reconciliation Commission (NPRC) into operation; to confer additional jurisdiction on the Commission, including its investigative powers; and to provide for the terms of office.' The Act operates in line with the constitutional mandate to establish a Commission. Commissions of inquiry may investigate the conduct of any civil servant or inquire into the management of departments of public service; their primary purpose is to investigate, to educate, and to inform the society (Gomery, 2005). However, Gomery (2005) explains further that the tenets of a commission, once appointed, are that it must have a high degree of independence and autonomy. This method of transitional justice has been applied widely, with South Africa's TRC being one of the renowned commissions, while in Rwanda's case, the International Commission of Investigation of Human Rights Violations was established pursuant to the UN Security Council Resolution 1013 (United Nations, 1995). Prior to the establishment of the NPRC, Zimbabwe has had Commissions of Inquiries into Gukurahundi.

Eppel and Raftopoulos (2009) refer to the 1982 Dumbutshena Commission of Inquiry into events surrounding the Entumbane clashes between the ZIPRA and ZANLA ex-combatants; and the 1983 Commission of Inquiry into the Matabeleland Disturbances. The latter is commonly known as the Chihambakwe Commission. Although commissions of inquiry excel in fact-finding, which is useful in truth-telling and reconciliation, as argued Tutu, the question is: to what extent do commissions of inquiry contribute to peacebuilding? Zimbabwe's case highlights some of the pitfalls of this method. Following the inquisitions of the Dumbutshena and Chihambakwe commissions, the Catholic Commission for Justice, Peace in Zimbabwe (CCJPZ) and Legal Resources Foundation (IRF) (1997) note that the Zimbabwean government refused to make public the findings and reports that were produced. In this case, neither the assertion that commissions of inquiry have a high degree of autonomy nor the argument that they serve to inform the public applies.

Additional challenges to the NPRC Act's purpose are the gap between legal provisions and their implementation. Part II of the NPRA provides its functions in detail, which are, *inter alia*, to ensure post-conflict justice, healing, and reconciliation; to develop and implement programmes to promote national unity, and to bring about national reconciliation by encouraging people to tell the truth. Truth-telling as a concept of transitional justice, for instance, rely more on the Commission's ability to regain the trust of the victims and survivors to extents where they are confident to confide in the Commission. Therefore, concepts of truth-telling and reconciliation require individuality and must not be homogenised.

Reconciliation: a process and an outcome

In line with reconciliation, a concept of non-judicial transitional justice, the NPRC Act's title suggests that reconciliation is central to the enactment and implementation of this framework. Further, the aim to achieve reconciliation is reiterated in section 252 of the Constitution of Zimbabwe (2013). Reconciliation as either a process or an outcome, as presented by Archbishop Tutu, ought to encompass the acknowledgement and injustices caused as violations of both the social and criminal codes. This acknowledgement is not divorced from peacebuilding processes of truth-telling, reparations, dialogues and consideration of the needs and expectations of the victims. There is a growing consensus in the existing literature that top-down approaches to transitional justice are insufficient in ensuring reconciliation. For example, the 1988 declaration of amnesties by Mugabe, who was the former prime minister and then highest authority as the president of Zimbabwe suggested a top-down approach. These amnesties have been classified herein as negative peace because they proved insufficient to reconcile and integrate the Zimbabwean society.

Other impediments are the lack of acknowledgement of wrongdoing, which Clark (2008) argues is a decisive part of the reconciliation dynamic. In relation, Gukurahundi, post-conflict responses in Zimbabwe suggest political denialism, Rwafa (2012) notes that the massacres were described by former President Mugabe as merely a moment of madness'. Moreover, the government has repeatedly suppressed information regarding the 1980s massacres, denied its role or responsibility for the crimes, and even labelled the Gukurahundi a 'Western conspiracy.' It is upon these connotations of denialism that Zimbabwe's post-conflict reconstruction process has its foundation. While others could argue that the denialism approach was predominant during Mugabe's presidency, contemporary events suggest the maintenance of this tactic under President Mnangagwa's tenure, who as justice minister argued against the disclosure of the Dumbutshena and Chihambakwe commissions stating that:

> As long as the first respondent [Robert Mugabe] declines to publish the Reports on the basis of the interest of the State and safety of other persons, he cannot be compelled to publish the Reports… the findings and recommendations were solely for use by the Government and Government had no legal duty to divulge the findings to the general public. He added, 'I am of the view that no good cause has been shown for the above Report to be published and that, in any case, it

cannot be published when it cannot be found.

(Patriotic Front Zimbabwe African People's Union v Minister of Justice, Legal and Parliamentary Affairs, 1985).

In a similar fashion, the NPRC Act does not articulate what will be done with the findings of the Commission's investigations and the history of commissions of inquiry in Zimbabwe point to them serving those who appoint these commissions rather than the people. The above quotation creates a nexus between peacebuilding through transitional justice and institutional reforms. Reconciliation in Zimbabwe, therefore, is limited by the lack of acknowledgement of wrongdoing through the criminalisation of violent acts, denialism of injustices meted against civilians, limited political and judicial will to encourage the disclosure of fact-finding commissions, thereby challenging truth-telling. The NPRC Act is ambiguous when it comes to the course of action after its investigations. It follows that this legal framework flouts the foundational tenets requisite for reconciliation to be realised.

Reparations

This study also explored reparation as a concept of transitional justice. The conceptual framework referred to the use of this concept in South Africa, Sierra Leone, Morocco and Rwanda, among other Africa contexts. In South Africa's case, Fernandez (1999) observes that the TRC made provisions for the President's Fund, a reparative mechanism, while in Rwanda, the state assumed responsibility for the welfare of genocide survivors under Law n° 02/98 of 1998 and Law n° 69/2008 and established the Genocide Survivors Assistance Fund (FARG), offering monthly reparative grants. The rationale for reparation as argued in the conceptual framework, is that victims of human rights violations have the right to reparation and rehabilitation because of losses they would have suffered, including financial and physical loss. On the one hand, Zimbabwe has a precedent of employing this mechanism, evidenced by the recompense and welfare benefits given to war veterans. Chaumba, Scoones and Wolmer (2003) account that some veterans have received expropriated farms as benefits. On the other hand, victims of the Gukurahundi massacres, which date to 1983 – 1987, have never been recompensed financially or with material.

The contrast in Zimbabwe between who is recompensed and who is not evinces an intrinsic dilemma of the concept of reparation, which is that the budget for welfare, including reparative grants, is the result of a political process of allocation and prioritisation, hence political support or threats posed by the lack of doing so, is often a decisive factor. Within this perspective, reparations as a concept depend on institution reforms, as in Rwanda's case where the Tutsi-led RPF government took charge from the Hutu-led government after the latter's defeat, subsequently resulting in the end of the 1994 genocide. In the absence of a changed regime, political and judicial will are indispensable. Despite perceived shortfalls such as the insufficiencies of reparations in meeting the expectations of the victims, the NPRC Act of 2018 does not stipulate the incorporative of this restorative justice measure.

Amnesties: lets 'Forget' our way to reconciliation

The conceptual framework presented herein explored amnesty as a restorative justice technique. At the advent of Zimbabwe's independence in 1980, Prime Minister Robert Mugabe's inaugural speech proclaimed that all parties should 'let bygones be bygones', and this proclamation was followed by Amnesty Ordinances that gave, firstly, blanket amnesties to the Rhodesian government and the liberation movements (Carver, 1993; Mashingaidze, 2010). Secondly, Doran (2017) notes that amnesty without trial was granted in April 1988, after Gukurahundi and the 1987 conjoining of ZANU-PF and PF-ZAPU into one party. It follows that amnesty ordinances laid the foundation for peacebuilding processes in newly independent Zimbabwe. However, these amnesties are limited in redressing the causes of conflict, particularly ethnic tensions amongst the black community.

In line with ethnic tensions, this chapter referred to contestations regarding the classification of Gukurahundi as genocide, while some authors opt for politicide. Regardless, the role of ethnicity in massacres cannot be overlooked. The historical origins of ethnic enmity in Zimbabwe date as far back as King Mzilikazi's era, around the 1860s; thus they are outside the remit of this research. However, it is important to note that ZANU and ZANLA or ZAPU and ZIPRA had tribal affiliations, which were exacerbated by increasing regional recruitment and mutual antagonism, leading to a growing association of ZAPU with the Ndebele speakers, whereas ZANU was predominant in the Shona regions, as observed by Harber (1985). These tensions worsened after independence as former ZANLA and ZIPRA combatants clashed at *Entumbane* camp, which was a catalyst for the large-scale defections of ex-ZIPRA combatants from the Zimbabwe National Army (ZNA) (Alexander & McGregor, 2017).

Under the pretext of disciplining the military dissidents who had defected from ZNA and those who were purported to succour them, an estimated 20,000 people were killed in an operation code-named Gukurahundi (CCPJZ/LRF, 1997; 2007). Based on the above historical account of deeply entrenched ethnic tensions, amnesties alone, though advantageous in garnering support for fact-finding and truth-telling, are inadequate. In fact, Article 6 of Protocol II Additional to the Geneva Conventions of 1977 encourages authorities to grant amnesties as 'gestures of reconciliation,' meaning that this is not an independent concept; it must be viewed in line with reconciliation and forgiveness of the offender by the victim.

While the NPRC Act does not explicitly declare amnesties, its lack of criminalisation of Gukurahundi evinces the lack of censure of an act that some scholars classify as a genocide, a heinous crime against humanity.

Overall, institutional reforms proved a common ground for the effective implementation of restorative concepts, including reconciliation, on which the NPRC Act is centred. The key difference of post-conflict peacebuilding in referenced cases is the shift in governance. In South Africa, the declaration of democracy in April 1994 marked the end of the segregating apartheid regime, the Nationalist Party, *Nasionale Party* in Afrikaans, which was the perpetrator, was disbanded in 1997 (Giliomee, 2013). Similarly, the end of the 1994 genocide in Rwanda marked a complete shift in political affairs. Dallaire (2009), former Force Commander of the United Nations Assistance Mission for Rwanda (UNAMIR), the peacekeeping force for Rwanda between 1993 and 1994, states that by July 1994, the RPF had eventually defeated the genocidal government, forcing the interim government to flee into Zaire.

As a result, the ruling RPF in Rwanda can adopt an assertive and retributive justice system, as provided by its Constitution and the Organic Law (1998), whose main purpose, as articulated in Article I, is to prosecute because it was not the main perpetrator of the genocide. In the South African political sphere, the ruling African National Congress (ANC), although it is gradually losing its grip as the dominant party, is not implicated as a perpetrator of apartheid. In Zimbabwe's case, however, the perpetrators of Gukurahundi massacres were the Fifth Brigade, a special unit of the military, whose chain of command by-passed 'the intermediate levels observed by the rest of the army' (Berkeley & Schrage 1986) and only answered to then Prime Minister Robert Mugabe of the ZANU-PF party, which rules Zimbabwe to date. The lack of institutional reform in Zimbabwe's political leadership has implications on legislation and peacebuilding.

In the same light, the establishment of the National Peace and Reconciliation Commission was a constitutional mandate through the Constitution of Zimbabwe Amendment 19 of 2008 and annexed in the amended constitution of 2013. Yet, the ZANU-PF party contested the approval of the NPRC Bill resulting in the NPRC Act's enactment in 2018, about ten years later. Moreover, in relation to retributive justice, which views the state as the custodian of the rights of its citizens, and the administer of punishment in cases where the criminal code is flouted, the delay in legislative processes created an impasse in initiating state-led peacebuilding processes. Although 2017 marked a shift in Zimbabwean politics when the long-serving president Robert Mugabe was removed from power, this political shift is not as significant compared to the cases of South Africa after apartheid and Rwanda post-1994.

The limited institutional reform, a shift from Mugabe to the Mnangagwa regime, both of the ZANU-PF party stands as a stumbling block to efforts towards peacebuilding as the state often relapses into its oxymoronically unusual yet usual way of using violence. Moreover, Coltart (2018) states that the current President, Emmerson Mnangagwa and his Deputy, the retired army general Constantino Chiwenga were directly involved in the Gukurahundi massacres. Both held influential positions during Mugabe's regime, and they have top government positions at present, making the idea of retributive justice even more elusive. Nonetheless, the existing, although limited institutional reforms have allowed the enactment of the NPRC Act. However, for peace and reconciliation to be realised it takes more than a deficient legal framework.

Dealing with dehumanisation and memorialisation

While dehumanisation, as defined in the previous sections, involves perceiving a person as non-human in ways such as reducing them to an animal, or a sub-human and erasure of empathy for another person, memorialisation can redress or reinforce dehumanising psychological traumas. Memorialisation is the organisation of collective events by political agents and other role players in a manner that is not only remembered but also influential (Amadiume et. al, 2000). Throughout Zimbabwe, places, where significant historical events occurred have been recognised; for example, the memory of the liberation struggle is preserved at the National Heroes Acre, whose construction commenced as early as 1981, according to Duri (1985). At present, several monuments have been erected, including a museum, showcasing artefacts, photographs, documents, and other paraphernalia from the liberation wars. Despite controversies over who deserves and is buried at the national shrine, and the politicisation of the 'hero' title, this example evinces that the ZANU-PF led government is conscious of the need to preserve history.

In contrast, the Gukurahundi massacres are intentionally omitted from the educational curriculum, which impedes the citizens' right to know the truth about the atrocities. De la Rey (2001) argues that truth-telling is an important element of reconciliation and restorative justice, thus, attempts to conceal the memory of Gukurahundi reduce the viable peacebuilding options that Zimbabwe could consider and subsequently confines the NPRC and the NPRC Act in its quest to resolve the burdens of the past violence, which is a constitutional mandate. Nonetheless, scholars who explore traditional justice initiatives in Zimbabwe argue that there are memorialisation processes at the community level. Ncube (2018) discloses that in Maphisa, a rural area in Zimbabwe's Matabeleland region, there are several mass graves and memorial sites, which the community members know. However, these memorial sites are not officially recognised by the state, creating yet another shortfall of measures excluded in the NPRC Act.

In line with memorialisation, Dabengwa, one of the ZAPU leaders who were present at the signing of the Unity Accord of 1987, later likened it to a 'marriage of convenience,' explaining, in part, the cessation of ZAPU's operation under ZANU-PF in 2008 and to reassuming its title (Doran, 2017). Musiyiwa (2008) states that the ZANU-PF party and war veterans take the spotlight at the Unity Day celebrations, making it more difficult for victims to establish sincerity from the state. For victims of Gukurahundi, Unity Day is a reminder of the massacres, because no justice has been delivered for this injustice, and the NPRC has not shown much commitment to change the *status quo*, particularly on the justice for the victims front. Although there is no law that explicitly prohibits the commemoration of Gukurahundi in Zimbabwe, there is not one that allows and legitimises it, either. The NPRA, as a legal framework on peacebuilding, does not incorporate this as a vital part in its 'resolving past violence' agenda.

Memorialisation, therefore, though argued by Amadiume and An-Na'im (2000) to have the potential to aid the process of reconciliation, can be used as a political tool to subjugate other members of the society, thus hindering reintegration and reconciliation. For example, the memory of the liberation struggle, preserved at the Heroes Acre monument and museum, is often used to deflect criticism of the ruling ZANU-PF party's failures. The liberation rhetoric remains a cornerstone of ZANU-PF's policy to give a single-sided narrative of the struggle for independence. Therefore, it might be that non-state-sanctioned measures are likely to yield lasting peace and closure than sanctioned and yet choreographed.

Bandwagoning or intended action?

The bandwagon effect, described in the introductory paragraphs, is a psychological phenomenon whereby the rate of uptake of beliefs, ideas, and trends increases with respect to the proportion of others who have already done so (Myers, Wojcicki & Aardema, 1977). In essence, as normative processes of peacebuilding are adopted and receive credit elsewhere, others 'hop on the wagon'. This chapter assessed Zimbabwe's legal framework on peacebuilding, the NPRC Act in reference to negative and positive peace. Previously adopted peacebuilding methods such as the use of amnesties proved inadequate in redressing entrenched ethnic animosity; hence this measure was classified as negative peace.

Further, this chapter attempted to align the NPRC Act with the United Nations Convention on the Prevention and Punishment of Genocide (UNCPPCG); however, the applicability of this international framework is challenged by contestations regarding the classification of Gukurahundi in local and international literature. Further, the UNCPPCG criminalises the act and attempts to commit genocide, and domestic frameworks on peacebuilding in Rwanda, for instance, mirror this provision, which anchors the corrective justice system. In Zimbabwe's case however, the NPRC Act does not criminalise Gukurahundi; thus, this chapter referred to the United Nations' Transitional Justice Framework, which incorporates judicial and non-judicial methods of peacebuilding.

The NPRC Act aligns with the non-judicial restorative mechanism, under which measures such as reconciliation, reparations, institutional reforms, and amnesties fall. While exploring these concepts of restorative justice, the NPRC Act fell short on reconciliation owing to denialism of Gukurahundi, while reparations proved a viable method, which has been employed for recompensing war veterans. However, this method has not been incorporated in the NPRC Act to enhance its potential to realise its primary objectives of attaining peace and reconciliation. Institutional reforms proved lowest in Zimbabwe compared to Rwanda and South Africa, where there were regime changes from the genocidal or apartheid governments, respectively. Previous methods thrived in the use of amnesties, but this only yielded negative peace.

Cognisant of the challenges mentioned above, it will be remiss to disregard the progress which preceded the NPRC Act. For example, state-led initiatives under the Organ for National Healing, Reconciliation, and Integration (ONHRI) such as the History of Conflict in Zimbabwe Research Project; the Zimbabwe National Policy Framework for Peace and Reconciliation (ZNPFPR); and Traditional Mechanisms, Approaches and Systems for Peacebuilding, Conflict Resolution and Reconciliation (TMASCRR). Although the NPRC Act has been criticised here for not incorporating traditional methods in its legal provisions, President Mnangagwa gave a directive for traditional leaders to spearhead the exhumation and reburial of victims of Gukurahundi massacres in the Matabeleland region and Midlands province.[4] Moreover, writings by Eppel (2014) show that reburials have been carried out by CSOs such as Ukuthula Trust with neither the government's approval nor direct censure.

Overall, Zimbabwe's peacebuilding processes present a hybrid of institutionalised and non-institutionalised processes. First, CSOs such as the Ukuthula Trust have incorporated peacebuilding methods unguided by the NPRC Act, which only came to existence in 2018. Second, non-state-led traditional practices appear to have had an impact on restorative justice, particularly offering closure to the victims. Therefore, the NPRC Act must be implemented with urgency to address the state's shortfalls in their participation in redressing violence in Zimbabwe. While it is difficult to establish whether the enactment of the NPRC Act is intended action

---

4 'Zimbabwe Peace Commission Shocked After Mnangagwa Snub in Gukurahundi Reburials'. All Africa, 6 December 2020.

aimed at regulating pre-existing peacebuilding initiatives by CSOs and fostering collaboration with the government, the examples provided herein show that this legal framework is deficient in its theoretical provisions, affecting implementation.

Recommendations

The possibilities of alternative peacebuilding and restorative transitional justice methods in Zimbabwe have since been explored by academics such as Vambe; Benyera; Murambadoro; and Ndlovu, among others. Murambadoro accentuates the importance of the government acknowledgement of Gukurahundi, which includes an official apology to the victims whilst Vambe (2012) argues for the issuance of communal reparations. These two academics highlight that without positive institutional change, national peace and reconciliation may remain unrealised. Further, Benyera (2014) posits that Zimbabwe needs to investigate indigenous traditional justice systems, which the local communities are already familiar. These traditional mechanisms include *gwava* (bringing the deceased's spirit back to the realm of the living), and *nyaradzo* (memorial services), and must be incorporated in state-led peacebuilding initiatives. In the same light, this chapter recommends the following:

- Reviewing the NPRC Act of 2018 after three-year intervals to assess whether its provisions, implementation and aims are coherent. This review will enable the possibility of introducing interventions to address perceptible shortcomings so that efficiency can be enhanced.
- In addition to reviewing the NPRC Act, the Commission (NPRC) is only meant to last for a period of ten years, as stipulated in Section 251 of the Constitution. This time is insufficient to inquire into decades of conflict, state-orchestrated violence, and mass human rights violations. Therefore, an extension of the Commission's tenure paired with increased efficiency is recommended.
- It is recommended that both the Act and the Commission must view transitional justice concepts as complementary rather than individual processes. As such, bringing in aspects of retributive justice may facilitate the NPRC Act's potential to reach its mandate by bringing closure and justice to the victims. Moreover, the restoration of the victims' dignity through dignified reburials must be institutionalised.

Overall, while this study explored examples from other African post-conflict contexts, including Rwanda, Sierra Leone, Morocco, and South Africa, it would be remiss to propose a 'one-size-fits-all' measure of the NPRC Act as peacebuilding methods should be adopted in relation to the specific context in which they will be applied. However, there are prerequisites for enhanced efficacy of peacebuilding initiatives hence the exploration of international norms for establishing positive peace after conflicts. Justice for both the victims and the offenders, either restorative or punitive, is an important ingredient to the peacebuilding process. Although the NPRC has adopted the reconciliation mantra, reconciliation without justice is deficient. Finally, it is recommended that the NPRC should propose resolutions to the Zimbabwean government, which include both restorative and retributive mechanisms and enhance its efficacy in order to avoid failing at its basic premise, which is to drive national 'peace and reconciliation'.

3

The Gukurahundi Transitional Justice Deadlock in Zimbabwe

Pedzisai Ruhanya and Bekezela Gumbo

Introduction

The Gukurahundi genocide from 1983-87 continues to threaten Zimbabwe's future peace (Ndlovu 2019; Gusha 2019; Alexander 2021; Dube 2021).[1] An estimated 20,000 citizens were slain, some of whom were buried in mass graves in sites in Tsholotsho or abandoned mines like Bhalagwe in Kezi. In 1984, the Mugabe administration appointed the Chihambakwe Commission to investigate these atrocities but suppressed the disclosure of their report (CCJPZ and LRF 1997; Ndlovu-Gatsheni 2008; Huyse 2003). To resolve these atrocities, this chapter argues that Gukurahundi has to be classified as a transitional justice (TJ) issue and be resolved following this principle.[2]

The only attempt to resolve the question following the Gukurahundi years was the amnesty that followed the 1987 Unity Accord between the Zimbabwe National Union Patriotic Front (ZANU-PF) and the Patriotic Front Zimbabwe African

---

1   Gukurahundi is a Shona term for the first rains that cleanse all the dirt; and in this context it is used to refer to ethnic cleansing (genocide).

2   The United Nations defines transitional justice as a 'full range of processes and mechanisms associated with a society's attempt to come to terms with a legacy of large-scale past conflict, repression, violations and abuses, in order to ensure accountability, serve justice and achieve reconciliation' (OHCHR, https://www.ohchr.org/en/transitional-justice, ; See also, S/2004/616). It is not just justice but a special variant of justice. Thus, we argue that attempts to give justice and healing to victims of Gukurahundi falls within the TJ conceptual framework. Attempts in academia and policy to sideline Gukurahundi from the TJ framework is in itself an injustice.

Peoples Union (PF-ZAPU). This gave immunity to dissident and state agencies for atrocities committed mainly on unarmed Ndebele-speaking citizens (CCJPZ and LRF 1997). No full transitional justice has occurred to date. Victims continue to experience the consequences of Gukurahundi. This has made the topic a source of grief, pain and hatred that require resolution.

The Gukurahundi issue is a question of dealing with past human rights violations and injustices perpetrated by the ZANU-PF government and the military against the people of Matabeleland and sections of the Midlands region. This is especially significant because the atrocities were tribal, regional, and partisan in nature (Kalley et al. 1999; Huyse 2003). The state's efforts to resolve it ought to end the identity politics and hatred created between the victims, the Ndebele and the Shona who were supporters of ZANU-PF, the party that orchestrated the Gukurahundi massacres (Mashingaidze 2010; Gusha 2019; Alexander 2021; Dube 2021). The telos is to reconcile the nation, heal the victims, ensure forgiveness and encourage government legitimacy within those regions where the victims and their families still live.

Despite the Mnangagwa administration's rekindled efforts towards achieving some form of justice, the securocratic state and its patronage networks, which include the ZANU-PF perpetrators, remain in charge of the state. They cannot be judges in their own case. Transitional justice, as part of a democratic transitional process, relies on other democratic processes such as free and fair elections (Lederach 1999; Rigby 2001; Kasapas 2008). Such measures have been successively blocked by the securocratic state (ZDI 2017; Ruhanya and Gumbo 2022). Therefore any form of justice for the victims of Gukurahundi has been incapacitated by the absence of an enabling democratic, political and institutional framework.

International law statutes such as the 1948 Convention on the Prevention and Punishment of the Crime of Genocide, the Convention against Torture and Other Cruel, Inhuman or Degrading Treatment or Punishment, the 1949 Geneva Conventions, and the Rome Statute of the International Criminal Court (ICC) have established a legal framework that supports transitional justice and obliges states to prosecute perpetrators of international crimes such as genocide, torture or violation of the laws of war. According to these statutes, the ZANU-PF government's imposition of food embargoes, deprivation of registration documents, and rape during Gukurahundi represents a genocidal atrocity (CCJPZ and LRF 1997). The nation expected the Unity Accord to lead to a comprehensive TJ programme but such expectations have not been met.

Many studies have shown evidence of the military's capture of key state institutions and use of violence to block democratic transitions (Rupiya 2005; Tendi 2013; Moyo 2014; Maringira 2017; 2021). Many also show that the military elites form a supreme power-bloc that uses ZANU-PF as its infrastructure for maintaining its stay in power and manufacturing legitimacy to govern (ZDI 2017; Ndawana 2020; Ruhanya and Gumbo 2022). The military elite has been decisive in all key critical junctures in Zimbabwe's transition. Examples include, the 1975 Mgagao Declaration in Tanzania that authored the tutelary in the replacement of Ndabaningi Sithole by Mugabe as leader of ZANU-PF; military tutelary in the Lancaster House negotiations, which gave birth to Zimbabwe's independence (Chung 2005); military dominance in the Gukurahundi operation (1983-87); the June 2008 run-off Operation Mavhoterapapi[3] where the military killed many opposition supporters to(re-)install ZANU-PF after losing the March 2008 elections to the opposition; the overthrow of Mugabe in 2017, and the 2018 post-election protest when the military shot and killed unarmed civilians. Each of the foregoing serve to prove the continuation of the securocratic state (Maringira 2017, 2021; Ndawana 2020). In all the cited cases, the military elite blocked potential democratic transitions using armed violence to (re-)install ZANU-PF. In other words, party and military elites exist as a single entity wherein the latter is a decisive power-bloc (Ruhanya and Gumbo 2022).

This chapter employed a thematic analysis of secondary data from newspaper articles, reports and journal articles from Zimbabwean organisations such the Zimbabwe Defence Industries (ZDI), the National Transitional Justice Working Group (NTJWG), the CCJPZ and dissertations as cited in the bibliography. We also analysed articles from international organisations such as the the United Nations (UN). Thus we were able to identify recurring conduct, objectives and events to deduce themes and meanings which offer answers to three main questions: what is the role of the securocratic state in the resolution of the Gukurahundi transitional justice deadlock? Given that we have an intransigent securocratic state, how do we explain the Mnangagwa regime's apparent commitment to justice? To what extent is TJ achievable in the current context?

The securocratic State in the Gukurahundi transitional justice deadlock

Three intertwined conditions allow an enabling political system for successful TJ these are: i) an emerging regime following a regime change; ii) legitimacy of the new regime; and iii) their capacity to handle the process (Fischer 2011). The first refers to a need for the state to transition from the old order to the new one committed to democratic transition and the rule of law (Kritz 1995; McAdams 1997; Thoms et al. 2008). In other words, a transitional justice policy can only be implemented by leaders with a respect for democratic values and/or a regime that is not implicated

---

3 Meaning 'where you placed your vote'. In other words, an operation to punish those who did not vote for the ruling party.

in past injustices. Capacity refers to the need for a reformed judiciary, legislative and executive institutions, which are democratic and independent of the control of perpetrators of past injustices and war crimes. There must also be strong safeguards and protection for witnesses and victims due to sensitivity of the information they disclose (USIP 2008; Kasapas 2008; Fischer 2011). The independence of the justice system is necessary because '… if one party to a conflict prevails and initiates prosecutions against members of the losing faction, the latter will claim that the trials are acts of revenge rather than justice' (USIP 2008: 4). The third condition, that is, legitimacy of the justice system, refers to the consent and support that the victims give to the post-conflict TJ systems and processes (Elster 2004; USIP 2008; Kasapas 2008).

The Gukurahundi massacres are an example of the outcomes of government by military operations, a feature peculiar to the securocratic state. It is therefore unlikely that perpetrators will preside over crimes, which they committed, and expect the victims to truly reconcile with them and heal. The state under which the Mnangagwa regime operates, lacks the capacity, legitimacy and 'emerging regime' status required to give Gukurahundi victims genuine transitional justice. Four key pillars upon which the securocratic state is organised and deployed are: i) military capture of the ruling party and hybridization of military rule; ii) militarisation of state institutions responsible for TJ; iii) capture and deployment of traditional leaders within the infrastructure to coerce rivals and manufacture legitimacy to rule and; iv) capture of state resources.

Capture of the ruling party and hybridization of military rule

The main pillar of the Zimbabwean securocratic state is the continued capture of the ruling ZANU-PF party by military elite for use in hybrid military rule. This ensures that successive ZANU-PF civilian leaders become conduits of the military elite or a retired component within this decisive power-bloc. This has ensured that transitional justice for Gukurahundi victims lacks the requisite political will or judicial independence as the ZANU-PF leaders who have vested interests in maintaining the *status quo* are still in control of the state. Operation Restore Legacy, which overthrew the late former president Robert Mugabe, succeeded in (re)installing a leader who was implicated in Gukurahundi as the Minister of State Security. This has inhibited any possible prosecution that might have been achieved by a less partisan successor.

The capture of ZANU-PF for the purposes of preventing any genuine resolution of past military atrocities is traceable to the war of liberation from 1975. The most important event being the Mgagao Declaration (1975) used to remove the Revd Ndabaningi Sithole as president of ZANU-PF and replacing him with Mugabe (Chung 2006; *The Patriot* 2017; *The Sunday Times* 2019). From that moment, it is clear that the military elite had begun infiltrating ZANU-PF directly through the decision-making process, and the secondment of its chosen civilians into powerful positions (ZDI 2017). In other words, they captured the party, and a securocracy was established in Zimbabwe well before independence. Key decision-making positions in ZANU-PF and the government – including Gukurahundi TJ processes – were filled directly by the military elite, or indirectly through its civilians within ZANU-PF structures.

Something similar occurred during the 1979 Lancaster House negotiations in Geneva. Fay Chung (2006: 160) a key member of the party, notes that:

> The military routinely suspected all those who had spent some years in the United States of having pro-American sympathies and of having ties with the CIA, and Zvogbo was not exempt from this suspicion.

Subsequently, in 1980, ZANU-PF, a securocrats' party, went on to assimilate its equally militarised rival, PF-ZAPU after subjecting it and its members to seven years of military violence during Gukurahundi (Stauffer 2009; *The Sunday Times* 2019). In 1987, the two political movements transmuted into one party, ZANU-PF (Raftopoulos and Mlambo 2009). Thereafter the war of liberation remained their main source of political legitimacy. The majority of the political elite(s) doubled as former military officers in the bush war while retaining political leadership of their respective parties. Mugabe himself was the President of ZANU-PF and overall leader of the armed guerrillas (Chung 2006). Mnangagwa, who became Mugabe's vice president in 2014, is currently president of ZANU-PF and President of Zimbabwe but he was also a senior member of the Zimbabwe African National Liberation Army (ZANLA) in charge of the CIO during the years of the Gukurahundi atrocities. The implication of such infiltration, capture and manipulation of ZANU-PF by the military elite is that a Gukurahundi transitional justice policy is calculated to protect the perpetrators within ZANU-PF.

The military/ZANU-PF conflation in the form of the ZANLA high command during the pre-independence era was developed into the Joint Operations Command (JOC), and it was central in the restructuring of the national army into what is now called the Zimbabwe Defence Forces (ZDF) that participated in Gukurahundi massacres (Ndlovu-Gatsheni 2006; Maringira 2017, 2021; Ndawana 2020). The JOC is a group of military elites drawn from the heads of all security organs (army, air force, prison service, intelligence, and police) (Alexander and Tendi 2008; Tendi 2013). Their omnipotence has been displayed in its decisive role in transition politics both in ZANU-PF and government. In the June 2008 presidential election run-off, after Mugabe lost the 29 March presidential election to MDC leader Morgan Tsvangirai, the JOC deployed violence and fraud to help Mugabe and

ZANU-PF win the run-off (Alexander and Tendi 2008; Masunungure 2011) – an outcome which was dismissed by the international community. The most notable military manoeuvre was effectively the coup justified as a move to 'restore legacy' in November 2017 (Asuelime 2018; Maringira 2021). Indubitably, in Zimbabwe, the military will always step in and commit atrocities to save their party, ZANU-PF. Transitional justice under the Unity Accord took the form of state and non-state perpetrators of Gukurahundi violence being given amnesty; a reassuring tactic meaning that violence is always pardoned and thus can always be replicated because they offer a sense of impunity.

Militarisation of state institutions responsible for transitional justice

Gukurahundi TJ has been hindered through militarisation of key state institutions, which in principle ought to support it. Having liberation struggle credentials and/or attracting such credentials to oneself by parentage or association has for a long time been a most important pre-requisite for senior political positions in key institutions. For instance, General Constantine Chiwenga stressed his intention to instruct the ZDF to disobey Morgan Tsvangirai if Mugabe, a leader with liberation war credentials, lost the elections.[4] Justification that Mnangagwa was the most qualified candidate to succeed Mugabe as president following the 2017 coup spoke clearly to this fact. Thus, government institutions lack conformity to principles of independence, legitimacy and victims' trust needed to ensure success of the Gukurahundi TJ processes. From the head of state responsible for appointing judges and independent commissioners to the executive responsible for the Gukurahundi TJ policy, there is a traceable link to the perpetrators of atrocities (CCJPZ and LRF 1997; Ndlovu 2019).

The military in the securocrats' group has also displayed its power in various spheres of the state e.g. the ZANU-PF commissariat, which campaigns, and the Zimbabwe Electoral Commission (ZEC), which administers elections (ZDI 2017; CiZC 2018). In addition, military personnel occupy positions in ministries such as agriculture, land, justice and economic development (ZDI 2017). Retired members of the military with a liberation background have been appointed judges of the High Court as, for example the current Judge President retired Major General Justice George Chiweshe (Pindula 2021). Effectively, therefore, all decision-making is partisan. Thus, Zimbabwe has a strong political system which outwardly appears to be a civilian system but effectively it is a military junta.

In short, this chapter demonstrates that the securocratic state has made transitional justice unachievable because (i) the military elite captured a dominant

---

4 Gama, L. 2008. "Chiwenga threatens coup if Mugabe loses election." SW Radio Africa, March 10. http://www.swradioafrica.com/News_archives/files/2008/March/Mon%2010%20March/lg-general-threatens-coup_1.html.

political party and appoints securocrats to govern as civilians although all they do is rubber-stamp decisions made behind closed doors by the JOC; (ii) the apex decision-making body of the securocratic state is the military elite which governs through a the ruling political party; (iii) the military factor intervenes directly in politics in cases of emergency when, for example, its legacy is threatened by the opposition or from within its civilian conduits; (iv) a patronage network of securocrats is dispersed across key strategic communities, decision-making and economic spheres in order to protect the interests of the military. In systems with a weak legislature, which undermine the constitution and the rule of law, the military stifles dissenting voices, and emerges as the most powerful player capable of defining the direction of transition politics (Diamond 2008; Acemoglu et al. 2010). The perpetrators of the Gukurahundi genocide have no superior force to compel them to assume responsibility for past human rights violations or subject them to a vetting process that could reform the whole security sector.

Transitional justice: a theoretical framework

The resolution of Gukurahundi injustices falls within the TJ sub-sector of peace-building and is conceptualised as a post-conflict judicial and non-judicial process. These are the practices that follow a period of conflict, repression and strife and are aimed at acknowledging, prosecuting, compensating for and forgiving past human rights abuses (Roht-Arriaza 2006; Clark 2009; Kasapas 2008; UN 2014). Transitional justice is a post-conflict government policy that seeks to build sustainable peace and the rule of law in the nation and foster the transition from an authoritarian to a democratic order (Lederach 1999; Elster 2004; Kasapas 2008; UN 2014). Judicial measures involved in transitional justice include trials and legal reforms whilst non-judicial measures include truth commissions and compensation schemes (Elster 2004; Kasapas 2008). Transitional justice is predicated on the notion that grievances tend to engender hatred the longer they remain unresolved, frustrate the victims and create a cause for aggrieved identity politics that can lead to violence (Lederach 1999; Rigby 2001; USIP 2008; Kasapas 2008). There are three possible TJ scenarios: i) following a or as part of a democratic transition; ii) one that is externally or internationally driven, and iii) one following a non-liberal transition (Hansen 2011).

Transitional justice in democratic transitions

Case studies show that a TJ deadlock such as that of Gukurahundi is better resolved after the authoritarian regime responsible for the crimes has been removed from power and replaced by a liberal and/or democratic regime (Kritz 1995; McAdams 1997; Barahona de Brito et al. 2001). This is the orthodox, normative and/or liberal typology of transitional justice peculiar to countries experiencing transition from authoritarian regimes to democracy. In such cases TJ seeks to install democratic norms and standards on a post-authoritarian nation. Transitions in certain Latin American countries in the eighties or in central and eastern Europe following communist rule offer good examples (Hansen 2011). The 1994 Truth and Reconciliation Commission in South Africa presided over by the African National Congress regime after defeating the apartheid regime in elections is one of the best examples of the conceptual framework followed in transitional justice. The Zimbabwean regime that came to power following the regime change in November 2017 does not meet the basic requirement of 'replacement' of an authoritarian regime by a democratic one.

Externally or internationally driven transitional justice

There are some cases where TJ has been internationally driven and such cases can offer a ray of hope. The International Criminal Tribunal for the former Yugoslavia (ICTY) established in 1993 by the UN which prosecuted war crimes committed during the Yugoslav wars (1991-2001) is one example. In Africa, the 1994 UN's Security Council's International Criminal Tribunal for Rwanda is another. However, strong Chinese and Russian support for Zimbabwe's securocratic state led them to veto the Security Council Resolution to impose sanctions on Zimbabwe following the June 2008 electoral violence.[5] Such interventions make externally driven transitional justice very unlikely in Zimbabwe.

Transitional justice in non-liberal transitions

Transitional justice in non-liberal transitions entails processes undertaken by an authoritarian regime that took power from an authoritarian predecessor, although the former disapproves of the latter (Hansen 2011). The Zimbabwean transition in November 2017 fits this description. The adjudication of more than 5,000 victims' cases in Nicaragua by the Sandinistas after a military victory over the Somoza dictatorship in 1979, the Ethiopian criminal trials following the overthrow of the Mengistu regime in 1991, and the Chadian Truth Commission set up by President Idriss Déby after overthrowing Hissène Habré in 1990 offer good examples of this variant of transitional justice (Reyntjens 2004; Waldorf 2009; Hansen 2011). A common factor in these illiberal transitions is that the former authoritarian regime was replaced by a 'new' dictatorship. This made it possible for the latter to prosecute the previous regime. However, the transition from the Mugabe to the Mnangagwa regime removed certain key players but did not alter the military factor (as discussed above). Thus, this power bloc remained untouched. Thus, unlike the examples cited

---

5 This decision by the China and Russia governments was motivated by their hostility to the west, their history with the Mugabe regime, particularly the support they gave to liberation forces fighting an anti-colonial war, and protecting their lucrative forest and mining interests in Zimbabwe.

above, the Mnangagwa dispensation lacks the fresh moral prosecuting power to resolve the Gukurahundi TJ deadlock.

The ideal transitional justice mechanisms for Gukurahundi massacres

A genuine TJ policy ought to address the following questions: How can an emerging regime peacefully integrate both the supporters and the victims of a former regime? How should it approach justice and reconciliation, human rights crimes, and the search for truth? Five programmes have been widely adopted as key pillars of a transitional justice process that answer these fundamental questions: i) criminal prosecutions; ii) truth and reconciliation commissions; iii) vetting process; iv) reparations and compensation (Lederach 1999; Rigby 2001; Kasapas 2008; Fischer 2011; UN 2014).

Prosecutions

In some cases, TJ has been implemented through the prosecutions process, the most direct form of accountability for atrocities and war crimes, and means of providing retributive justice in the aftermath of violent conflict (Hansen 2011; Fischer 2011; UN 2014). However, local courts tend to suffer from a lack of finance and expertise, and lack the independence and/or legitimacy to handle prosecutions that are politically sensitive and/or partisan. This is the case with regard to the Gukurahundi TJ process as the courts have no capacity or independence and do not have the victims' trust. Where national courts suffer such challenges, hybrid courts that draw in local, independent and international judicial experts are preferred. Such tribunals were set up in East Timor, Sierra Leone, Cambodia, Bosnia and Lebanon to bridge the judicial capacity and legitimacy gap. This route is supported by the Convention on the Prevention and Punishment of the Crime of Genocide, the Convention against Torture and Other Cruel, Inhuman or Degrading Treatment or Punishment, the Geneva Conventions, and the Rome Statute of the ICC. These oblige states to prosecute perpetrators of international crimes such as genocide, torture or violation of the laws of war.

The ICTY implemented by the UN offers an example of international prosecutions and a mechanism for retributive justice (Meernik 2005; Nettelfield 2006; Orentlicher 2008). Despite the success of the ICTY in achieving the restoration of peace and reconciliation, it remains controversial.[6] That said, the tribunal sent a clear deterrence message to possible future perpetrators and broke the cycle of violence (at least temporarily) (Minow 1998; Bell 2000). The ICC has also offered recourse

---

6 This approach remains controversial because it is contingent on the full support of the veto powers in the UN Security Council and it has been lambasted for being subject to manipulation by powerful countries.

to victims of high-level political violence while providing an opportunity for them to speak truth to power and have their grievances addressed. This is considered a healing procedure (Fischer 2011). Transitional justice prosecutions should ensure that victims of past atrocities trust that any new government will protect them and prevent the repetition of similar atrocities.

In countries where non-liberal transitions occurred, the new authoritarian order has to be different from the old one for it to have the political will and legitimacy to prosecute perpetrators of atrocities who served in the old order (Reyntjens 2004; Waldorf 2009; Hansen 2011; UN 2014). This is not the case with the Mnangagwa regime which is led and controlled by the same military elite who presided over the Gukurahundi atrocities under Mugabe's regime. This partly explains the government's failure to set up a prosecuting tribunal but opted for a public consultation forum in the name of the National Peace and Conciliation Commission (NPRC).

The Mnangagwa regime has insisted on its mantra of 'let bygones be bygones' which is inimical to the spirit of transitional justice, as it prevents accountability for past atrocities. The let's forget and put all behind us form of TJ is often preferred when there is no clear winner but negotiated compromise between the members of the old and the new order leading to collective amnesia (Boraine et al.1997; Pankhurst 1999). This may be appropriate within a context where there has been violence and suffering among or caused by both parties. The Gukurahundi was not a 'mutually hurting' scenario – only one side suffered violence. Moreover, the decision to employ this tactic, this mantra, derived from a unilateral decision by one party/government. Under such circumstances, being encouraged to 'forget' cannot lead to reconciliation and sustainable peace (Boraine et al. 1997).

Truth commissions

Truth commissions have been considered as the 'third way' between prosecutions and collective amnesia. Although, they lack the power to punish perpetrators (Kasapas 2008; Fischer 2011), they enable restorative justice and they give victims a chance to air their grievances, have them investigated with the facts documented, plus the relief of hearing perpetrators take responsibility for their past crimes. The South African Truth and Reconciliation Commission (TRC), the Sierra Leone Truth and Reconciliation Commission and the Commission for Reception, Truth and Reconciliation in Timor-Leste serve as good examples. They have helped in counteracting cultures of denial and providing official exposure of truth. This enhances individual and social healing and reconciliation (Hayner 1994, 2001). The requirement for these commissions to be independent from parties to the past conflict is sacrosanct. It gives the process legitimacy and effectiveness (USIP 2008; Fischer 2011). Extensive public consultations, outreach and engagement are required to ensure that the commissions collect as much truth as possible. However, they can suffer politicisation, intimidation, lack of authority and their recommendations are sometimes ignored (Kasapas 2008). Unlike the TRC, the Zimbabwean NPRC has been crippled by the lack of the 'truth' in its mandate, which is too broad, so that the question of Gukurahundi TJ has been given limited and distorted attention. For instance, Commissioner Obert Gutu, the spokesperson of the NPRC noted that:

> Gukurahundi is just a very small, tiny fraction of the various other disputes we are talking about. It's a pity that normally people look at the commission as only dealing with one issue of Gukurahundi. I think Gukurahundi is just a small, tiny fraction of the various other disputes we are talking about. We are talking of issues that happened in 2005; Murambatsvina, you are talking of various other issues, some dating back to pre-independence times (NTJWG 2021).

The magnitude of deaths and atrocities related to Gukurahundi require a special commission created solely to resolve the matter. Including Gukurahundi with a range of other atrocities reduces the scale of the outrage. It also sidesteps solutions by enabling perpetrators to divert attention to pre-independence injustices suffered under the Ndebele kingdom in the nineteenth century. The NPRC also lacks independence. Its commissioners are said to have links to the appointing authority, who themselves may be culpable.

Vetting process

The UN (2010) emphasised the importance of vetting saying, 'public institutions that helped perpetuate conflict or repressive rule ... should be transformed into institutions that sustain peace, protect human rights, and foster a culture of respect for the rule of law.' Transformation of the state after conflict or authoritarian rule is essential. Vetting enables the new regime to transform the state by creating public institutions that are legitimate, trusted by victims and prevent the possibility of including abusive officials in the public administration thereby preventing a recurrence of enabling impunity. Security sector, judicial and bureaucratic reforms ae essential to the vetting process (Fischer 2011). Mani (2002) notes the importance of focusing vetting and reform on the 'crucial tripod': the judiciary, military and police-prison system as the *sine qua non* for the establishment of the rule of law. Although vetting is not a judicial action, it works best in cases where past atrocities were committed by government officials in the army, police, judiciary and executive. A fair and transparent vetting procedure ensures that such tainted officials do not remain in office in the new dispensation.

Reparations and compensation

Reparations and compensation processes include giving victims payments or services as 'compensation for the harm they or their loved ones have suffered during a period of conflict' (USIP 2008; Kasapas 2008; Fischer 2011). Reparations serve as a mechanism for distributive justice which seeks to 'tackle the roots of the unrest by addressing the structural factors that led to the escalation of conflict to violence' (Mani 2002: 7-11). Reparations ensure that harm suffered by victims is recognised and repaired, such that it restores their property rights and their dignity, and rebuilds trust and solidarity among communities to the satisfaction of victims (Rigby 2001; Kasapas 2008). This is the most often demanded recourse for past atrocities yet most difficult to achieve due to limited resources. Thus, reparations and compensation programmes go together with truth commissions as they require identification of victims and quantification of their losses. International law recognises that victims of systematic human rights abuses are entitled to prompt, adequate and effective reparation and that states have a duty to provide comprehensive reparations. Compensation can be achieved through symbolic programmes such as memorials, national apologies or in-kind services (such as free health or education benefits) or monetary life support schemes. However, compensation and reparations cannot be achieved if perpetrators do not acknowledge and account for their past wrongs. This has been the greatest predicament in Zimbabwe's Gukurahundi TJ attempts.

Conclusion

This chapter concludes that the Gukurahundi TJ question has been hindered by the absence of a permissive political order. The chapter focused on the three conditions that are essential if genuine Gukurahundi transitional justice is to be achieved. These are: a regime change from the old order to the new, legitimacy of the regime presiding over the Gukurahundi process, and the capacity of the state to handle the process. Many case studies reviewed in the chapter have revealed that a regime change is needed before instituting TJ. The November 2017 transition from the Mugabe to the Mnangagwa regime lacked two key ingredients: it failed to change the old order and the securocratic system continued unchanged or reformed; thus the resultant regime lacked the necessary democratic commitment. These deficiencies have resulted in lack of political will and commitment to truth telling, prosecutions and security sector and judiciary reforms, which must form the basis of a Gukurahundi TJ process. The NPRC that has been created to handle transitional justice issues has been bedeviled by an overcrowded mandate, partisan appointment of commissioners and lack of political will. The failure to appoint a commission to deal with Gukurahundi injustices reveals the ZANU-PF government's unwillingness to embark on a genuine resolution of the Gukurahundi genocide. This chapter argues that the stalemate is caused by the military elite that has captured ZANU-PF and used it to form a securocratic state that was implicated in the Gukurahundi atrocities and is thus unwilling to prosecute, humiliate and/or reform itself out of power.

4

Sexual Violence: Gukurahundi's Public Secret

Sibonginkosi Moyo-Mpofu

Introduction

Sexual violence has been a hallmark of war since time immemorial and women and girls have largely been the primary target (Leatherman 2011). The Gukurahundi genocide is no exception. Much research has been conducted on the atrocities perpetrated against the people of Matabeleland and the Midlands during this period, 1983-87, when the ruling Zimbabwe African National Union Patriotic Front (ZANU-PF) waged a war on defenceless Ndebele-speaking supporters of the Zimbabwe African People's Union (PF-ZAPU), its erstwhile liberation war rival. While there is evidence that sexual violence as a weapon of war was used by the Fifth Brigade, and to some degree by the dissidents (CCJPZ and LRF 1997; Hodzi 2012), little investigation and documentation of these crimes has taken place, just as little has been done to redress these particular atrocities. The subject of sexual violence has also been a difficult area of study because the majority of victims are reluctant to come forward and speak for reasons that include shame, fear of being blamed or not believed, and at times being mistreated.

The chapter is written in the context of promises made by President Emmerson Mnangagwa's regime after controversially grabbing power from Robert Mugabe in November 2017. As noted in other chapters in the volume, the Mnangagwa regime, which labelled itself a 'Second Republic', promised Zimbabweans a 'new dispensation' which would, among other pressing issues, facilitate acceptable redress of the Gukurahundi genocide. The subject of Gukurahundi has gained national attention as a result of these promises, yet the suffering of women remains relegated to the side-lines, with focus being paid to other genocidal crimes, perceived as 'more grave', which include murders, disappearances, assault and arson.

Research indicates that sexual violence has serious physical and psychological consequences as well as devastating social and economic impacts on the lives of victims, their families and communities (Jones, et al. 2007; PLoS Medicine Editors 2009), yet these have yet to be investigated within the Gukurahundi context. Moreover, testimonies from survivors suggest that a significant number of children were born as a result of rape by the Fifth Brigade yet little if any work has been carried out to understand the experiences and needs of these mothers or their children.[1] Indeed, gender justice remains elusive in terms of transitional justice in Zimbabwe, although as Nowrojee (2012) argues, the inclusion of gender-violence in post conflict justice settings would contribute towards the condemnation of the horrors experienced by women and girls while also ensuring that perpetrators are held to account and such crimes are not repeated in future.

Using data from five focus group discussions and interviews carried out with Gukurahundi victims and from the documentary film *'I Want my Virginity Back'* (Asakhe Films 2020), this chapter explores narratives of sexual violence experienced in communities affected by Gukurahundi.[2] Narrative inquiry is used to examine how people speak about such experiences and how they reference the social, cultural and institutional context (Clandinin and Rosiek 2007). There remains a clear need to record the data on the magnitude and impact of sexual violence during Gukurahundi in order to facilitate effective interventions to address the needs of victims and to remove the cloak of secrecy. My argument is threefold: first there is not much attention about conflict-related sexual violence (CRSV) that occurred during the Gukurahundi genocide in current public discourses and activities aimed at addressing the genocide. This has, in turn, led to and is mirrored by a noticeable absence of research on the subject, and thirdly, victims themselves, for many reasons that I explore, find it difficult to open up about their experiences or are reluctant to do so even when approached.

Method

Data were collected from five focus group discussions (FGDs) held in an area directly affected by Gukurahundi i.e. Tsholotsho in Matabeleland North province. The FGDS were conducted by a Bulawayo-based NGO as part of their programming and the author was one of the facilitators. Community leaders were asked to invite

---

[1] Although not the subject of this chapter, this is a problem that has a long history in Zimbabwe, which betrays society's attitudes towards sexual violence against women in conflict situations.

[2] This is part of an ongoing Ph.D. research done by S. Mpofu. More field research is yet to be carried out.

up to twenty community members to these discussions. The call was aimed at people interested in talking about their Gukurahundi experiences and the groups contained eight to twenty participants and were a mixture of men and women. In some of these meetings, younger people who did not experience the atrocities also participated. The 2020 Asakhe Films documentary *I Want My Virginity Back* was also used.

Data from both the discussions and the documentary were analysed to assess how and when people speak about sexual violence during the genocide. The two sources of data differed in that the FGDs did not necessarily focus on sexual violence *per se*, while the documentary's main focus reflects the experience of sexual violence.

What is sexual violence?

Sexual violence is an act of a sexual nature by force or threat of force or coercion, a sexual act performed in a coercive environment and against someone incapable of giving genuine consent (ICC 2011; WHO 2012). Rape is the most common form of sexual violence (Leatherman 2011) – one where 'the body of a person is invaded, resulting in penetration, however slight, of any part of the body of the victim with a sexual organ or of the anal or genital opening of the victim' (ICC 2011). Sexual violence also includes the physically forced penetration, however slight, of the vulva or anus using other body parts or an object. It can also include other forms of assault involving a sexual organ such as forced contact between the mouth and penis, vulva or anus (WHO 2012). Rose (2015) argues that rape is not a sexual act but it is an act of violence.

Conflict-related sexual violence

Conflict-related sexual violence (CRSV) includes rape, sexual slavery, forced prostitution, forced pregnancy, enforced sterilisation, forced marriage and any other form of sexual violence of comparable gravity perpetrated against women, girls, men or boys and is directly or indirectly linked to a conflict (UN 2021). According to this report, the perpetrator is often associated with a state or non-state armed group while the victim is often identifiable through their actual or perceived link to a 'persecuted political, ethnic or religious minority group…'

Within the context of Gukurahundi, innocent civilians mainly women were sexually assaulted (i) for political reasons because they supported PF-ZAPU and (ii) for ethnic reasons because they were Ndebele. Women became the symbolic, indeed real, battlefield upon which the power of the state and the Shona was made manifest over defenceless civilians. However, women also suffered at the hands of dissidents, who were mainly Ndebele; they were caught between being accused by dissidents of helping the Fifth Brigade and accused by the latter of harbouring or sleeping with dissidents (Asakhe Films 2020).

Studies indicate that sexual violence is not a new phenomenon and continues to be a characteristic of conflict[3] (Chappell 2003; Leatherman 2011). It has, for example, been used as a weapon of war in countless conflict-ridden countries. These include Rwanda (estimated 250,000 to 500,000 women and girls), Bosnia and Herzegovina (approx. 60,0000 women and girls), Sierra Leone (over 50,000), the Democratic Republic of Congo (once referred to as the rape capital of the world) 200 000 since 1998. In Zimbabwe, testimonies have revealed horrendous sexual violations of female combatants by their male counterparts in guerrilla camps (Muwati et al. 2010; Nhongo-Simbanegavi 2000; Zimbabwe Women Writers 2000). Many civilians, especially *chimbwidos* – young women who ran errands, cooked and cared for guerrillas who operated in their areas – are said to have suffered the same fate (Zimbabwe Women Writers 2000).[4]

Although there is extensive literature on the subject of sexual violence, it is almost always gender-blind. Nowrojee (2012) notes that in many post-conflict settings, gender justice often remains the exception rather than the rule. As a result, victims of sexual violence in conflict have not had the opportunity to find healing, or for their voices to be recognised as part of the collective narrative of conflict and post conflict. Writing about CRSV in Zimbabwe's war of liberation, Muwati, Mheta and Gambahaya (2010) observe that official historical accounts systematically suppress women combatants' brutal experiences of sexual violence at the hands of guerrilla commanders, in order to promote narratives of heroism and 'patriotic' history.[5] Within the Gukurahundi context, neither the prevalence nor the impact of sexual violence on victims, their families and their communities have been investigated extensively, thus it remains a public secret almost forty years on.

Sexual violence in conflict has gained global attention in the last two decades following the establishment of the international criminal tribunals of the former Yugoslavia (ICTY) (UN Security Council Resolution 827 in 1993) and Rwanda (ICTR) (UN Security Council Resolution 955 in 1995). The ICTY was the first to include rape as a crime against humanity (Njoroge 2016; Tompkins 1995). The ICTR was the first war crimes court to deliver verdicts against crimes of genocide in Rwanda and to prosecute, convict and sentence perpetrators of sexual violence

---

3   'Sexual Violence, the Weapon of War That Has Ceased to Die'. *Huffington Post*, 13 2014.

4   More recently, former combatant and ZANU-PF MP Margaret Dongo testified that women combatants endured unspeakable sexual abuse in ZANLA guerrilla camps in Mozambique, mainly at the hands of their commanders. She lamented that most of the women have been systematically silenced. 'Margaret Dongo lifts the lid', *Newsday* 11 August 2022 [https://www.newsday.co.zw/2022/08/dongo-lifts-lid-on-liberation-war-sex-abuses/] accessed 26 August 2022.

5   In 2006, Fay Chung's book, *Reliving the Second Chimurenga* exposed some of the abuses of female combatants in ZANLA liberation camps and even fingered some senior Zimbabwean national heroes. In relation to this chapter, these testimonies reveal that ZANU-PF exported and deepened a serious culture of sexual violence to Matabeleland and the Midlands during the Gukurahundi.

in a genocide (Njoroge 2016). More importantly, it was the first to not only define rape in international criminal law, but also to recognise it as a means of perpetrating genocide (Njoroge 2016). This led to crimes of sexual violence (CRSV) being recognised internationally as a gross human rights violation (Duggan and Jacobson 2009; PLoS Medicine Editors 2009; Simic 2018).

As a result, sexual violence in conflict is no longer seen as an inevitable by-product of war but as a defining tactic of modern conflicts that is both preventable and punishable (DioGuardi 2016; UN Peacekeeping n.d.) These tribunals also led to the inclusion of sexual violence crimes in the Rome statute of the 2000 Rome Treaty of the International Criminal Court (ICC). Many countries globally have ratified numerous treaties on the recognition of sexual violence in conflict as a crime against humanity yet few have gone on to put into practice what they signed up for (Boesten 2014). Thus, CRSV remains on the periphery of transitional justice efforts; a very public secret, as knowledge of its occurrence is known yet the violations remain absent from public and human rights discourse.

Sexual violence is a cheap and readily available weapon of war yet its effect on target communities is long-lasting (Maciejczak 2013). It is a weapon (Jones et al. 2014; Leatherman 2011; Park 2007) which serves a fundamental purpose. It is not just men seeking sexual gratification from women. Rather, it serves a greater purpose, which is the humiliation of the target population. While it is the individual woman who is sexually violated, the family and the community, its identity as well as its social relationships and status, are also attacked through the individual (Boesten 2014; Jones et al. 2014, Human Rights Watch 1996). Gottschall (2004: 131) aptly posits that war time rape is 'a coherent, coordinated, logical, and brutally effective means of prosecuting warfare'. Systematic rape is used as a war weapon for ethnic cleansing and its ultimate goal is to erode the community fabric, and in a way that few weapons can (Domingo et al. 2013; Human Rights Watch 2011). The incidents of rape are often unpredictable thus serving to not only terrorise the community but also to deter any efforts towards resistance or attempts at protection (Moser and Clark 2001).

Men see themselves as protectors of women in their communities, from their wives and daughters to their mothers and relatives and are, in this way, also targeted for humiliation and from being powerless to protect their women and children. Bernard (1994 in Maciejczak 2013) outlines six strategies of sexual violence as a weapon of war: (i) it can facilitate ethnic cleansing by forcing people to flee their homes (ii). It can demoralise the enemy [target], (iii). It signals the intention to break up the community, (iv). It inflicts trauma and psychological damage on the enemy, (v). It provides psychological benefits to the enemy [the attackers/occupiers] and (vi). It inflicts a blow against a collective enemy if the target group is of high symbolic value. Bhattacharyya (2008), notes that rape accounts show that it is designed to terrorise the whole community. It is 'symbolic defilement' (p. 109) meant to show the enemy that they are powerless and that the perpetrator can humiliate them as they please. Bhattacharyya (2008: 109) sums it up: 'War rape is an address to the enemy – 'look at us violate your people, look at us contaminate your stock and make your children ours, look at how helpless you are before our brutality.'

Brownmiller (1975) notes that men's attitude towards the raping of women is that it is inevitable. As long as men are fighting for the acquisition of new land, for the subjugation of new people, then 'unquestionably there shall be some raping' (Brownmiller 1975: 31). She notes that this has been the case throughout many religious wars, wars of revolution, World War I and II, the Vietnamese war, etc. While in the twentieth century, rape has been condemned as a criminal act, it still continues to be a common weapon of war, with women seen as regrettable casualties. Rape in war is possible as a result of society's pre-existing socio-economic and culturally shaped gender-relations with women's experiences of insecurity predicated on a range of socio-economic and political factors that view the status of women as lower than that of men (Leatherman 2011; Ni Aolain 2013). Kirby (2011) notes that it is feminist scholars who championed a view of sexual violence as a form of social power characterised by gender dynamics, and this effectively politicised it and forced it into the public domain.

Sexual violence during the Gukurahundi genocide

The Gukurahundi, also known as the 5 Brigade or the Fifth Brigade, was made up of mostly Shona-speaking soldiers and there is anecdotal evidence suggesting that they claimed their goal was to destroy the Ndebele ethnic group because they supported Joshua Nkomo, the leader of PF-ZAPU. The Fifth Brigade were deployed in Matabeleland North in 1983 and in Matabeleland South in 1984 and they wreaked havoc in these communities, with an estimated 20,000 civilians being killed, hundreds disappeared, and thousands more severely assaulted (CCJPZ and LRF 1997; Cameron 2018). Oral testimonies indicate that a significant number of women and girls were raped or sexually violated in one form or another. These violations occurred in public and private spaces (Asakhe Films 2020). Women and young girls were either raped in front of their families or communities or forcibly taken to the Gukurahundi bases ostensibly to cook for the soldiers but instead subjected to rape and other forms of sexual assault. One of the participants of the focus group discussions wonders 'what kind of cooking takes place at night?' an indication that he was aware that the women were not cooking but undergoing something far worse. Although no direct links have been made, the sexual assault of women in military bases which took place in Matabeleland has a history in

ZANLA military camps in Mozambique. Muwati, Mheta and Gambahaya (2010) contend that the main reason why women were not at the battlefront as guerrillas was that they were domesticated in the rear (the camps) for the sexual gratification of commanders. Tragically, women's bodies became sites of abuse, exploitation and violation not by Rhodesian forces, but by the nationalists.

Moser and Clark (2001) also posit that in many conflicts, girls are taken to camps by soldiers ostensibly for cooking, laundry and cleaning, while in reality they are needed for the amusement of the soldiers. In the context of Gukurahundi, abductions and rapes were a systematic war strategy. Moser and Clark bring out another element of war-time rape which is important to consider in the context of Gukurahundi, which was the transfer of assets from women. In most African communities, women have little control over physical assets such as land, their assets are their productive and reproductive labour. Abducting women from their homes to cook and clean for the soldiers removed this contribution and was a secondary act of demoralisation. Moser and Clark suggest several aspects of reproductive labour, motives and consequences to the act of rape: women being raped so that they give birth to 'enemy' children, thereby preventing them from becoming mothers within their own communities, while often also making them unacceptable to their neighbours and families; or injuring them physically so they are unable to bear children. They give as a case in point in the Rwandan context:

> Women of child-bearing age were targeted as reproducers of society. They were not killed as war booty or collateral damage. Rather they were targeted as part of a policy specifically encouraged and directed to further the goal of the genocide leaders which was to destroy all Tutsi as a social group. (Moser and Clark: 59).

Similarly, during the Gukurahundi genocide, women were raped and sexually assaulted as part of a strategy to destroy the Ndebele as a social group.

Many of the children born as a result of Gukurahundi rape have no knowledge of their fathers and in some cases even of the tragic circumstances of their birth. As noted in some chapters in this volume, some of these children, who are now adults, were not able to obtain birth certificates which are necessary to write public examinations at school, to get national identity cards and to enjoy most citizenship rights in Zimbabwe, which in many cases has cascaded to their offspring. Apart from a plethora of social and cultural problems, such children found it difficult to integrate in society as young adults. Many joined the hordes of young people from the region who trekked to neighbouring countries such as South Africa in desperate search of a living. Ultimately, the development of the Ndebele and their region is negatively impacted, as Mpofu and Makombe argue in this volume. In many cases, children born of rape served as constant reminders of the horrors that befell their mother (see Baker 2016).

In the documentary 'I Want My Virginity Back', a young woman recounts how her father hated her sister who was born through the rape of her mother by Gukurahundi soldiers. Later, the sister committed suicide owing to the ill-treatment from her step-father, which the mother was powerless to stop. Another victim of rape narrated that her husband had accused her of willingly sleeping with the soldiers, and thus the couple had an acrimonious relationship until the husband died. Knowledge of a woman being raped during war, often results in domestic abuse post-conflict as the man struggles to cope with what happened (Anderlini 2011).

The rape of girls and women as well as boys and men has gained not only media attention but also attention from NGOs and INGOs, human rights groups and scholars (see Maedl (2011). This has unfortunately not been the case with Gukurahundi-related sexual violence four decades on. The CCJPZ report documents only a few reported cases of sexual violence and acknowledges that this is because very few people would have been comfortable reporting such cases. As a result, sexual violence during the genocide has been conspicuously missing from public discourse.

Sexual violence as a public secret

Historically, experiences of sexual violence are often shrouded in silence and secrecy (DioGuardi 2016; Tombs 2016). Public secrecy entails what Taussig (1999) aptly refers to as 'unsecret secrets' that you have to pretend not to know and that everybody pretends not to know. Victims and witnesses alike tacitly keep hidden what is known for fear of negative social consequences of speaking out. Zerubavel (2006) speaks of a 'conspiracy of silence' around issues that individuals and communities are reluctant to discuss publicly. To borrow from Zerubavel, there is a 'conspiracy of silence' around sexual violence resulting in mutual denial. Silence plays a fundamental role in how communities remember the past (Stone et al. 2012). People are able to speak at length about a specific period in their lives yet leave out certain aspects of that experience. The silence is a result of various factors, including fear, shame, embarrassment and pain (Zerubavel 2006). A group of people collectively partake in the denial, thereby preventing that subject from entering public discourse, i.e. effectively silencing it.

This appears to be the case with sexual violence perpetrated during Gukurahundi. Narratives abound on the killings, abductions, and arson that obtained yet little is revealed about experiences of sexual violence. It is not just the victim who keeps silent but the whole family and community tacitly agree to keep mute for reasons that include shame, thereby implicitly silencing the subject (Delic and Avdibegovic 2015; Zerubavel 2006). CRSV does not become part of the collective narrative of the community. Where it surfaces, it is more visible as a mass crime or as impersonal narratives, for example: *they were raping women, many women were raped.* The individual characteristics are minimal, they are rarely specific, personal narratives around what happened or how it happened.

Rape and other forms of gender-based violence are marred by severe social stigma and this leaves women not only physically and psychologically scarred but also burdened with isolation and ostracisation (Human Rights Watch Report 1996). The majority of women will not publicly reveal their experiences for fear of rejection and failing to reintegrate into their communities. Thus women are pressured into staying silent. Moreover, women who were publicly violated, are more at risk of failing to get married because everyone knows about their 'shame'. A Gukurahundi rape survivor in 'I Want My Virginity Back', testifies how the father of her child would not follow through on his promise of marriage because after being raped numerous times by the Fifth Brigade and the dissidents, the man's parents told him he could not marry her because she was a 'prostitute' who was 'sleeping with soldiers':

> The boy who got me pregnant had not broken up with me but his parents ended up telling him that he should not marry the […] prostitute. She has been sleeping with the Gukurahundi at Gomoza. … I am a prostitute because I am forced to sleep with whoever wants to sleep with me. Another one comes and forces himself on me in the bush. (Asakhe Films 2020).

Stigmatisation and isolation often make it difficult for women to speak publicly about sexual violence (DioGuardi 2016). One can only extrapolate that this is also the case with Gukurahundi victims because so little research has been done in this regard. Interestingly, the documentary *I Want My Virginity Back* portrays mostly elderly women speaking openly about their experiences with the use of such language as … 'my husband is dead so I can speak'. Mostly younger women (in their late forties and fifties) interviewed in the documentary are unidentifiable, their faces are blurred.[6] This indicates that elderly women are 'de-sexualised' and therefore have nothing more to lose, they can thus share their experiences, something they would not have been able to do when they were younger. A vast majority of rape survivors, especially younger women, will hide their experiences if they can so as to preserve their livelihoods and remain part of families and communities (Moser and Clark 2001).

Interestingly, Zimbabwe appears too comfortable to endorse this silence as evidenced not only by the lack of efforts to address sexual violence in the Gukurahundi genocide. The institutionalised silence on the subject and the refusal to investigate its horrors is also borne of the reality that a number of the perpetrators remain in

---

6   This observation was also confirmed in interviews with producers of the film in August 2022.

powerful positions and an investigation would not serve their best interests (Eppel 2004; Killander and Nyathi 2015; Doran 2017). Furthermore, the wider prohibition of discussion about Gukurahundi in Zimbabwean society (Eppel 2004) also entailed prohibition of talk about sexual violence, thereby creating two layers of silence.

There has been little effort in Zimbabwean national law to address sexual violence during Gukurahundi. The Government of National Unity (GNU) established the Organ on National Healing, Reconciliation and Integration (ONHRI), which was headed by three ministers, one each from the three parties to the Global Political Agreement. Hodzi (2012) notes that the ONHRI paid little to no regard to gender dynamics of political violence. The 2013 Zimbabwe constitution established the National Peace and Reconciliation Commission Act (NPRCA). It provides for a Gender Unit that will, among other things 'investigate the use of sexual violence during armed conflict'. In this regard, a Victim Support, Diversity Management and Gender Committee (VSD and GC) was established by the commission, its role being to advise on strategies and methodologies for responding to gender provisions of the law. Despite this positive and promising endeavour, to date, there has been no concerted effort to address crimes of sexual violence during Gukurahundi, meaning that there is still no opportunity for justice and reparation for survivors, and with only less than a year before the termination of the NPRC mandate.

In 2019, the VSD and GC conducted women 'safe spaces' meetings around the country, including in Tsholotsho, Bulawayo and Maphisa. While these were meetings targeting women and focused on issues affecting them such as access to critical services, sexual violence was not included on the agenda. It was the women themselves in these meetings who chose to speak about their experiences during Gukurahundi, which only confirms their desperate need of safe spaces to narrate their experiences and explain how it has affected their lives or the welfare of their communities.

The secrecy and silence around sexual violence during Gukurahundi goes beyond the shame and trauma felt by survivors to that of the patriarchal anger also felt by their communities. There is the shame and anger associated with men's 'failure' to stand up to the perpetrator to protect 'their' women from being sexually assaulted. There is also the notion that men's honour has been compromised because their women were assaulted in front of them, and by Shona men, injuring both their masculinity and their pride. Leatherman (2011) posits that women's standing in society plays a fundamental role in how they recount or fail to recount their experiences of sexual violence; the views, feelings and reactions of their society are a major priority and influence.

Gukurahundi's survivors of sexual violence therefore do not 'own' the anger and the shame of being raped. The environment in which they live does not allow them to do so. They have to bottle it up together with their pain and pretend the violation never happened so as to protect the dignity of the patriarchy. One may even go as far as arguing that they are simply reminders of the injury committed against the men in the community. Such social pressure forms a dominant part of the silencing mechanisms that prevent women from speaking out, resulting in what Leatherman argues contributes to incomplete histories of rape narratives and analyses.

The conspiracy of secrecy and silence about CRSV during Gukurahundi also spilled into the academic world where there is little mention of it. Much has now been written about the period, ranging from reasons resulting in the genocide to the horrors that obtained during that time and these are covered in much detail (CCJPZ and LRF 1997; Eppel 2004; Killander and Nyathi 2015). Nonetheless, sexual violence has never been investigated to the extent it deserves. Zerubavel (2006) argues that what we avoid socially is also avoided academically. If this is the case, one cannot help but question the role of academic research if it is not to unpack and analyse a country's history, no matter how controversial. The work that has been done to unearth the silence on CRSV in Zimbabwe's liberation war is a case in point.

The CCJPZ report (1997: 4) cites the need to 'promote greater openness to certain truths, currently denied…' and further states that 'There is a significant chunk of Zimbabwean history which is largely unknown' (CCJPZ and LRF 1997: 3), stating:

> Apart from murders, many other atrocities took place in Zimbabwe between 1982 and 1988, such as destruction of homesteads or even entire villages, mass detentions of civilians, and the physical torture of civilians, including rape and the phenomenon of mass beatings (CCJPZ and LRF, 1997: 6).

As a case in point, the report cites a family who reported their two minor daughters being taken from their home into the forest by the Gukurahundi soldiers, where they were *beaten* then returned home. Reading between the lines suggests that the girls were taken to the forest and raped yet the family's account is censored. This censorship could be interpreted as the family actively convincing itself that the heinous crime of rape was not perpetrated on the innocent girls. They are silent because they are trying to protect themselves from the pain as well as the shame that comes with rape and their failure as parents to protect their minor children. It is difficult to know whether the girls were only subjected to beatings, but from other accounts of young women or girls being taken away, it is likely that if any sexual violence occurred it was suppressed in the parents' accounts, or was not pursued by the interviewers. In the ZWW's (2000) anthology, one of the former female candidates explains that often, they did not report sexual assault quite simply because doing so was futile. It is therefore important that this silence around sexual violence be interrogated, it is the responsibility of researchers to investigate. Often, families of victims of sexual violence protect themselves from the pain and the shame by suppressing the experience when they narrate events.

As Simic (2018) notes, many women may not want to have their histories repeated in public, at least not with their names mentioned, for fear of stigma and ostracism as well as the likely negative reactions from their husbands and families. Yet many feminists understand the importance of documenting women's lives and experiences, and for many women, it is important that their voices be heard in the public domain. Porter (2007) sees the articulation of women's narratives about sexual violence as important to traumatized women because they promote the search for truth and healing. Simic (2018) concurs with this view as she argues that documentation is important, for at least seeking justice for women's suffering. Muwati, Mheta and Gambahaya (2010) argue that in relation to Zimbabwe's liberation war history, documenting the voices and experiences of women creates 'a gender-based trajectory of memory' (p.171), which turns gender into a vital resource that can be employed to challenge historical authoritarianism and discourse. In so doing, women are empowered to articulate experiences of their resilience in dehumanising conflicts. Simic's approach is that instead of asking women questions about their experiences, rather let them tell their stories, uninterrupted, let them tell what they think is important for them to share. But sexual violence has been so much a secret for too long it does not naturally come up even during Gukurahundi talk. ZWW's (2000) approach – having victims interviewed by women – is also worth considering.

Narratives of silence

As has been noted, most conversations and narratives of Gukurahundi experiences are mostly silent on sexual violence incidents, focusing mostly on killings and some other forms of violence. A look at some of these conversations shows that victims are reluctant to speak of personal experiences of sexual violence and tend to speak of it in general terms or as something that happened to other people. This includes such examples: '*They were raping our women*'. This is a blanket statement which on the one hand acknowledges that women were being raped yet on the other paints rape not as an individual crime but a mass crime. One could argue that it is part of the masking of sexual violence crimes because it gives no room for intervention for the victim(s).

Narratives from focus group discussions analysed for this chapter seem to reinforce this point, as discussions focused largely on other genocidal crimes to the exclusion of sexual violence. Participants spoke at length about the murders of family members and neighbours, abductions, torching of homes, the many meetings they were forced to attend and the many people who abandoned their homes in search of safety mostly in the city of Bulawayo. In almost all the discussions, participants did not speak about sexual violence at all. In the few cases where it was raised, it would be from an individual and none of the other participants followed up on the issue.

Below, are some of the excerpts of the testimonies of women given during the focus group discussions:

- They would take the women in the evenings to go and cook for them and they would return in the morning, what kind of cooking takes all night
- There was no sexual violence in our area fortunately … They met my mother coming from the fields with her pots and plates and accused her of cooking for the dissidents… they called a community meeting and forced her to strip naked and walk up and down in front of everyone.

These two quotes raise interesting questions, which underline the difficulties victims experience when attempting to confront the reality of rape. The second one further brings into light people's different perceptions of what sexual violence constitutes. This woman was not raped but was forced to strip naked in public, obviously intended to shame and humiliate her. While this was a degrading, embarrassing situation, the daughter's sentiments indicate that she had never thought of her mother's experience as sexual assault until she was asked if she did not think her mother was sexually assaulted. From this, one could argue that it is the secrecy around the subject that limits people's understanding of and ability to question such events.

- They took my daughter with them one evening…. She says that in the morning when she unzipped the sleeping bag, there was a snake next to her. She says she was so scared because she could have died.

This woman chooses to ignore the possibility that her daughter had unconsented sexual intercourse with the soldiers. Focusing on the incident with the snake helps her focus on something that she believes is beyond her control, a snake, which is naturally wild and dangerous.

- They did it to me.

In 'I Want My Virginity Back' one victim speaks of her experience of rape at the age of seventeen at the hands of a soldier:

- I was called by this soldier…. I didn't know anything, I was a child… He dragged me into a ditch… if you deny me what I want I will kill you…Right there he did what he wanted with me even though I was a child.

This is another way of speaking about rape, *it*, almost euphemistically. It is difficult for this woman to say what it is but listening to her story makes it clear that *it* refers to rape.

Conclusion

The subject of sexual violence during Gukurahundi remains cloaked in silence almost forty years on. Granted, Gukurahundi itself has been cloaked in official silence for over three decades, only burgeoning into the limelight recently. The same cannot be said of sexual violence. Affected communities live with this public secret, with many victims in desperate need of support. Only when the lid is lifted from this silence can victims and their communities be able to heal and rebuild their lives.

5

Dismembering Memory of a Genocide: Contestations over Bhalagwe Mass Graves Memorial Site

Mbuso Fuzwayo, Samukele Hadebe and Dion Nkomo

Introduction

Zimbabwean authorities have tried, albeit with little success, to either deny or distort the macabre events euphemistically called Gukurahundi, which in essence constituted crimes against humanity involving ethnic cleansing and genocide in Matabeleland and Midlands provinces. Gukurahundi is 'a taboo topic for discussion and debate insofar as such debates threaten hegemonic notions of national unity and expose the ruling Zimbabwe African People's Union – Patriotic Front's (ZANU-PF) violent incorporation of the Zimbabwe African People's Union (ZAPU) to entrench its rule' (Nyambi 2014: 2). There remains a veil of secrecy and heavy censorship over the period, notwithstanding efforts by some writers and artists to keep the matter alive. In its futile attempts to manipulate the remembering of the genocide, the Government of Zimbabwe (GoZ) and the ruling party, ZANU-PF, are in a way engaged in efforts to dismember the memory of the genocide and instead, create a positive image of these otherwise cruel and tragic events. For Christiansen (2005: 9), the unity founded on the state's strategic remembrances of the massacres is 'installed as the sign by which memories of the violent past could be turned into an obligation to forget.' Similar efforts have been witnessed in other post-genocide contexts such as Namibia and Rwanda (Jessee 2017). However, forced forgetting and selective remembrance would be difficult for victims whose pain and hurt remain unacknowledged and unatoned.

This chapter explores contestations over the memory of Gukurahundi genocide, with particular reference to the Bhalagwe memorial site. It draws on the work and experiences of Ibhetshu Likazulu and relevant communities on the one side and on the other, ZANU-PF and its ex-guerrilla veterans. Ibhetshu Likazulu is a community-based human rights organisation which was founded in 2005 to address issues of concern to the communities of Midlands, Bulawayo, Matabeleland North and Matabeleland South provinces, which were the primary target of Gukurahundi. From 2017, the organisation has been at the forefront of efforts to remember the victims of the genocide who remain buried in disused Bhalagwe mine shafts in Matobo district, Matabeleland South.

Not enough scholarly attention has been paid to concerted attempts by authorities to erase the memory of the genocide, and this has perpetuated a culture of violence with impunity in Zimbabwe. Nor has there been documentation of the efforts by communities and community-based organisations such as Ibhetshu Likazulu to resist the distortion and erasure of the genocide memory. By using Bhalagwe as a case study, we seek to demonstrate the conflictual memories of Gukurahundi by the Zimbabwean government and Ibhetshu Likazulu. By authoring this as collaborative reflections led by Mbuso Fuzwayo, the secretary general of Ibhetshu Likazulu, we evoke some aspects of autoethnography to give the organisation a voice that has continually been silenced by government, as it shall be seen in this chapter. Inspired by Chimamanda Adichie, Jessee (2017) exposes the danger of a single story regarding the memorialisation of the Rwandan genocide, which the Kagame regime has striven to monopolise.

Autoethnography is described as:

> ... a research method that uses personal experience ("auto") to describe and interpret ("graphy") cultural texts, experiences, beliefs, and practices ("ethno"). Autoethnographers believe that personal experience is infused with political/cultural norms and expectations, and they engage in rigorous self-reflection—typically referred to as "reflexivity"—in order to identify and interrogate the intersections between the self and social life (Adams, Ellis and Jones 2017: 2).

From an autoethnographic perspective, the voice of Ibhetshu Likazulu shares the organisation's experiences of navigating the repressive space where its activities are deemed illegal. Adams, Ellis and Jones (2017: 3) assert that autoethnographic accounts 'speak against, or provide alternatives to, dominant, taken-for-granted, and harmful cultural scripts, stories, and stereotypes'. This speaks to the Zimbabwean context where the government dominates the public sphere and delegitimises any subversive voices. Organisations such as Ibhetshu Likazulu rely on alternative media platforms to express their concerns. While both the organisation and the

GoZ claim to be driven by the desire to bring peace and healing in the aftermath of Gukurahundi, their versions and activities nonetheless markedly contradict each other. It is these contestations that are dealt with in this chapter, with the focus being to offer another side of the story that accounts for the experiences of Gukurahundi victims as represented by Ibhetshu Likazulu. This is a rare opportunity for Ibhetshu Likazulu to define itself as a human rights advocacy organisation in a genocidal context that is characterised by the monopolisation of memorialisation of the country's past including the war of liberation and the genocide that ensued afterwards. Relevant literature is used to indicate that Ibhetshu Likazulu's tussles with the GoZ are not unique but prevalent in post-genocide contexts.

Memorialisation of genocides: a brief literature review

Reflecting on the writings about the Rwandan genocide, Small (2007) regards the memorialisation of genocides as the duty of memory. Yet genocide memorialisation is always characterised by contestations that result in 'sites of aggressor-victim memory' (Kosicki 2007: 24). Jessee (2017) also captures this precisely in her analysis of the complexity of researching post-genocide remembrances in Rwanda. At the core of such complexity is the generally perverse genocide denial by aggressors (Bilali, Iqbal and Freel 2020, King, 2010; Sibanda, 2021). It took 107 years for Germany to acknowledge her responsibility in the Namibian genocide. While obstinate and resistant to any efforts of memorialising the genocide, the same government ironically continued to adore and protect monuments commemorating German colonial soldiers in Namibia. While tributes were paid to German soldiers of the genocide era at various monuments, 'indigenous soldiers [including those who perished in the genocide] are rarely listed on such monuments' (Steinmetz and Hell 2006: 117).

The literature on the Namibian genocide is replete with examples of the lopsided nature of 'power and means ... in the struggle over memorialisation' of genocides (Niezen 2018: 554). One apt example pertains to the Kramersdorf cemetery in Swakopmund, a coastal city to the west of Windhoek. The cemetery has two sections which exhibit a striking contrast. Lyrefelt (2020) paints a scenic picture of the German section with graves marked by tombstones, names, location, date of birth and death of each soldier. Around the graves are flourishing, green irrigated plants and well-constructed paths. The section where genocide victims are buried provides a stark contrast that closely mirrors that of the Zimbabwe's national heroes acre and the Bhalagwe mass graves.

> Instead of tombstones, the graves are marked with sand heaps. Sometimes there is a wooden cross or just a rock on top of the sand heaps. There are no names, dates, place of birth/death wherever you look (Lyrefelt 2020: 31).

The lopsided nature of power against genocide victims frustrates the commemorative efforts of victims and relevant advocacy organisations. Their memorialisation activities are regarded as unprogressive, divisive and undesirable for nation-building and economic development. They are resisted because they evoke what Jeftic (2019) calls 'dangerous memories'. Fears of dangerous memories strike authorities who attempt to suppress the unpleasant genocidal experiences. In Namibia, Sam Nujoma, the independent country's inaugural president declared that 'The new Namibia and the new Germany are no longer concerned with the past. We are leaving the sad history behind us and are working progressively together' (Die Welt 2002). On their part, the German Namibians have expressed their disdain towards the Herero and Nama activities. For example, they protested the culturally symbolic mounting of a bull skull on a Herero chief's grave at the Kramersdorf cemetery, complaining to the police that it was stinking (Lyrefelt 2020: 31-2; Steinmetz and Hell 2006: 168). Here the victims are denied a culturally appropriate way of mourning and remembering their departed who perished in the genocide. Literature from other contexts such as Rwanda indicates that activities of memorialising genocides are criminalised, repressed and dealt with through brutal operations that are themselves reminiscent of the genocides that the victims would have survived (Jessee 2017). As it will be seen, the contestations of Gukurahundi genocide in Zimbabwe are characterised by government's repressive and violent response to memorialisation activities by Gukurahundi victims and advocacy organisations.

Steinmetz and Hell (2006: 375) use the concept of co-optation to show how, faced with the futility of attaining forced forgetting from the victims, those in power attempt to appropriate aspects of genocides for their own political capital. The Namibian government has conveniently appropriated originally Herero and Nama commemorative days to make them national holidays, especially the Herero Day and the Heroes Day. The former, previously called the 'Red Flag Day' (Lyrefelt 2020; Niezen 2018; Steinmetz and Hell 2006; Kössler 2007) was initially a Herero commemoration of Samuel Maherero who led the Herero revolt against the Germans, culminating in the genocide. The latter is a celebration of Henrick Witbooi, who was originally celebrated by the Nama following his murder during the genocide in 1905. Kössler (2007: 375) views both commemorative days as 'clear and explicit instance[s] of shifting emphasis to a national perspective' from the groups who are genuinely aggrieved by the genocide. These remembrance holidays and monuments have not appeased the disenfranchised communities who regard them as 'little more than lip service in bronze, brick, and stone' (Niezen 2018: 556). Contestations thus continue, with the Herero and Nama continuing to use the days to protest the genocide and its enduring legacy. Ultimately, while genocides are commemorated, memorialisation activities are not only separate, but they are also different. Often, victims mourn their departed while the aggressors celebrate their role in ending genocides which they presided over and yet continue to absolve themselves. Niezen's report (ibid.: 559) 'strategic avoidance' of the Namibian government's participation in the programmes organised by *Oturupa*, a Herero network called which runs campaigns for genocide justice.

What the literature reviewed here shows is the complexity of memorialising a genocide. In the case of the Namibian genocide, the contestations involve three parties, with the victims yearning for their justice, on the one hand, pitted against the perpetrators in the form of Germany (and the German Namibians), as well as the collaborating post-independent Namibian government, on the other hand. It is on this account that the Namibian victims have declared their struggle for justice as 'fighting against two governments' (ibid.: 550), with both governments having different benefits from the memory erasure of the genocide. Germany has been accused of hypocrisy for memorialising the holocaust (ibid.: 550; Steinmetz and Hell 2006; Lyrefelt 2020), which scholars regard as no different from the Namibian genocide. Olusoga and Erichsen (2010) regard the latter as Germany's own holocaust. As it will be shown in the remainder of the chapter, Gukurahundi remains the GoZ's own holocaust that would ideally be wished away by the authorities who continue to profit from its legacy.

Challenges in researching the Gukurahundi genocide

Researching genocides is generally difficult because the perpetrators always deny the occurrences and invest heavily towards concealing their crimes and destroying any relevant evidence. Jessee (2017) has already noted that regarding the Rwandan genocide. Official narratives do not acknowledge genocides. In Zimbabwe, two government commissioned reports on Gukurahundi, the Chihambahwe Commission Report and Dumbutshena Commission Report, have never been made public. Nonetheless, academic papers, dissertations and books continue to be published on various aspects of the Gukurahundi years. Some notable works on Gukurahundi include the Catholic Commission for Justice and Peace (CCJPZ 1997) and Legal Resources Foundation (LRF 1999), Alexander et al (2000), Lindgren (2002), Eppel (2004), Mashingaidze (2005), Ndlovu-Gatsheni (2008), Scarnecchia (2011), Moorcraft (2012), Muchemwa (2015), Ndlovu (2017) and Ngwenya (2017).

Notwithstanding the growing corpus of literature on Gukurahundi, the understanding of events still remains clouded by multiple narratives about who drove the conflict and for what reasons. This fuzziness may be because there is still unease among those who experienced it and a fear of speaking out as well as a lack of unfettered access for comprehensive research on the ground. The many questions that remain unanswered and not easy to research within the prevailing political atmosphere in the country have given room to imagination, conjecture and in some cases, outright distortion. Very little memorialisation work has been done to date, except, arguably, the commemorative event of 22 December 1987; the date when the unity accord between PF-ZAPU and ZANU-PF was signed, which was declared a national holiday, Unity Day. Even still, this commemoration qualifies as a case co-optative remembrance that is akin to those reported in Namibia (Lyrefelt 2020; Niezen 2018; Steinmetz and Hell 2006; Kössler 2007).

Interestingly, creative work, especially fiction, has popularised the subject of the genocide and kept it at the forefront of the public eye. As with academic publications, fiction has tended to focus on either detailing the brutalities or speculating on the causes and apportioning culpability. Two distinguished artistic works drew national and international attention, that is, Owen Maseko's *Sibathontisele* (Let's drip on them) paintings in 2010 and the *ULoyiko* (fear) theatrical performance in 2017 by the Cape-Town-based Siphesakhe Youth Organisation. Maseko was arrested and charged with violating Section 33 of the Criminal Law and Codification Act, a law that punishes anyone who 'insults or undermines the authority of the President'. He was also charged with Section 42(2): 'Causing offence to persons of a particular race, religion, etc.[1]) Since incarcerating artists could not apply to the foreign *Loyiko* troupe, it is alleged that agents of the Zimbabwean state offered them a bribe to stop the drama but to no avail[2].

Yvonne Vera's *Stone Virgins* (2002) is one fictional work of significance that popularised the genocide. Less known but equally historic novels are David Magagula's *Sasisemeveni* and Ezekiel Hleza's *Uyangisinda Lumhlaba* (1992). Ndlovu (2001) suggests that such works were products of distortion by the Zimbabwe Literature Bureau, which solicited and screened literature to make it pro-establishment before and after independence (cf. Chiwome 1996). Christopher Mlalazi's *Running with Mother* (2012) is also a powerful work, and so are several poems, e.g. 'We Bhalagwe' (Zondo 2018) and Siziba's (2017) 'Ode to the nameless', which are performed at Gukurahundi commemorative events or published online. Also, of importance in pioneering protest art against Gukurahundi is Lovemore Majayivana Tshuma through his many Ndebele songs that tended to subtly allude to the genocide and the subsequent marginalisation of the people of Matabeleland (Hadebe 2001).

Alexander (2021: 763) describes the constrained voices of the Gukurahundi victims as 'forced silence'. This forced silence has meant that many works on the genocide were published abroad by writers and academics who often never had

---

[1] 'Art, censorship and the Gukurahundi', **Pambazuka News**, 23 October 2010.
[2] 'Zapu applauds ULoyiko Play on Zimbabwean Gukurahundi Genocide', **Bulawayo 24 News**, 3 July 2016.

the opportunity to talk to survivors or visit concentration camps or mass graves. Notwithstanding, the works by Timothy Scarnecchia (2011), Hazel Cameron (2018) and Stuart Doran (2017) that utilised de-classified diplomatic sources, which were previously inaccessible, have revealed more about certain actors that had either gone unnoticed or whose roles were not fully explained. Still, the Matabele genocide memorialisation remains under-researched and information is scant despite the efforts of some writers, artists, journalists and organisations like Ibhetshu Likazulu.

The story of Bhalagwe

Although there is still no certainty about the number of the Gukurahundi casualties, the disappeared and those maimed from the brutality of the genocidaires, the worst atrocities were in Matabeleland North province where the murderous Fifth Brigade of the Zimbabwe National Army was initially deployed. The most affected districts in Matabeleland North were Tsholotsho, Lupane and Nkayi, and later parts of Midlands like Silobela, Zhombe and Lower Gweru, where the crack force left a bloody trail of destruction characterised by mass rape, torture, burnt homesteads and mass murder. However, surprisingly, the largest mass grave is not in Matabeleland North but in Bhalagwe, Matabeleland South (Alexander 2021). That this is so attests to the sinister efforts to destroy evidence. Foreign media had reported on the massacres of women, children and defenceless men, and the burning of villages especially in Tsholotsho, Lupane and Nkayi. Unfortunately, in his discussion with Peter Preston and Donald Trelford, the then editors of *The Guardian* and *The Observer* respectively, Prince Charles of the UK dismissed the Matabeleland massacres as exaggerated (Cameron 2018: 29). Probably in order to conceal the atrocities, the GoZ had to ensure that no trace of their murderous trail remained.

As the Fifth Brigade advanced to Matabeleland South, it rounded up civilians from villages in Matabeleland North, Midlands and Matabeleland South and ferried them by army trucks to concentration camps, with Bhalagwe becoming the largest, with no less than 6,000 people. Once a ZPRA military base, Bhalagwe had a disused mine close by which became handy for dumping victims of the Fifth Brigade, either dead or alive, down the mine shafts. Subsequently, it was not easy to ascertain the identity of all the victims as they came from various districts in different Ndebele-speaking provinces. To an extent, the killers almost succeeded in concealing or destroying evidence as the secrets of Bhalagwe were not known outside the area until a mining company tried to resuscitate the mine in 1991. During their preparatory work of digging out rubble and pumping out water, to their horror, they discovered decomposed bodies, and skeletons (Alexander 2021). One of the most memorable being a woman with her baby still strapped to her back (RFI 2019).

Memory work by Ibhetshu Likazulu

One of the preoccupations of Ibhetshu Likazulu has been memorialisation through lectures, prayers, commemorative events and memorial plaques. Some of the lecturers include the Rogers Nikita Mangena Lecture, Mgagao Memorial Lecture, Lookout Masuku Lecture, Njini Ntuta Lecture, Makhathini Guduza Lecture and Archbishop Henry Karlen Lecture. The lectures paint a picture of victimhood at the hands of the GoZ. Ibhetshu Likazulu carefully selects the subjects of its commemorative events not just to tell the other side of the story but to point to the ruling party and the government' agency in the killing and suffering of the people of the region. For example, the Mangena Lecture commemorates the Zimbabwe People's Revolutionary Army's (ZPRA's) best commander and military strategist, Rogers Nikita Mangena, whose life was cut short when his vehicle struck a landmine in Zambia in 1978.

Although the Mgagao Massacres occurred in 1976, the perpetrators were not necessarily Rhodesian soldiers but fellow liberation war combatants, i.e., ZANLA guerrillas with the support of their Chinese instructors and Tanzanian soldiers. Indeed, the genesis of Gukurahundi genocide is traceable to Mgagao when 50 unsuspecting ZPRA recruits, who were dishing out porridge early in the morning, were gunned down by ZANLA recruits. Although caught by surprise, they were able to disarm some of their attackers and fight back while others escaped to safety but with huge losses. Thus, the Mgagao Memorial Lecture is intended to rekindle the memory of the treachery of ZANU-PF against the people of Matabeleland.

Lookout Masuku was ZPRA's last commander who, after being inducted into the Zimbabwe National Army as Lieutenant-General, was arrested and charged with treason together with ZPRA's former intelligence chief, Dumiso Dabengwa and other former senior cadres. Although acquitted by the courts, the GoZ nevertheless reincarcerated them;[3] Masuku was released when he became seriously ill and he died in 1985. The people of Matabeleland accused the GoZ of his death, which was perceived as having been part of the genocide.

Njini Ntuta, ZAPU secretary for defence, was murdered execution style in 1984 allegedly by anti-government ZAPU dissidents, though suspicions remain that it was the work of state agents. A commemorative lecture for this ZAPU stalwart was a reminder of the many Ndebele leaders who were eliminated. Makhathini Guduza, a renowned ZAPU nationalist, was responsible for facilitating Joshua Nkomo's escape from his residence in Pelandaba suburb, Bulawayo as the Fifth Brigade, who attempted to assassinate him (Guduza, no date). In his unpublished autobiography, Guduza recalls that he became a wanted man, and he sought refuge at Dukwe Refugee

---

3 '6 in Zimbabwe cleared of treason, jailed again', *The New York Times*, 28 April 1983.

Camp in Botswana. However, the Zimbabwean authorities succeeded in snatching him from the camp and brought him back to Zimbabwe where he suffered torture and imprisonment (Guduza, no date).

We should note that among the churches, it was the Catholic church that spoke out most strongly against the atrocities of Gukurahundi (CCJPZ and LRF 1999). Indeed, it was the CCJPZ (with the Legal Resources Project) that provided the first researched documentation of the genocide.[4] The Catholic bishops even wrote to then Prime Minister Robert Mugabe, expressing their concern over security conditions in Matabeleland and parts of Midlands (CCJPZ and LRF 1999). Archbishop Heinrich Karlen of the Roman Catholic Church in Bulawayo (1994-97) was one of the first people to alert the world to the Gukurahundi atrocities and spoke out strongly against its human rights abuses (Todd 2007). This made him regarded by the government as an enemy. Hence, Ibhetshu Likazulu's lecture in honour of Archbishop Karlen serves to remind people of the service of the Roman Catholic Church during those terrible years.

Perhaps the memorial lectures have not stirred as much controversy and the wrath of the state as the commemorative holidays have done. Ibhetshu Likazulu commemorates Independence Day (18 April), Heroes Day (8 August) and Unity Day (22 December). For many people in the Matabeleland region, (save for ruling party supporters) these holidays are reminders of a painful past. So, it is in this context, that Ibhetshu Likazulu has subverted them to commemorate the victims of Gukurahundi, in the same way the Herero and the Nama respectively celebrate the Herero Day and the Heroes' Day in Namibia in contradistinction to the government authorities. For example, the Unity Day is largely perceived as 'surrender day' by many activists in the Matabeleland provinces, irked by the comparative absence of development in their region. The Unity Agreement was signed by Joshua Nkomo on behalf of PF-ZAPU and Robert Mugabe on behalf of ZANU-PF on 22 December 1987, and it marked the superficial cessation of hostilities between anti-government dissidents and government forces in what the latter deemed a 'civil war'.

However, since Nkomo and PF-ZAPU never publicly acknowledged that the dissidents were under their instruction, the general perception remains that there were no, or very few, real dissidents, and that this role was assumed by agent provocateurs sent by the government itself. We should recall that during the struggle against the Smith regime, the Selous Scouts had masqueraded as guerrilla fighters only to betray those who genuinely supported the freedom fighters. The actions of the so-called dissidents were often reprehensible, which fuelled the suspicions that they might have been state-sponsored agents. Moreover, rarely did the dissidents

---

4 *Breaking the Silence: Building True Peace, A Report on the Disturbances in Matabeleland and the Midlands 1980-1988.*

and the government forces engage in battle. Further, as Todd (2007) recounts, some of the 'dissidents' had the contact details of senior police officers. Unlike the ZPRA guerrillas of the liberation struggle, the 'dissidents' were mainly undisciplined bandits who cared little about the security of communities. Their destruction of property that served communities such as schools, libraries, buses, etc. led the people of the affected regions to believe that the destruction was meant to impoverish and underdevelop their provinces. Ibhetshu Likazulu now observes 22 December annually as the day of remembrance for the thousands of innocent civilian lives that perished between 1983 and 'Unity Day' in 1987. Not surprisingly, the usual official fanfare and speeches associated with this public holiday do not mention the Gukurahundi atrocities. What is extolled by the government is the unity and peace brought about by Zimbabwe's liberation icons, Nkomo and Mugabe. ZPRA and ZAPU war songs, which are rarely played, are aired around the Unity Day holiday. While Nkomo's liberation credentials are either unacknowledged or at best minimised, he is usually favourably portrayed for his role in the unity agreement, with the name UMdala Wethu amplified in remarkably similar ways to the derogatory names and hate speech that he suffered during the Gukurahundi (see Maseko and Nkomo 2022, in this volume).

Ibhetshu Likazulu have been irked by the official celebration of Unity Day and the praise-singing of Nkomo and Mugabe as having brought peace. This, in their view, unashamedly disconnects from the realities of violence by the Fifth Brigade and the dissidents. Nothing is ever mentioned about past suffering, continued trauma and lost opportunities to the impoverished population of Matabeleland. It is the selective amnesia behind the memorialising of the Unity agreement, while obscuring the accompanying violence that birthed it, which Ibhetshu Likazulu decided to challenge.

In defiance of official narrative, Ibhetshu Likazulu converted the 22 December celebration to one that commiserates and commemorates the death and destruction for which the Fifth Brigade and the dissidents are responsible. Since 2005 the organisation urges people to wear black to symbolise the mourning for the dead and disappeared every 22 December. As expected, the Zimbabwean authorities did not ignore that challenge to their choreographed memory event, they attempted to disrupt Ibhetshu Likazulu commemorative gathering. For example, on 22 December 2016, Mbuso Fuzwayo, had to seek a court order to proceed with the event which the police had surreptitiously barred claiming double booking of the venue at the Stanley Square, Makokoba in Bulawayo. Ibhetshu Likazulu's activities have predictably become regular running battles with the Zimbabwean police.

Perhaps what angers the authorities is the subversion of a day intended to celebrate their achievements, but which is now doing the opposite. The activities organised by Ibhetshu Likazulu on the public holiday normally begin around 8.30 a.m. at Joshua Nkomo statue in Bulawayo. Actually, the erection of the statue was not without controversy and it had to be covered up immediately afterwards due to public anger. Some simply disliked the idea that the government commissioned statue was carved by North Koreans who are disliked in the region for training the genocidal Fifth Brigade. Others complained that the statue was standing on too low a pedestal. It was also argued that because the statue was facing in the direction of Mashonaland, it implied submission which was an insult to the people of Matabeleland.

By congregating at the Joshua Nkomo statue, the mourners apparently usurp its symbolism in defiance not submission. Then, singing defiant songs, the activists then march along Joshua Nkomo Street, and join the main activities: the church service, solidarity speeches, poetry and songs that take place at Stanley Hall. This hall, in Bulawayo's oldest suburb of Makokoba, is the cradle of African nationalism and resistance to colonialism. Public meetings have been held there for over a century and, by using this historic venue, Ibhetshu Likazulu connects its defiance to the militant tradition of resistance associated with Bulawayo and Matabeleland region.

For the record, no other group has ever memorialised Gukurahundi in this way. Ibhetshu Likazulu has been a pacesetter, earning its accolades from practical struggles on the ground, in most cases on shoe-string budgets from well-wishers. The various donor-funded human rights advocacy organisations operating in the region dare not provoke the wrath of the state.

Moreover, from 2016-18, Ibhetshu Likazulu commemorated the six tourists who were allegedly abducted by dissidents and subsequently murdered. It was this incident that was used by the GoZ, with an already trained and armed Fifth Brigade, to start operation Gukurahundi under the guise of hunting down dissidents. In its leaflet advertising the commemorative event, Ibhetshu Likazulu states:

> As part of its activities in memorializing the victims of Gukurahundi and bandits, Ibhetshu Likazulu has chosen this year 23 July 2016 to remember the six tourists; Kevin Ellis, Brett Baldwin, Tony Bajzelz, William Butler, James Greenwell and Martyn Hodgson. True healing and reconciliation necessitate truth telling of what happened to the six men and why it happened. For the affected Matabele communities, these six in a way became intricately part and parcel of the history and memory of the affected region by their unfortunate victimhood. Their lives were cut short in Matabeleland in a conflict about the Matabele. Their names and their very innocence in that conflict shall remain indelible reminders of all those innocent lives lost. With the permission of families of the six and their respective governments, Ibhetshu Likazulu would

like the Insuza community in Bubi to erect a plague in their memory and honour on 23 July 2016, the anniversary of the day of their kidnapping and disappearance in 1982.

However, at the time of writing, the plaque has not yet been erected. Mbuso Fuzwayo was convinced that his organisation would erect the plaque as planned as well as many others. As a grassroots organisation, Ibhetshu Likazulu has remained determined to bear the overwhelming work of memorialisation of the genocide with neither government nor massive donor support on its shoulders. Unfortunately, some stakeholders who might be expected to play a contributory role have not done so. For example, few opposition leaders have honoured invitations by Ibhetshu Likazulu to participate in the memorial events. Annually invitations go to many leaders and leading opposition politicians even those from Harare, but none have attended, perhaps demonstrating the country's ethnic fissures where the genocide issue is perceived not as a national problem but a regional one.

In 2017, Ibhetshu Likazulu petitioned the Bulawayo City Council to rename the famous soccer stadium, Barbourfields, to Lookout Masuku Stadium. Mbuso Fuzwayo wrote:

> Renaming the Barbourfields Stadium to 'Lookout Masuku Stadium' in honour and memory of his heroic role and distinguished service in the liberation and peace building in our nation. Our considered choice of Barbourfields was based on its significance as Bulawayo's premier venue in hosting artistic, sporting and cultural events where citizens normally gather for such important events and occasions. It would be a befitting honour to the legendary ZIPRA icon and a deserved memorialisation of one of Bulawayo's distinguished sons whose sacrifice for our dignity and humanity remains unparalleled. Lastly, by honouring the memory of Lookout Masuku, Bulawayo would have taken the lead in not only preserving the legacy of ZIPRA men and women, but in drawing from it inspiration for peace building, loyalty and service for generations to come.

To the amazement of the petitioners, the opposition-led Bulawayo City Council turned down the request. It argued that Masuku had had nothing to do with soccer; instead, they renamed the stadium after Tafi Moyo, a businessman, and one of the funders of Highlanders Sports Club. While no one doubts Moyo's credentials, honouring him was perceived as intentionally spiting the original petitioners. Hence, the memorialisation of counter narratives is often a fraught objective: hurdles derive not only from the state but also sometimes from supposedly progressive stakeholders, such as the Bulawayo City Council, who are expected to be sympathetic with the Gukurahundi victims and survivors.

Memory as a site of contestation

As already shown above, and further discussed below, there are contradictions about how Zimbabwe remembers or forgets Gukurahundi or aspects of it. Contradictions in that not only does the official narrative face counter-narratives, but it is also revisionist. Memory is recovered for a purpose and it would seem that the recollection of Gukurahundi has contradictory purposes. This is not unusual as Confino (1997) states that 'National memory ... is constituted by different, often opposing, memories that, in spite of their rivalries, construct common denominators that overcome on the symbolic level real social and political differences to create an imagined community'. This is also attested to by Jessee (2017) in the case of Rwanda. Memory-making is undoubtedly an important aspect of nation building, that is, if properly done. However, as shown in the literature review, the sincerity of nation-building during the Namibian and Rwandan governments' efforts in this direction have been questioned by scholars who argue that a major motivation is scoring easy political points (Jessee 2017; Kössler 2007; Lyrefelt 2020; Niezen 2018; Small 2007; Steinmetz and Hell 2006).

Halbwachs (1992) notes that the collective decides what it is valuable to recall. However, the Zimbabwean authorities would wish the nation to remember the supposedly peaceful resolution to a conflict through the Unity Agreement, while some elements within the affected communities take a different view. It is, therefore, not unusual for historical memories to be manipulated according to the expected benefits of the various groups (Assmann 2007). The memory of a genocide is subject to intense competition to control the narrative not just between government and oppositional forces, including civil society organisations, but also among the various civic and political actors in the Matabeleland region.

While memories can promote a more critical self-image, they can also lead to dissension by tearing open old wounds and reanimating inveterate conflicts (Assmann 2007; Jessee 2017). Indeed, the Zimbabwean authorities have for long silenced voices on the Gukurahundi genocide for fear of the potential rupture and worsening political and ethnic polarisation. On the one hand, they seem to prefer anti-memory, which is understood as 'buried or repressed remembrance' (Lyrefelt 2020: 22) and selective remembrance on the other hand. With the officially sanctioned remembrance of Gukurahundi, which smacks of the victor's recall, and claims an absolute and exclusive interpretation of history (Assmann 2007), there should be reasonable expectation of a counter-selective narrative by pro-Mthwakazi groups that will run in parallel if not in conflict with the official line.

Furthermore, the selective memory of Gukurahundi purportedly by victim communities tends to offset their own possible guilt by minimising their share in it to the point where they may make it disappear entirely (ibid.), magnifying their sense of injury and the guilt and culpability of the other. The example of Gukurahundi confirms that 'historical memory does not remain passive knowledge' but can be exploited by political elites to strengthen or subvert nation-building (ibid.). Hence, regarding 'the past as a unifying force' can become either 'a useful tool or dangerous weapon when used in political context' (Ohorchak 2011: 13). Warning against a single story, Jessee (2017) regards genuine collaborative memorialisation, founded in truth-telling, as a desirable ideal. As experiences from other contexts show, this appears to be currently an unattainable ideal regarding Gukurahundi.

Contestations over Bhalagwe memorialisation

As already discussed, Gukurahundi remains a sensitive, controversial subject and a site of contested memory. It would appear a contradiction that on the one hand we have claimed that there is silencing and forced forgetting of Gukurahundi, while on the other, we claim that there is memorialisation of the same. This is the nub of the contestation. The Zimbabwean state manipulates the memory of the genocide to suit its political aims that of claiming national unity.

The Bhalagwe mass graves exemplify both the act of silencing and of manipulation. Therefore, we now turn to exploring the tussle over the memorial site by local communities and pressure groups led by Ibhetshu Likazulu, on the one hand, and by the Zimbabwe Republic Police (ZRP), the ruling party ZANU-PF, and a section of ex-guerrilla veterans, on the other. Although the mass graves are now a public secret, community members have not yet dared to go to there. Apart from the bones that were discovered by a mining company when trying to resuscitate the mine, stirring public attention to the embarrassment of the GoZ, no one dared to visit the defiled area again (Alexander 2021: 773). Even the mining venture was quickly abandoned.

Then in 2017 Ibhetshu Likazulu organised a prayer service to be conducted in Bhalagwe, to remember the thousands killed and disappeared. In compliance with Zimbabwe's strict rules on public gatherings, the organisation duly informed the provincial police headquarters. A convoy of vehicles left Bulawayo destined for Bhalagwe. For the protection of the local community from victimisation, it had been previously arranged that those coming from Bulawayo should be the first to congregate at the site and thereafter the locals would join them. It was reasoned that it would be more difficult to pursue the former than it would the rural populace who tend to be highly vulnerable to victimisation by violent ruling party agents.

The convoy of vehicles from Bulawayo had not travelled more than twenty kilometres from the city centre before a police roadblock stopped them and the police refused to let the main minibus proceed. While this may have been a routine police procedure, the concerned travellers perceived it as a deliberate harassment.

Still, the real showdown came when the convoy was stopped again about three kilometres from the site by heavily armed police who told them that the Bhalagwe mass graves were out of bounds and the government had not sanctioned the prayer service.

Amongst the delegation to Bhalagwe was the late veteran politician, Dr Dumiso Dabengwa, former Home Affairs minister and then president of revived ZAPU. Although not the organiser of the prayer meeting, his attendance as a respected, senior liberation figure, meant that he attracted public attention. Since the ZRP blocked the participants from reaching the site, they decided to offer a short prayer *in situ*. But the police would not allow them to do this either. Still, candles were lit by Dabengwa but the ZRP kicked them aside. Video footage of this act of disrespect went viral and heightened public anger in Matabeleland[5].

After the forced resignation of Robert Mugabe as state president on 21 November 2017 and the subsequent rise of Emerson Mnangagwa, the state somewhat changed its attitude when the new president stated that the issue of Gukurahundi could be publicly discussed and lasting healing be found. An example expressing this position is Mnangagwa's interview at the World Economic Forum in 2018, where he still refused to take refused to apologise to the people of Matabeleland[6]. Immediately afterwards, Ibhetshu Likazulu organised once again a prayer service at the Bhalagwe site, and it was permitted to go ahead but with heavy police presence.

Thereafter, in 2018, Ibhetshu Likazulu together with the local community erected a memorial stone to honour the memory of the Bhalagwe victims of the genocide. Although the police would not allow the memorial stone to be placed close to the mass grave sites, they nevertheless allowed its erection some distance away. For this and other logistical reasons, the NGO took almost nine months to complete the monument which was inscribed as follows:

> THIS PLAQUE WAS ERECTED ON THE 25TH OF MAY 2018
>
> IN LOVING MEMORY OF OUR INNOCENT & DEFENCELESS CHILDREN, MOTHERS & FATHERS
>
> WHO PERISHED DURING THE GUKURAHUNDI, MATEBELELAND GENOCIDE 1983-1987
>
> SIYALIKHUMBULA.
>
> **INSERTED BY IBHETSHU LIKAZULU**

Since then, the contestations over the memorialisation of Gukurahundi at Bhalagwe have played out in no less than four episodes of memorial plaques erected by Ibhetshu Likazulu being vandalised and razed to the ground. As the secretary-

---

5 'Former Home Affairs Minister Dumiso Dabengwa surrounded by Police', Twitter, 23 October 2017, https://twitter.com/lilomatic/status/922371943633948672.

6 'One-on-one with Zimbabwean President Emmerson Mnangagwa', *Youtube*, 26 Jan 2018, https://www.youtube.com/watch?v=zi-HIf1dYV4.

general of Ibhetshu Likazulu, Fuzwayo wrote a protest letter to the National Peace and Reconciliation Commission (NPRC) accusing war veterans aligned to the ruling ZANU-PF party, and the police who had been hostile to the erection of the monument, of destroying the memorial. At the time of writing, no one has officially been held responsible and arrested. The remarks made by the Deputy Chief Secretary, Presidential Communications, George Charamba on 17 January 2022 following the fourth time vandalisation of the Ibhetshu Likazulu's memorial plaque, confirmed the government's disdain towards the memorialisation of Gukurahundi George Charamba. Following the destruction of the memorial plaque for the fourth time early in the year, Charamba declared that the erection of the monument was arbitrary and illegal, and the police and government were not bothered to bring the culprits to book.[7] Alexander (2021: 772) demonstrates that the contestations over Gukurahundi memorialisation, are nothing new, and reports how the community 'effort to create a memorial at a mass grave in Lupane in 1997' was shut down by the CIO'. According to her, the contestations have been a case of 'a noisy silence'.

In the light of the above, while it may never be known who destroyed the Bhalagwe memorial, what precisely their motivation was, or whether they were simply obeying orders, suspicions pointed to ZANU-PF and the war veterans associated with the ruling party. When Ibhetshu Likazulu publicised its intention to place a memorial stone at Bhalagwe, the former erected a plaque in honour of victims of the anti-colonial struggle, although nothing occurred in that area during the liberation struggle that demanded special mention. Unfortunately, their plaque was also destroyed as soon as it was put up. However, although Ibhetshu Likazulu had been opposed to a shrine at Bhalagwe memorialising victims of the struggle on the grounds that it would obscure the genocide, the organisation issued a statement condemning the vandalism. Ibhetshu Likazulu's position is that there should be no rivalry over the memorialisation of the victims of either the anti-colonial or post-independence violence since the same communities that suffered under Rhodesian forces' repression suffered similarly under Fifth Brigade atrocities. To give prominence to one memory over another presumes that some violence is more justifiable than the other.

Dismembering genocide memory

By using the same Bhalagwe site to honour the dead of the anti-colonial war and not of the genocide, it could be alleged that the Zimbabwean authorities and their supporters seek to eclipse the memory of the genocide with that of liberation war victims. Not that a memorial to the latter, particularly in Matabeleland, really matters

---

7 'Charamba Silences Gukurahundi Pressure Group', *All Africa*, 18 January 2022, https://allafrica.com/stories/202201180612.html.

to the ruling party but it suggests that they are progressive and pursuing peace as opposed to the violence of war, while simultaneously suppressing memorialisation of the Gukurahundi.

The official celebration of 22 December Unity Day, also distorts the years of atrocity that brought about the signing of the Unity Accord between PF-ZAPU and the ruling ZANU-PF. The official narratives around Unity Day paint a picture of two liberation parties whose differences resulted in civil strife, which was ended by the unity agreement. Joshua Nkomo and Robert Mugabe are therefore celebrated for their supposed wisdom in unifying their warring parties. This has created an impression of two rivals who were equal in arms and equally culpable for violence in the country. It disguises the fact that it was not an interparty conflict but a government using all the apparatus of violence at the disposal of a state to unleash untold suffering against defenceless civilians. The violence was not countrywide but concentrated in Matabeleland and the Midlands and mainly targeted Ndebele-speaking citizens.

Since the GoZ has consistently refused to acknowledge the genocide, it has consequently failed to offer an apology. Robert Mugabe once referred to the genocide as 'a moment of madness'. But instead of then taking responsibility for it, he apportioned blame to both perpetrators and victims by saying 'we killed each other'. Given that there is no record of villagers in Tsholotsho or Lupane or Nkayi ever fighting back and killing even a single soldier, hence, Mugabe's wilful duplicity in offering a revisionist narrative. In terms of its genocide denial, it resembles the words on the memorial stone of the Herero and Name victims of Namibian genocide which state that the victims 'perished under mysterious circumstances' (Lyrefelt 2020: 31).

It can be argued, therefore, that the attempts at obliterating the memories of the Gukurahundi genocide by the Zimbabwean authorities are calculated, premeditated and implemented according to a plan. Since there have been no prosecutions either for members of the Fifth Brigade or for the so-called dissidents, a culture of impunity has been entrenched in Zimbabwe with the country's record of human rights violations remaining a cause for concern. Perhaps, the late poet Siziba (2017) aptly captures the mood of forced amnesia that devalues even the memory of the victims of Gukurahundi to nothingness:

> *Mass graves are the abodes*
> *Of figures condemned to die*
> *Without names*
> *Without tombstones to mark their resting place*
> *The nameless and unknown have many names*
> *One of the names is Gukurahundi.*

Conclusion

This chapter has drawn from Ibhetshu Likazulu's work on memorialising the Gukurahundi genocide in general and Bhalagwe site in particular to demonstrate the politics of remembering and forgetting in Zimbabwe. While official narratives tend to obscure, distort and sometimes outrightly deny genocide memory, counter narratives challenge state-sanctioned memory-making. In Matabeleland it is unavoidable that any 'memory worth talking about – worth remembering – is memory of trauma' (Antze and Lambek 1996: xii–xiii) and a counter memory to the official narrative fostered by the state. Without an acknowledgment of the genocide and hence investigations and prosecutions, the full truth behind the Gukurahundi genocide against the Ndebele might never be publicly known, at least not during the ZANU-PF's rule and its revisionist 'patriotic history' (cf. Ranger 2004). Memorialisation of the genocide, as has been the case with the attempts around the Bhalagwe mass graves, will remain a challenge not only due to lack of adequate information about what actually happened but also due to the Zimbabwean state's obstruction of truth-telling and dislike of divergent remembering and forgetting. However, Ibhetshu Likazulu and other human rights defenders should find inspiration from the Herero and Nama activists in Namibia, that superior state power and resources do 'not always stop activists from pressing for public space and artefacts of memory to commemorate their historical causes and represent their experiences of suffering' (Niezen 2018: 554).

6

The Linguistic Dimensions of Gukurahundi in Zimbabwe

Busani Maseko and Dion Nkomo

Introduction

This chapter explores the linguistic dimensions of Gukurahundi to address claims that the operation was anything other than a genocide. When discussing genocide, Lang (2020) reveals the connection between genocidal acts and language. Writing on the Nazi Holocaust, Lang (2020: 155) lays bare the nexus between genocides and language:

> To escape the consequences of language, for worse or for better, would require an impossible step outside history for its speakers or writers no less than for its audience – and whatever else we discover about the Nazi genocide. The background to this claim is broader than the specific evidence of the role of language in the Nazi genocide. The existence of a causal relation between language and history, between linguistic practice and events in the social context, would be disputed only on the view of language as neutral and transparent medium. Testimony comes from many different sources of the history of language as 'real' history, evolving in direct relation to features of the historical and social context. On general grounds, it is predictable that linguistic developments which occurred at the time of Nazi genocide would disclose features resembling those of the process of genocide itself; it would be difficult to understand how the latter might occur without corresponding changes in language (Lang 2020: 155).

Lending credence to Lang's (2020) assertion is the reality that genocides are not merely biological killings. They also involve cultural obliteration of particular groups of people, together with virtually everything that defines their identity, their soul and spirit as a cultural entity, including the repository of their tradition, folklore, music, literature and language (Bowring 2014; Devonish 2010; Lemkin, 1953; Skutnabb-Kangas 2000). For its purposes, this chapter concerns itself with two major linguistic dimensions of Gukurahundi, namely the language of genocide and linguistic genocide. Unpacking and illustrating these dimensions exposes how language was used before, during and after Gukurahundi in order to justify it, as well as the vital place of the language question in post-genocide nation-building efforts.

A recent paper in the *Journal of Literary Studies* by Sibanda (2021) compellingly demonstrates how the language that was used before and during Gukurahundi betrayed the genocidal intentions of the Zimbabwe African National Union-Patriotic Front (ZANU-PF) government in the early days of independence from Britain. Just like the violence that it accompanied, the language was so damaging that it left ethnic scars that continue to haunt and undermine national building as the country heads towards the golden jubilee of its independence. The insincerity of the Zimbabwean government's national healing and reconciliation programmes has not ameliorated the situation, resulting in the perpetuation of the Gukurahundi legacy which manifests itself in, among others, linguistic genocide as another linguistic dimension that is analysed in this chapter.

While connections can be made between it and the language of Gukurahundi in that it usually ensues as part of the physical violence, linguistic genocide has transcended the military deployment in Matabeleland. According to Devonish (2010) and Skutnabb-Kangas (2000), linguistic genocide refers to the imposition of a specific language over speakers of other languages which threatens inter-generational transmission of their native languages with real risks of language death. In non-genocidal contexts, a more appropriate term would be linguistic imperialism, a term that was initially used by the Ghanaian linguist Gilbert Ansre (Ansre 1977) before it got popularised by Robert Phillipson (Phillipson 1992) to refer to the worldwide spread of English. The linguistic genocide that is discussed in this chapter is deeply rooted in the Gukurahundi genocide and perpetuates the same ideology that resulted in the massacre of largely Ndebele-speaking citizens by a largely Shona-speaking ZANU-PF-led government.

An analysis of the linguistic dimensions of Gukurahundi in Zimbabwe facilitates an understanding of the nature of violence that was deployed as a nation-building mechanism in Zimbabwe along tribal lines. While the physical violence of Gukurahundi might have ended, part of its enduring legacy manifests itself through the imposition of Shona as Zimbabwe's *de facto* official language and the unmarked symbol of 'Zimbabweanness' (Ncube and Siziba 2017a). We argue that this practice is a subtle form of Gukurahundi, intended to legitimate and naturalise structures of inequality, which resonate with Bourdieu's (1991) concept of symbolic violence. Gukurahundi has become a metaphor for the structural violence and subjugation experienced by Ndebele speakers in post-genocide Zimbabwe.

The genocide and language nexus

The term *genocide* was coined by the Polish-born jurist and scholar, Raphael Lemkin, in the 1940s. The *Encyclopedia Britannica* states that *genocide* is a compound term derived from the Greek term *genos*, which refers to group identity markers such as race, tribe or nation and the Latin term *cide* for 'killing' (https://www.britannica.com/topic/genocide).

Accordingly, *genocide* is defined as 'the deliberate and systematic destruction of a group of people because of their ethnicity, nationality, religion, or race' (https://www.britannica.com/topic/genocide). Among other identity markers, language is often implicated in the determination of the ethnicity and nationality of genocidal target populations. Language is used in various ways in the context of genocide, including before, during and in the aftermath. In the next few paragraphs we attempt to situate our contribution within existing scholarship that projects the nexus between genocides and language.

Firstly, language boundaries are exploited between the in-group and out-group members who respectively commit and suffer from genocides. Although Bourdieu (1991) notes that language boundaries are sometimes more imagined than real, Toivanen (2007) exemplifies such an exploitation of language boundaries between Russian and Ukrainian politicians in the execution of the Soviet genocide. Language boundaries, which sometimes coincide with national, racial and ethnic boundaries, present ready-made fault lines that are exploited at the various stages of instituting a genocide. In terms of Stanton (2016), cited in Sibanda (2021), this exploitation starts at the classification stage of a genocide, where there is discrimination between the in-group and the out-group.

Secondly, language is then actively used to discredit and criminalise members of out-group populations through what Gordon Allport, in his theorisation of the nature of prejudice, terms antilocution (Katz 1991). In her appraisal of Allport's legacy, Katz (1991: 132) acknowledges the vital role of the 'conditioning of negative responses to minority group images, facilitated by linguistic tags and other cues'. At this stage, members of the out-group are not only accused of political, religious or cultural crimes, for which they should pay the ultimate price, they are also dehumanised through hate speech in a manner that justifies genocidal atrocities. This one linguistic dimension is pursued at length by Sibanda (2021)'s publication. Sibanda (2021) offers a thorough and diligent treatise of the language of Gukurahundi from the onset and demonstrates how hate speech and name calling, which prevail in other genocide contexts (see also Cole 2014; Donohue 2012; Lemkin 1953), featured prominently in Zimbabwe.

Thirdly, apart from being identified by means of their language, among other sins, members of out-groups are victimised or even killed for using their language and coerced to speak the language of the aggressor, which language often gets systematically imposed on the genocide survivors at the expense of their own language, even in the post-genocide era. Lemkin (1953) observes that while the 1930s Soviet genocide targeted the Ukrainian intelligentsia and peasantry for systematic killing, it also sought to obliterate the national soul and spirit of being Ukrainian in the form of tradition, folklore and music, literature and language.

Accordingly, 'the Russian language itself is implicated as the bearer of genocide' (Bowring 2014: 69). What makes the language question remain politically charged in Ukraine today is the fact that while 'there are no Ukrainian medium schools in Russia, the Russian language still dominates as a medium of instruction in over a thousand schools in Ukraine' (Bowring 2014: 65). Language practices in Zimbabwe, particularly as they relate to Shona and Ndebele languages, resonate with the Ukrainian experience whose roots are traceable to the Soviet genocide. In terms of Skutnabb-Kangas (2000), this is called linguistic genocide (see also Devonish 2010; Lemkin 1953). In this contribution, we see linguistic genocide as an extension of the military genocide as it perpetuates the initial genocidal ideology of obliterating anything that defines the victims and survivors of the genocide.

Finally, language plays a critical role in the denial of genocides by the perpetrators and accomplices. Bilali, Iqbal and Freel (2020: 284) note the 'pervasiveness of genocide denial by perpetrator groups', largely owing to the fact that 'committing atrocities threatens the in-group's moral integrity and its social image'. Open admission of committing genocidal acts is rare, with excuses and euphemistic language being preferred in order to ameliorate the crimes. Inversely, the term genocide itself becomes an unpalatable taboo whose utterance may invite further violence for genocide survivors. Accordingly, this chapter explores how the Zimbabwean government has used language to address Gukurahundi. It is in this respect that Bourdieu's (1991) notion of symbolic violence is evoked. According to Bourdieu (1991), violence does not always have to be physical. It can manifest itself in the power differential between social groups, and in the aftermath of physical violence, it is often manifested through an imposition of the norms and values of the group with greater social power on those of the subordinate group (Bourdieu 1991). The remainder of this chapter now delves into the Gukurahundi operation and its linguistic dimensions.

The operation, the operators and the operated

Since 1980, the ZANU-PF-led government has adopted violent operations as the *modus operandi* when dealing with political difference. Apart from Gukurahundi, the Land redistribution exercise, codenamed the Third Chimurenga or *Hondo yeminda* in Shona, Operation Murambatsvina, and most recently, Operation Restore Legacy are some prominent examples of violent politically-driven operations. The latter turned out to be a sanitised *coup d'état* that ended Robert Mugabe's 37-year rule, having been camouflaged as an operation that 'targeted criminals around the (then) president'. Ironically, the criminality that instigated the operation seems to have escalated with dire political and economic impacts.

However, in terms of scale, gruesomeness and impact of its violence, Gukurahundi remains the worst of them all. The report by the Catholic Commission for Justice and Peace in Zimbabwe (CCJPZ) (1997) remains the most comprehensive documentation of Gukurahundi atrocities and it is recommended for general reading on matters that are beyond the scope of the present discussion. Narratives of victims, including pregnant women whose wombs were ripped open ostensibly to remove unborn 'dissident children', abound on online social media platforms. The victims were literally 'operated' without administering any anesthetic, thereby subjecting them to agonising pain and death. Thus, the use of *operation, operators and the operated* to refer to Gukurahundi, its perpetrators and the victims respectively in this chapter constitutes an unapologetic pun. While the *operators* refer the Fifth Brigade forces that executed the Gukurahundi genocide, it is unequivocally known that these forces operated under the instruction of the Zimbabwean government and reported directly to Mugabe who entered into an agreement with his Korean counterpart Kim Il Sung to train the Fifth Brigade immediately after Mugabe's announcement of the need to 'combat malcontents' (CCJPZ 1997).

As a point of departure for our analysis of the linguistic dimensions of Gukurahundi, we seek recourse from onomastics to unpack the name of this heinous operation. As the linguistic science of naming, onomastics enables us to understand the genocidal intentions of Gukurahundi and the one-party-state ideology that was central to Mugabe's government upon assuming office. Etymologically, Gukurahundi was named through a metaphorical extension of a Shona word whose basic sense is defined in *Duramazwi ReChiShona*, the 1992 published Shona dictionary as follows: *Iyi imvura inowanzonaya kana vanhu vapedza kupura* (this is the rain that falls after people have finished harvesting). To this denotative meaning, it is important to add that this rain washes away the chaff from the previous season to prepare for the new season before the main summer rains (see also Mpofu 2015; Ncube and Siziba 2017a; 2017b; Ndlovu 2018; Sibanda 2021; Sithole and Makumbe 1997).

The political appropriation of the word 'gukurahundi' officially began with the declaration of 1979 as 'Gore reGukurahundi' (The Year of the Storm), which was meant to see the intensification of the struggle to completely destroy the enemy (Sithole and Makumbe, 1997). At face value, the enemy could be assumed to be the Rhodesian settler regime. However, Ndlovu-Gatsheni (2012b) traces Gukurahundi as a defining political strategy that emerged with the formation of ZANU-PF in 1963. It is with respect to the post-independence Matabeleland massacres that the meaning of the metaphorical storm could be fully understood. What would otherwise be an innocent literal sense of the word got tainted with the blood of an estimated 20,000 mainly Ndebele speakers and perceived supporters of the opposition Patriotic Front-Zimbabwe African People's Union (PF-ZAPU) (Mpofu 2019; Ncube and Siziba 2017a; 2017b; Sibanda 2020; Sibanda 2021).

Akin to all other genocides in history, language acts were used in tandem with political and intelligence strategies to legitimise the Gukurahundi genocide. Sibanda (2021) aptly sums up the Gukurahundi linguistic strategies when he writes:

> …linguistic conventions used by state actors before and during [G]ukurahundi created two social climates, one that legitimised tribal and political hatred, thus eliminating any social sanctions preventing genocide and the other that unmasked the state-sponsored genocide clothed as a necessary military exercise … (Sibanda, 2021: 129).

The cunning inaugural Zimbabwean government typified by its sharp-tongued leader identified dissidents as the primary targets of Gukurahundi. Notwithstanding the general use of the term *dissident* to refer to 'a person who publicly disagrees with and criticizes their government' i.e., a dissenter (Collins Online Dictionary), the use of this term in the context of Gukurahundi seems to have been assigned to generally ethnically Ndebele-speaking Zimbabweans whose majority supported PF-ZAPU led by Joshua Nkomo. Most scholars have concluded that the 'dissident menace' was a fabrication and conspiracy to justify the heavy-handed, brutal response by the state (Moyo, Sibanda and Mazuru 2013; Sibanda 2020; Sibanda 2021; Killander and Nyathi 2015; Eppel, 2008). It is now generally agreed that the Gukurahundi operation had less to do with dissidents and more about punishing the perceived Ndebele-speaking supporters of PF-ZAPU in order to recalibrate their minds and psyche to capitulate to ZANU-PF's one-party state ideology (Ndlovu-Gatsheni 2008; Sibanda, 2020; Alexander 2021). In its operations, the Fifth Brigade conflated being a PF-ZAPU supporter with being 'Ndebele' and with being a 'dissident' (Eppel 2008:12). Because multi-party democracy was never part of ZANU-PF's political ideology, Mugabe's desire to morph Zimbabwe into a one-party state demanded that he find ways to liquidate the opposition PF-ZAPU (Killander and Nyathi 2015).

Tribal and political hatred was already rife, dating back to the formation of

ZANU-PF through largely tribal defections from PF-ZAPU in 1963 and subsequent tribal clashes in the training and military camps during the liberation struggle. The discovery of arms caches allegedly belonging to PF-ZAPU in February 1982 and the persecution of former Zimbabwe People's Resistance Army (ZPRA) forces in the Zimbabwe National Army barracks, as well as the detention without trial of Dumiso Dabengwa and Lookout Masuku thickened the Gukurahundi plot. ZANU-PF was unmistakably possessed by the *gukurahundi* spirit from Mugabe to his junior ministers and this rendered the political situation in independent Zimbabwe toxic. In their eyes and words, PF-ZAPU was a 'dissident party' while Nkomo became the 'dissident father'; a cobra that needed to be crushed to cleanse the new nation (Nkomo 1984: 2). As Sibanda (2021) rightly observes, calling Nkomo a snake did not only sanitise the Gukurahundi genocide, but it also glorified Mugabe as the hero for cleansing the country in order to build a new nation.

In one of his many infamous speeches, Emmerson Mnangagwa, the then Minister of State Security, now the current president, was quoted by the *Chronicle* newspaper on 5 March 1985 likening PF-ZAPU followers and the Ndebele speakers in general to cockroaches and bugs that deserved to be exterminated by using the deadly pesticide DDT.[1] A few remarks suffice here. Firstly, it is the disgust with which the government viewed Ndebele people. Secondly, it is the decisiveness of the pest-control method that uses DDT which paints a vivid picture of the brutality that the dehumanised Ndebele people experienced at the hands of the tribal ZANU-PF government. In this respect, parallels can be drawn between Gukurahundi and other documented and well-known genocides in human history. During the holocaust, Nazis branded Jews as 'rats', while in recent memory, the Hutus referred to the Tutsis as 'cockroaches' during the Rwandan genocide. In a similar manner, in Sudan the Janjaweed affixed dehumanising labels such as 'black donkeys' on their victims (Donohue 2012; Sibanda 2021).

While name-calling is rife in political discourse, the ZANU-PF government and the Fifth Brigade deployed overtly hateful tribalistic language during the Gukurahundi era. For example, the Fifth Brigade soldiers claimed in some instances to be avenging their Shona forefathers who suffered tribal humiliations at the hands of the Ndebele kings, Mzilikazi and Lobhengula during their pre-colonial raids into Shona territories (Lindgren, 2005). Joshua Nkomo was mocked as a self-styled but powerless Ndebele king, i.e., *zimuNdevere* (the big Ndebele) or *zvimuNdevere* (the useless or insignificant Ndebele) by ZANU-PF politicians and supporters, showing that their politics was more tribal than ideological. Enos Nkala, who was a senior minister during that period, would remind Ndebele people that Nkomo was not

---

1 'Gukurahundi ghosts haunt Mnangagwa', *Mail and Guardian*, 24 November 2017. Available at: https://mg.co.za/article/2017-11-24-00-gukurahundi-ghosts-haunt-mnangagwa/

even Ndebele but rather Kalanga. Being Ndebele himself, Nkala clearly did not want to be associated with Nkomo either politically or ethnically. Out of confliction, he expressed his disdain for his Ndebele identity when he stated that he would cleanse himself of Ndebeleness if it were possible. This was the price that Nkala had to pay to convince his ZANU-PF party that he was a fully committed collaborator in the execution of Gukurahundi as a synonym for 'Ndebele ethnic cleansing' (Ncube and Siziba 2017a). By denouncing his Ndebele identity, it would appear as if Nkala was setting an example of what Ndebeles needed to do to survive in Zimbabwe. It could be ironic that Joshua Nkomo transformed from being regarded as the father of dissidents or the 'Ndebele king' to being Father Zimbabwe after capitulating into the 1987 Unity Accord.

The language of the operation

The Fifth Brigade and other supporting state security agents were predominantly Shona speaking. Just as Russian was seen as the language of the Soviet genocide by Ukrainians (Bowring 2014), the Shona language was weaponised into the language of Gukurahundi because of the way it was used to torture its victims. In this section, we draw on testimonies of survivors that are available online to show how Shona became implicated as the language of genocide. The Gukurahundi operation supplied the Shona-led government with an opportunity to foist its language onto the non-Shona-speaking population in parts of the Midlands and Matabeleland provinces. It is also by no coincidence that the Fifth Brigade was composed of mainly Shona-speaking personnel. Available testimonies by survivors online show how Shona language was 'weaponised' and deployed as a tool for identifying would be victims. Most survivors have testified how they were brutalised for failing to speak, understand or heed the soldiers' instructions that were given in Shona. In the following excerpt, a survivor summarises the fatal outcomes of not being competent in Shona during Gukurahundi:

> What I experienced is this, now this is Matabeleland, when the soldiers spoke to the Matabele, they spoke in Shona. Then if you don't understand Shona, or don't answer in Shona, that's when you are a target. If you ever knew Shona, you are safe that way. If ever you can speak Shona, you are safe, you are always safe.[2]

The above shows how the weaponisation of the Shona language provided the supporting armoury for the genocide and was also manipulated in the service of threat construction and hatred during the genocide. Those who spoke Shona were usually spared the trauma while anyone who failed to speak Shona became a target. Another survivor narrates how her failure to understand Shona landed her in trouble

---

2   https://www.youtube.com/watch?v=boK7TKs9zOg

with the Fifth Brigade after it was interpreted as stubbornness:

> [...] *bathi wena ulenkani? Bekhuluma ngesiShona. Ngathi angizwa mina. Ngathi angilankani kodwa isiShona angizwa kahle. Bathi wena uzaqonda…bangitshaya lonyawo lwami khathesi angisahambi kahle. Bangitshaya khonapho ngimgumdlezane ngileviki ngibelethile* (They said to me are you being stubborn? They were speaking in Shona. I responded that I was not being stubborn, but I did not understand Shona well. They said they were going to fix me…They thoroughly beat me up and injured my leg. I can no longer walk properly as a result. I had just given birth a week earlier and I was breastfeeding).³

Most testimonies of survivors also show that Shona became associated with the language of the genocide. In some cases, however, Ndebele speakers who had ties to Shona speakers through marriage or by being neighbours were able to manipulate such relationships to negotiate with the soldiers to have their lives spared. One woman for example narrates how being a neighbour to a Shona speaker saved her life and the lives of her other neighbours.

> *Thina lapha eMaphaneni saze sancedwa ngomunye usalukazi unaZu. UCaiphus wayethethe khonale esiShoneni. Basebefika bethatha usalukazi lwana bamenza udadewabo. Bathi wena wawuzodingani emaNdebeleni? Usengudadewabo sekhuluma labo ethi baxoleleni…Hayi wasinceda ngokuthatha khonale emaShoneni* (Here at Maphaneni we were saved by an old lady named naZu. Caiphus had married a Shona woman. When they got here, they treated her like their sister. They were even asking her why she had chosen to stay in Matabeleland. As their sister she pleaded with them to forgive us and spare our lives. He really did well by marrying someone from Mashonaland).⁴

From the foregoing, it is no wonder why Gukurahundi was seen as an operation targeting Ndebele speakers who were then conflated with supporters of PF-ZAPU and of dissidents. In one testimony, a survivor also explains how Gukurahundi was perceived as a war against the Ndebele, who were also branded dissidents. He narrates how the Fifth Brigade soldiers arrived at his local school to announce the beginning of another war:

> When the headmaster asked what they wanted, they said well, the war has started again. When he asked what war? They said well, the Shonas are in Matabeleland … The thing is, the *ma*Ndebele are…there is this thing, I think you might have heard it, all the Matabeles are dissidents …⁵

---

3   https://www.youtube.com/watch?v=NaoGDBl_wyY.
4   https://www.youtube.com/watch?v=c9yPzOdlYys.
5   https://www.youtube.com/watch?v=boK7TKs9zOg.

The above testimony feeds into the enduring narrative that Gukurahundi was never about dissidents but a war against the Ndebele people in general who were long seen as supporters of PF-ZAPU. As we argued earlier, this view is now generally regarded as one of the credible explanations for Gukurahundi by many scholars researching genocide in Zimbabwe (Phimister 2009; Ndlovu 2018; Alexander 2021; Sibanda 2021).

Many testimonies of how Ndebele speakers were forced to sing and dance to Shona songs during 'pungwes' are available online. In one of these testimonies, a survivor recalls how they were made to sing and dance from morning to sunset at the soldiers' camps:

> *Sasivuswa ekuseni kuthiwe siyetshona sitshaya itoyi toyi,* everyday *sisiyakhona sisiyatshona sigida khonangale. Sitshaya idikondo di! Ngake ngagida khonangale ngizithwele.* (Every morning we were ordered to go and dance. We toi-toied every day. Dancing *dikondo di!* I was once forced to dance while pregnant).[6]

Another survivor recollects how the elderly were forced to sing and dance in celebration while soldiers shot and killed some younger men who had been rounded up:

> *Kwafikwa kwakhethwa amajaha kwathiwa thina sihlabele. Sabuza ukuthi sihlabele sithini? Kwathiwa sithi 'ndinokambaira semombe… ndinokambaira semombe'. Khonapho abafana sebebuthelelwa laphana. Nxa abafana bebuthelelwa laphana amajaha ama ngapha, abe*Fifth Brigade*, bonabana abamabheredi abomvu aqalisa ukukhombela abafana. Abafana babulawa egcekeni thina sihlabela* (when they arrived, they selected young men while we were ordered to sing. We asked what should we sing? They said we must sing the song that went, 'Ndinokambaira semombe… ndinokambaira semombe' (I'm walking aimlessly like a cow… I'm walking aimlessly like a cow). At that moment, the boys were being rounded up and grouped together. While the boys were being rounded up, the Fifth Brigade soldiers with their red berets started aiming their guns at them. The boys were shot in plain sight while we were told to continue singing).[7]

Another survivor also recounts how people were forced to sing and rejoice at the death of their relatives:

> People were forced to bury their relatives, some of them alone, then forced to sing Shona songs and dance on their graves, praising Robert Mugabe.[8]

All these testimonies speak of untold trauma and dehumanisation at the hands

---

6   https://www.youtube.com/watch?v=Q2b5iVGCDs0.
7   https://www.youtube.com/watch?v=_lAyoCyesww.
8   https://www.youtube.com/watch?v=boK7TKs9zOg.

of the Fifth Brigade. For instance, women were forced to sing and dance to 'Mai vaDikondo', a Shona song that devalued and stereotyped them as being of loose morals (see Ncube and Siziba 2017a on this stereotypical perception). The forced singing of 'ndinokambaira semombe' (I'm walking aimlessly like a cow) also dehumanised the victims by equating them to cows. This is certainly consistent with most genocides where the victims are deliberately devalued and made to appear less human to justify and rationalise the genocide (King 2010; Sibanda 2021). As it has been in other genocidal contexts, Gukurahundi victims were equated with animals, insects and diseases. These language acts were deployed alongside the physical violence to effectively dispense with any sense of humanity in the victims and to recalibrate the psyche of the Ndebele victims into submission.

Language planning and practices as reproductions of Gukurahundi

In the post Gukurahundi era, Ndebele speakers and their language continued to be disenfranchised and marginalised in domains of education, the media, politics and the criminal justice system (Ndhlovu 2006; 2008a) and newer forms of marginalisation continue to emerge every day. Central to this sense of disenfranchisement is the Shona language that has been made ubiquitous at the expense of Ndebele and other languages, such as Tonga, Kalanga, Shangaan and Nambya, which are spoken in Matabeleland areas.

Studies of language policy and practice have shown how 'official discourses play an important role in naturalising and normalising a certain language ideology…' (Lin 2000: 181). Language practices in education, the media, and other spaces in Zimbabwe legitimate and present Shona as the *de facto* national language owing to the numerical, political and economic superiority of its speakers (Ncube and Siziba 2017a). This has in turn accorded it symbolic power and dominance over other indigenous languages. The emergence of a Shona-dominated, ZANU-PF ruling elite in post-independence Zimbabwe played to the advantage of the Shona language, hegemonically presenting it as the uncontested marker of Zimbabweanness (Ncube and Siziba 2017a; Maseko and Matunge 2020). The state's disposition towards Ndebele language policies and practices both officially and un-officially, appear to foreground the Shona language even among those whose first language is either Ndebele or Tonga.

In consequence, some Tonga chiefs have taken the Zimbabwean government to task, even threatening to chase away Shona-speaking teachers who do not speak Tonga. Clearly, primary school children learning to read and write for the first time, are disadvantaged when their teachers cannot speak their home language. The deployment of Shona-speaking teachers in predominantly Ndebele-speaking areas of Matabeleland has also been a bone of contention. Misspelt Ndebele words and strange expressions in Ndebele language school textbooks and billboard advertisements[9] have also drawn the ire of Ndebele-speaking citizens, who view such practices as calculated to subvert their language. Consequently, Ndebele speakers and pressure groups such as Ibhetshu Likazulu and Mthwakazi Republic Party have also led protests against these practices, particularly against the deployment of non-Ndebele speaking teachers in predominantly Ndebele-speaking schools.

The contentious use of Shona where ordinarily the use of English, the country's *lingua franca*, would be considered inclusive, betrays the insincerity of the Zimbabwean constitutional provision, which recognises sixteen languages[10] on an equal footing. Despite this apparent parity, Shona is used by government officials and politicians even in non-Shona-speaking areas of Zimbabwe. Shona and Ndebele were identified as the only official national languages in Zimbabwe following Clement Doke's recommendations in 1931 (Ndhlovu 2006; 2008b). However, before and after the new 2013 Constitution was signed into law, observed practices attest to the preponderance of Shona over all other indigenous languages (Nkomo and Maseko 2017). Moreover, some scholars such as Ngara (1982) had argued that Shona would be the default replacement of English as Zimbabwe's official language after the country's independence. Ngara was proved wrong, owing to vociferous opposition from minority language activists from the Venda, Tonga and Kalanga Languages and Culture Association (VETOKA) (National Language Policy Advisory Panel 1998).

Nonetheless, Shona remains preponderant in the domains of government such as the Parliament of Zimbabwe, where Ndebele-speaking politicians have been sanctioned and humiliated for using their language. For example, Obert Mpofu, a former minister and loyal ZANU-PF politburo member was rebuked by the Speaker of Parliament for responding in Ndebele to a question posed to him in Shona by a fellow lawmaker.[11] The speaker, thereby, legitimated the use of Shona, while proscribing the use of Ndebele, i.e. 'some languages are more equal than others.'

Another example is that of Joshua Malinga, a ZANU-PF member and the former mayor of Bulawayo who was detained by the police for being 'rude and uncooperative' after using his native Ndebele language during an exchange with them in the predominantly Ndebele-speaking city of Bulawayo (Nkomo and Maseko 2017). Ndlovu (2009) also provides examples of Shona politicians who

---

9   'Outrage over Chicken Slice spelling boob', *Chronicle,* 16 December 2014.
10 The sixteen officially recognised languages of Zimbabwe are: Chewa, Chibarwe, English, Kalanga, Koisan, Nambya, Ndau, Ndebele, Shangani, Shona, sign language, Sotho, Tonga, Tswana, Venda, Xhosa.
11 'Zimbabwe: Speak in Shona, Speaker Tells Ndebele Minister', Available at: https://allafrica.com/stories/201407250757.html

exclusively use Shona during rallies held in Ndebele-speaking areas without the use of interpreters. Many similar cases have been recorded (see Nkomo and Maseko 2017).

The performing arts sector is not exempt from the structures of power in post genocide Zimbabwe. For instance, studies have shown how Ndebele-speaking citizens have had to 'perform in the oppressor's language' to be relevant and profitable in a Shona-dominated and regulated performing arts sector (Ncube and Siziba 2017a). The latter is Shona-centric and privileges Shona cultural products as the symbols of a Zimbabwean identity. This has compelled some Ndebele artists such as Sandra Ndebele and the duo of Afrika Revenge to infuse Shona lyrics into their productions as a strategy to survive in the music industry (Ncube and Siziba 2017a). Some artists have had to relocate to Harare, the Shona-dominated capital city, in order to collaborate with Shona musicians to appeal to this Shona-centric habitus (Ncube and Siziba 2017a). Although other artists have resisted this compulsion (Ncube and Siziba 2017a), their careers have taken irreparable knocks. The consumption and aesthetic taste of Ndebele music in Zimbabwe is restricted to Matabeleland while Shona music is presented as 'national'. Most popular Shona artists such as Jah Prayzah and Winky D have unbridled access to audiences in Matabeleland as most music promoters hail from Harare, but the reverse is not true. To cement the selective consumption of Zimbabwean music, and the privileging of Shona musical products, Jeyz Marabini, a Ndebele musician was booed off stage for singing in Ndebele during the inauguration of President Emmerson Mnangagwa in Harare in 2018.[12] The negative symbolism of this act accentuates the fact that culture within Zimbabwe has become exclusive rather than inclusive.

The expression 'Shonalisation of Zimbabwe' is used to signify the role Shona has appropriated in Zimbabwean society (Ndhlovu 2006; Ncube and Siziba 2017a). The legitimation of the language infects every facet of Zimbabwean life, and thrives through the proscription of Ndebele and other indigenous languages. We argue that this represents an act of symbolic linguistic and cultural violence that parallels the actual violence of Gukurahundi. The explicit and implicit pressure that drives the use of Shona effectively stifles alternative ways of expression and of being.

Retrospection and introspection

It is almost four decades since the 1987 Unity Accord concluded the Gukurahundi era, yet the state is still to publicly acknowledge the genocide. This means 'recognizing, admitting, or owning [the genocide] and accepting the authority of others [about the genocide]' (King 2010). However, as shown by Bilali, Iqbal and Freel (2020),

---

12 'Marabini booed for singing in Ndebele at Mnangagwa event', *Bulawayo 24 News*, 27 November 2017. Available at: https://bulawayo24.com/index-id-entertainment-sc-music-byo-123108.html

genocide denials are pervasive throughout the world.

The late former president and chief architect of Gukurahundi (Phimister 2009), Robert Mugabe contemptuously labelled the genocide as 'a moment of madness' (Ncube and Siziba 2017b) without saying who was mad. The same applies to his successor President Mnangagwa who has remained evasive, conveniently trying to persuade citizens to 'let bygones be bygones', as he did on 26 January 2018 at the World Economic Forum in Davos, Switzerland.[13] Like Mugabe before him, he avoided apologising. Instead, at a rally in Chitungwiza on 23 March 2022, he threatened various organisations that use – among other grievances – Gukurahundi to advocate for the self-determination of Matabeleland. Mnangagwa reminded victims of their painful experiences, delivering a chilling warning; 'You will be looking to shorten your life. You must walk a path that prolongs your life.'[14] Indeed, considering the period in retrospect, both Mugabe and Mnangagwa's attitude toward the genocide has been expressed through the language of hatred, violence and disdain as well as denialism or falsification as in the descriptive terms 'civil war' or Matabeleland 'unrest' and Matabeleland 'disturbances', but never genocide. The language of apology and conciliation that can be therapeutic and is essential in terms of nation building (King 2010) has remained unforthcoming.

The subject of Gukurahundi remains a political taboo outside government agencies such as the compromised National Peace and Reconciliation Commission. So tainted is the word in the metaphorical sense that Shona lexicographers could not accommodate it as an historical term in authoritative Shona monolingual dictionaries alongside others such as '*Chimurenga* – war of liberation'. In his poem 'Ode to the Nameless', the late poet and academic Gugulethu Siziba suggests that the term has been proscribed because it signifies the countless, nameless victims who were buried in unmarked graves without proper burial procedures. Instead, the attitude of the Zimbabwean government is to try and bury the word, the concept, the historical era so that they are out of sight and out of mind (see Chapter 5). For example, Owen Maseko, a visual artist, was arrested in March 2010 under the Public Order and Security Act for his exhibition of paintings portraying the Gukurahundi violence.[15] It is also exemplified in the arrests and torture of individuals who speaks out about it, while make it difficult for the victims to be exhumed and given proper reburials.

---

13 https://www.youtube.com/watch?v=zi-HIf1dYV4

14 'If you act like biblical Legion, you will end up cast into deep sea, Mnangagwa sends another chilling warning to MRP', *zwnews*, 24 June 2022. Available at: https://zwnews.com/if-you-act-like-biblical-legion-you-will-end-up-cast-into-deep-sea-mnangagwa-sends-another-chilling-warning-to-mrp/

15 'Artist arrested, genocide exhibit closed in Zimbabwe', *Global Press Journal*, 10 September 2012. Available at: https://globalpressjournal.com/africa/zimbabwe/artist-arrested-genocide-exhibit-closed-in-zimbabwe/

Overall, the language used with respect to Gukurahundi has been unrepentant, and reconciliation insincere. While Joshua Nkomo was relieved of the 'Dissident Father' tag, he only became 'Father Zimbabwe' and 'Umdala wethu' (our old man) in acknowledgement of his role in the signing of the Unity Accord, which saw his former 'dissident party' capitulate into ZANU-PF.

Conclusion

This chapter explored the linguistic dimensions of Gukurahundi to show the centrality of language before, during and after the genocide. We drew on online testimonies from survivors and statements from government officials as well as visible language planning and language practices in the post-Gukurahundi era. In doing so, we have shown how the Shona language was weaponised and continues to be deployed as a tool for perpetuating the legacy of Gukurahundi in symbolic forms. Languages are more than neutral instruments of communication; they reflect important symbolic and identity roles, particularly in post-conflict societies (Tannenbaum 2012). In post Gukurahundi Zimbabwe, the issue of language has remained topical as language is an important means of maintaining, legitimating, effectuating and reproducing unequal relations of power (Skutnabb-Kangas and Dunbar 2010). The foregoing suggests that the presentation of the Shona language within the Zimbabwean state, state-aligned institutions and in Zimbabwean society at large reflects the cultural and political antagonisms dating back to the pre-independence era. It is in fact a subtle form of violence which undermines everything that is different. As a continuation of conflict in symbolic and cultural ways in supposed times of peace, this has implications for processes of reconciliation (Skutnabb-Kangas and Dunbar 2010). Consequently, for victims and survivors, the term Gukurahundi has become a synonym and a metaphor for the structural violence and subjugation experienced contemporaneously. Mention of the word conjures images of all practices that seek to legitimate and naturalise structures of inequality in post genocide Zimbabwe. As Olusoga and Erichsen (2010: 352) observe, for 'the descendants of its victims, genocides are not a distant memory but an open wound that shapes their day-to-day existence' (Olusoga and Erichsen 2010: 352).

7

Public Media and Genocide: The Role of *The Chronicle* during the Gukurahundi Genocide in Zimbabwe

Bhekinkosi J. Ncube

Introduction

This chapter offers an examination of the role of the state-controlled media during the 1983-87 Gukurahundi genocide when over 20,000 mostly isiNdebele-speaking supporters of the then opposition party, the Zimbabwe African People's Union Patriotic Front (PF-ZAPU) were killed by the Fifth Brigade, a unit of the Zimbabwean army trained by North Korea. The chapter is therefore a study of the practice and politics of media production with particular focus on the role of public media in genocides. Research on the role of the media in state-sponsored violence in Zimbabwe has tended to focus on the post-2000 land invasions and political violence in general. Similarly, most writings on the role of media during genocides in Africa in general, have justifiably tended to focus on the role of the RTLM radio in the Rwandan genocide where close to a million Tutsis and moderate Hutus were killed in 100 days by Hutu extremists. Using *The Chronicle* newspaper as a case study, this chapter deploys critical discourse analysis (CDA) to explore the public media's role in the Gukurahundi genocide. Critical political economy theory, which holds that ownership among other things affect media messages that audiences receive, is also used. The chapter argues that unlike Rwanda where the media openly urged the killers on, the media in Zimbabwe was used to mask and justify the killings of thousands of innocent civilians. Zimbabwe Newspapers (Zimpapers) Group (Ltd) 1980 publishes *The Chronicle*. The newspaper is located in Bulawayo and it was established in 1884. The government of Zimbabwe owns 51% of Zimpapers shares through the Zimbabwe Mass Media Trust (MMT) whose board was dissolved in 2000.[1] The same trust owned a national news agency, Zimbabwe National News Agency (Ziana) that was responsible for distributing news.[2]

The Gukurahundi Genocide

The chapter is set against the overtures of the post-Mugabe government to open debate on the genocide, and by the growing demands for justice, commemorations, exhumations and reburials of Gukurahundi victims (Tshuma and Ndlovu 2020; Dube 2021).

Moreover, I grew up in rural Matabeleland where I witnessed the cruelties of the Gukurahundi soldiers. I vividly remember one day in 1984 when I was in Grade 3 at a rural school in poverty-stricken Plumtree which, years later, informed my interests in the study of the media in the genocide. Fifth Brigade soldiers, deployed in rural Matabeleland and Midlands in January 1983, came to our school just after the morning assembly and ordered everyone to the open space where the school held its morning assembly. Not being Ndebele speakers, they spoke through the headmaster and we were told to return home and call everyone – our parents, sisters, brothers, grandfathers and grandmothers – to school.

Two or three hours later, the whole school was gathered at the school's assembly point and we were directed to sit under a big tree, children and parents alike. The soldiers introduced themselves, and told us they were looking for 'dissidents' and that they were prepared to kill anyone who was not prepared to co-operate with them. They said they were also looking for PF-ZAPU supporters, those who remained blindly loyal to its leader Joshua Nkomo. They also introduced some people who said they were members of the press.

After some singing and dancing, the commander spotted a very old man – he might have been in his nineties – trembling and he went up to him and spoke

---

1 Appearing before a Parliament's Portfolio Committee on Information, Media and Broadcasting Services on 20 November 2019, the Permanent Secretary in the Ministry of Information, Publicity and Broadcasting Services, Mr Nick Mangwana said government was working on reviving the Zimbabwe Mass Media Trust and the full complement board of trustees was to be appointed soon (https://www.herald.co.zw/govt-to-revive-mass-media-trust/)

2 In 1981, the Zimbabwean government bought a majority stake in the Rhodesia Printing and Publishing Company, which was then owned by Argus Media, using a grant from the Nigerian government (Waldahl 2004; Saunders 1999). The MMT was set up as a buffer to prevent direct government control of the new company, Zimpapers. However, not long afterwards, the government began to use Zimpapers as its official mouthpiece, bypassing the weak MMT board (which they selected) and appointing party cadres into editorial positions.

in a language that I had not heard before. (Later I was told it was Shona.) He said: '*Mudara, maneta, mune nzara,* come on *imbai!*' (Old man, are you tired, are you hungry, come on sing). The old man was our neighbour. Because of his age or because he had a medical condition he was always trembling but he was a good man, a brave man. When the commander moved menacingly towards him, the old man attempted to stand up, staggered and was helped up by his equally aging wife. Someone from the crowd whispered, '*Uthi hlabela khulu*' (he is saying start a song) – and he sang: '*Dlala nkazana, dlala nkazana, dlala nkazana, sekusile. Ah yelele…*'[3] The shivering village responded: '*Jabulisa umoya wethemba lami sekusile*'. In all my eight years, I had never known that the old man could sing, but on that day, faced with a machine gun he sang, and ironically it was a song of celebration.

One can therefore infer that the Gukurahundi genocide in Zimbabwe is closely tied to issues of ethnicity, violence, political power and political identity. Political violence or killings in the country did not start with the Gukurahundi atrocities but violence has always manifested itself ethnically (Ndlovu-Gatsheni 2003). Indeed, there is serious ethnic polarisation in Zimbabwe, which has its roots in the pre-colonial and nationalist socio-political processes as well as in the post-colonial coercive nation-building project of the 1980s (Mamdani 1996). The struggle for control of the state as well as political legitimacy in pre-colonial, colonial and post-colonial Zimbabwe has always assumed an ethnic dimension, and as such it has always featured the Ndebele people, and it has been fiercer in Matabeleland and Bulawayo than in any other part of the country.

According to Mamdani (2001:21) ethnicity as a phenomenon articulates many concealed socio-economic and political issues ranging from contested histories and memories, political power dynamics, politics of belonging and hegemonic struggles. Moreover, as stated above, state-engineered and state-sponsored violence has been a recurrent feature of Zimbabwean political life since the first arrival of colonial settlers (Ranger 1995: 39; Alexander et al. 2000; Sithole 1995).

Zimbabwe's liberation war which pitted the nationalist liberation movements on one side and the settlers on the other also exhibited ethnic tendencies. These nationalist movements were PF-ZAPU (primarily Ndebele) and ZANU-PF (primarily Shona). Writing about this split, Sithole (1985: 122) observes that:

> Once ethnicity became a salient issue in the nationalist movement in the 1970s, PF-ZAPU became a minority party, a position that was likely to be maintained in the foreseeable future. Ever since the 1970s, PF-ZAPU retained loyalty mainly in Matabeleland North, Matabeleland South and the Midlands where Ndebele presence was significant. As such election manifestos meant little compared to

---

3   This is a traditional Ndebele love and celebratory song, which can be loosely translated as 'Dance little girl … dance little girl … It is now morning … Make my hopes and spirits rise … It is morning'.

the traditional loyalties. Moreover the fact that the areas of dominance fell among ethnic lines was not an accident and certainly not a matter to be ambivalent about.

Mombeshora (1990: 432) concludes that 'the seeds of the ethnic factor were derived from the pre-colonial past, [but] the colonial era provided fertile soil in which the ideology of tribalism (ethnicity) germinated, blossomed and was further propagated'.

The Gukurahundi genocide therefore refers to the slaughter of about 20,000 mostly Ndebele-speaking civilians in Matabeleland and some parts of the Midlands province by the Fifth Brigade. These killings began in 1983 mostly in Matabeleland North and spread to Matabeleland South in 1984 (Sibanda 2021; Kriger 2003; Alexander 1998). The soldiers had been trained by 106 military advisers from North Korea. The brigade was placed directly under the control of Mugabe outside army structures (Blair 2002: 30). Blair (2002) says of the Fifth Brigade:

> Its soldiers were drawn from largely Shona ranks of Mugabe's old guerrilla force, ZANLA. Step by step he was carefully preparing an onslaught. Later Nkomo would ruefully refer to Fifth Brigade as 'Mugabe's North Korea trained army' (Blair 2002: 30).

During this time a few acts of banditry were reported in Matabeleland but they did not warrant a wholesale assault by a brutal army unit (CCJPZ and LRF 1997). The murder and abduction of six young tourists along the Bulawayo-Victoria Falls road in July 1982 provided the spark that led Mugabe to unleash the Fifth Brigade under the command of Air Marshal Perence Shiri.[4] According to media reports, the tourist vehicle was stopped at a makeshift roadblock which the tourists – two Britons, two Australians and two Americans – assumed was manned by the army. Apparently, three female passengers and the driver were freed. Nonetheless, ZANU-PF accused dissidents (renegade ex-ZAPU soldiers who had refused to join the army) of the murders. Joshua Nkomo, the leader of PF-ZAPU, remained sceptical. Nkomo (1984: 240) insisted that one of the cars seen by the released female passengers was later used by the police to transport the driver of the damaged vehicle back to town. The car later disappeared.

According to the CCJP and LRF (1997) report on the genocide, the operations of the Fifth Brigade were marked by bases or torture camps at districts and missions, police stations, schools, and boreholes and even in the mountains. According to this report, soldiers also directed their energies to political re-orientation and mobilisation. This included forcing villagers to watch brutal torture and killing of

---

4 Arguably, the murder of the tourists was analogous to the Sarajevo incident which led to the First World War.

their loved ones and to ululate in support of their deaths. At times, whole families were slaughtered and homes were burnt down.

Stores and grinding mills were shut down and granaries were burnt under a dusk to dawn curfew which was declared in most of Matabeleland in early 1984 (ibid.: 77). Shops were closed and all forms of transportation were banned and drought relief supplies were suspended. This murderous starvation policy was meant to complement the efforts of the Fifth Brigade; if people could not be killed by the Fifth Brigade, they would definitely succumb to hunger.

Critical political economy and the hegemonic role of the media

The role of Zimbabwe's state-controlled media in the Gukurahundi genocide can be located within the political economy theory of the media. In other words, ownership, among other things, can affect the information the public receives; powerful institutions and interests act as 'primary definers', whereas journalists act as 'secondary definers', who simply translate into a popular idiom the interpretative framework furnished by accredited (government) sources (Hardy 2014). The theory holds that the structure of the industry influences content and its presumption is that there is an intrinsic relationship between ownership and content of media production (Curran and Gurevitch 1977; Curran 1992; Curran 1996).

For Hardy (2014: 7), different ways of organising and financing media institutions have implications for the range and nature of media content. According to Hardy (2014: 8) the goods produced by the media are at once economic and cultural, thus, it is important to explore the interplay between the symbolic and economic dimensions of the production of meaning i.e. the relationship of media and communication systems to wider forces and processes in society. It is, therefore, crucial to examine how the political and economic organisation of *The Chronicle* affected the production and circulation of meaning.[5]

According to Curran and Gurevitch (1977) early Marxist theorists viewed the media as part of an ideological arena in which various class views are fought out, albeit within the context of the dominance of certain classes (Curran and Gurevitch 1977: 4). According to this theory, media professionals enjoy the illusion of autonomy while in truth they are first socialised into and then internalise the values of the dominant culture. In other words, the media is not neutral but ideological (Hall 1977).

Downing et al. (1995: 76), ask such questions as: are the media free and independent to present views, news and entertainment just as they want? Are they free to offer a diverse range of views and have an independent opinion? Closely linked

---

5 Precisely because of the ownership structure of Zimpapers where government has 51% of the shares, most ministers assumed that Zimpapers must serve the interests of the ruling ZANU-PF party.

to this view are Althusser (1971) and Gramsci (1971)'s conception of the media as ideological state apparatuses largely concerned with the reproduction of dominant ideologies. Gramsci's (1971) theory of hegemony and the concept of ideology are also of central importance in this study. Gramsci was of the view that the ruling elite maintained control not just through violence and political and economic coercion but also ideologically, that is through an hegemonic culture in which the values of the ruling class become accepted as the values of all. The argument here is that the government and the state cannot enforce control over the people unless more intellectual methods are used. Gramsci also argued that the ruling class forms and maintains its hegemony in civil society by creating cultural and political consensus through the media. The latter is used to make inequalities and subordination appear natural so as to induce consent.

Media framing of genocide stories

A critical discourse analysis of five purposively selected *Chronicle* editorials and five front-page lead stories published between 1983 and 1987 was conducted. The former were chosen because editorials form the heart and soul of a newspaper as they analyse and evaluate important contemporary events, issues, and opinions. While editorials often profess objectivity and neutrality, they more often betray the opinions and beliefs of a newspaper's editors and publishers.

CDA stems from a critical theory of language, which understands its use as a form of social practice (Janks 1997: 329). This method of analytical research primarily studies the way social power is abused and dominance and inequality are enacted, reproduced and resisted textually and verbally in the social and political context (van Djik 1993).

CDA was used as a method of analysing *The Chronicle* editorials because it has been credited with providing a concrete means of understanding language, meaning and power. The context in which the editorials were written is also analysed as newspapers do not operate in a vacuum but exist within a particular socio-cultural and political framework.

In times of conflict or crisis such as genocide, the media especially under authoritarian regimes try to discursively manufacture consensus through the reproduction of certain stories. The media therefore functions 'cognitively through its schematic structure of manipulation' (van Dijk 1993: 253). Consequently, it is the textual features of news stories that play an active role in political and cultural relations of power. News stories can become active insofar as political ideology is concerned.

Fairclough (1993), a proponent of critical discourse analysis, argues that since the media, especially mainstream media, are connected to the market and their demands, they cannot claim to merely reflect reality but rather they seek to justify, preserve, rationalise, conceptualise and represent the interests of politically and economically dominant groups in a conflict at the expense of the minority. As a result, it can be argued that the language that the media use during a genocide is persuasive to the extent that 'news have a social, political and educational role, in that people try to understand and explain how events reported in the media relate to their own society and lives as a whole' (van Dijk 1988: 213). This, therefore, means that news is 'not an objective representation of facts (reality) [but] is cultural constructs that encodes fixed values… it is not the event but the partial, ideologically framed report of an event' (Caldas-Coulthard 2003: 273; Ncube 2017).

Entman (1993) is of the view that framing is a construction of social reality and that the media frames events through presenting images of reality in a particular or predictable way, in the process giving the story a preferred spin. Through framing, the media focus on certain events and then place them within a field of meaning, drawing public attention to certain issues or topics, while suppressing others. Therefore, one can see frames as abstracts that serve to organise or structure social meanings. Frames also influence the perception of the news by the audience (Tuchman 1978: ix). According to Hall (1982), the media are involved in the 'politics of signification', in which they produce images of the world that give events particular meanings. Hall's argument is that media images (stories, pictures, captions, headlines) do not simply reflect the world but they re-present it; that is, instead of reproducing the reality out there, the media engage in practices that define it.

Discussion

A CDA of the five editorials and five lead stories by *The Chronicle* reveals that the newspaper denied that the Fifth Brigade soldiers were killing innocent civilians. Neither did it make a distinction between dissidents and innocent civilians; indeed, it subtly participated in the genocide by masking or justifying the killings.

The way *The Chronicle* stories are packaged reveal that the production of texts is a result of a selection process from the paradigmatic choices at the disposal of the editors. In all five lead stories analysed, the source is an unnamed police spokesman or a government spokesman. The Minister of Home Affairs or the then Minister of National Supplies Enos Nkala dominates.

According to *Breaking the Silence, Building True Peace* (CCJPZ and LRF 1997), less than a month after the Fifth Brigade deployment, over a thousand innocent civilians had been killed, but this was not reported in *The Chronicle*. The report presents gruesome accounts of the events surrounding the Gukurahundi genocide but *The Chronicle* offers not a single mention of it. Denials, encouragement to re-deploy the Fifth Brigade, and claims that dissidents were killing ZANU-PF supporters and farmers dominate.

The report states that:

> At the same time as 5 Brigade was sent into the area the government had introduced a strict curfew on the region. This prevented anybody from entering or leaving the area, banned all forms of transport, and prevented movement in the region from dusk to dawn. A food curfew was also in force with stores being closed. People caught using bicycles or donkey carts were shot.... During the early weeks, 5 Brigade behaved in a way that shows that it had clearly been trained to target civilians. Wherever troops went they would routinely round up dozens, or even hundreds of civilians and march them at gunpoint to a central place, like a school or borehole. There they would be forced to sing Shona songs praising ZANU-PF at the same time being beaten by sticks. These gatherings usually ended with public executions.... It is clear 5 Brigade was following orders when it targeted civilians in this way because the pattern is similar throughout the regions affected (CCJPZ and LRF: 91).

Instead of focusing, for example, on the killings in Matabeleland and the hunger throughout Zimbabwe, but especially in drought-prone Matabeleland in 1982-83 due to the effects of the curfew, the newspaper remained silent. Instead, the newspaper is littered with headlines such as: 'Dissidents burn bus in Nkayi' (12 January 1984), 'Robbers set 3 buses alight in Nkayi' (17 January 1984), with the source almost invariably the 'police spokesman'. In both these stories, there is no comment from the passengers about what they saw. As a result, the headline is designed to paint a picture of lawlessness in Matabeleland in order to justify the deployment of the Fifth Brigade.[6]

One of the tenets of good journalism is to champion a citizen's human rights, but on 4 February 1983, *The Chronicle* led with a banner headline, 'Curfew imposed in Mat South: Move aimed at flushing out bandits'. The story is replete with details of the restrictions and a map showing the affected areas. That these were drought years and the closure of stores and banning of all traffic (including donkey-driven scotch carts) in and out of the region meant that villagers would starve was neither disclosed nor discussed by the newspaper because 'it was necessary to destroy the infrastructure that nurtured the bandits' (5 March 1983).

Just nine days after the curfew was imposed the paper boldly declared: 'Dissident activity on the decline' (13 February 1984) and went on to claim that a considerable number of dissidents had been captured due to the effects of the curfew. No figures or names were given, although in the same issue there is a story headlined: 'Militias to fight banditry'. Why, if there was a decline in the number of dissidents was there a

---

6 As the buses were burnt during the afternoon in an area where the Fifth Brigade were dominant, questions have been raised as to who set them alight, and who suffered as a result.

need to form militias to fight them? I argue that such stories were simply planted to support a curfew that had disastrous effects on the lives and livelihoods of innocent civilians. This is why on 24 April 1984 the paper led with the story: 'People in curfew areas now helping the army'.

The Acting Commander of Five Brigade, Brigadier Edzai Chanyuka said since the relaxation of the curfew two weeks ago, the army has seen 'smiling faces come forward to assist by reporting the presence of dissidents. Some have come forward to applaud our presence here saying they were happy we were winning the war against the dissidents and also weeding them out of their environment'.

The Chronicle did not mention the untold suffering caused by the army and by extension the government's starvation strategy. It is clear that the argument within ZANU-PF, one supported by *The Chronicle*, was that if the people could not die at the hands of the Gukurahundi then hunger would deal with them. The above quote reveals the newspaper's intention to hoodwink readers into believing that people in curfew areas supported the curfew, as also reflected in another story headlined, 'They want army not to move', (6 May 1984) in which villagers of Kafusi in Gwanda are said to have begged the Fifth Brigade to stay. The newspaper further opined, 'The crowd also appealed for ZANU-PF membership cards. People also appealed to the government not to lift the curfew because dissidents would be reactivated'.

And, indeed, people might have appealed for ZANU-PF membership cards not because they supported the party, but because they had become a passport to life.

In another story, 'Five Brigade is here to stay' (12 February 1983), *The Chronicle* writes:

> There are reports that the Five Brigade has killed 1000 'innocent' civilians in Matabeleland. Such statistics are of course hard to swallow. Also people sheltering, feeding and at times 'entertaining' dissidents can hardly be called innocent... The Five Brigade was never going to be popular but if it gets the job done, the country is the better for.

The implication of the above reductionist argument is that PF-ZAPU was sponsoring and supporting dissidents, and since PF-ZAPU was supported by Ndebeles, Ndebeles were therefore dissidents. *The Chronicle's* position is, however, that the Fifth Brigade is there to protect people against PF-ZAPU, and dissidents, and therefore must stay. That people were being indiscriminately killed by this army unit is not mentioned. The editors of the paper appear to wholly support ZANU-PF's attempt to violently crush PF-ZAPU in order to achieve a one-party state.

The Chronicle's support of the government strategy is consistently apparent. For example, the use of the word 'entertaining' (above) suggests that PF-ZAPU supporters are willingly supporting dissidents and must, therefore, also be eliminated. This line of thinking is evident in the story headlined: 'Minister defends Five Brigade' (5 March 1983). Then Minister of State (Security) Emmerson Mnangagwa, likening the dissidents to cockroaches and bugs said the bandit menace had reached such epidemic proportions that the government had to bring in 'DDT' (Five Brigade) to get rid of the bandits.[7] He said:

> The Govt had two options to deal decisively with the dissident menace. One was to burn down all the villages infested with dissidents and the other was to bring in the Five Brigade. The Govt chose the latter… It was necessary to destroy the infrastructure that nurtured the bandits. Dissidents can only survive where there was fodder for them (*Chronicle* 5 March 1983).

In an editorial comment of 28 November 1985 headlined, 'The locals are helping', the editor writes:

> But they [dissidents] cannot operate without the help of the locals, that much is obvious. Whether through fear or support they swim together like fish in familiar waters. Thereby lies their weakness. The dissidents must be deprived of the water that they swim in.

The editorial continues:

> There is one simple reason for this: they are receiving much support from the locals… This in effect makes them accessories to the crime; and in this case it is particularly heinous crime. They then should be treated to the same fate as the perpetrators when facing the wrath of the law.

Justification for killing the people of Matabeleland with impunity is sought through such statements. Likening PF-ZAPU supporters who coincidentally are Ndebele to cockroaches and bugs betrays the desire by the government to kill them. The newspaper does not openly declare war against the Ndebeles but 'DDT', a chemical used to destroy pests, is not selective about which ones i.e. the Fifth Brigade will kill indiscriminately.

Equally the water that the dissidents have to be deprived of was the innocent Ndebele civilians that had to be killed. For nowhere in the history of fishing have fisherman scooped out water to get fish. This view of seeing PF-ZAPU supporters and therefore Ndebeles as dissidents was amplified by Prime Minister Mugabe himself:

---

7 Interestingly, 39 years later in 2022, the Zimbabwe Vice-President Constantino Chiwenga used similar language while talking about the opposition party Citizens' Coalition for Change (CCC) and he said: 'I have heard others here saying down with triple C, let me assure you that there is nothing that it can achieve, you see how we crush lice with a stone'. https://allafrica.com/stories/202202280110.html

> Where men and women provide food for dissidents, when we get there, we eradicate them. We don't differentiate when we fight because we can't tell who is a dissident and who is not. Dissidents have no distinguishing marks (*The Chronicle* 6 April 1983).

What emerges from our analysis is the complimentary ideological role that the state media employed in rehearsing and justifying the logic and the arguments of a repressive state. By providing a platform and enabling the rhetoric, the story became an acceptable myth. Barthes argues that 'myths work to naturalise history… it [myth] always promotes the interests of the dominant classes by making the meanings that serve these interests appear natural and universal (cited in Fiske 1987: 135).

That *The Chronicle*'s role in the genocide becomes apparent in the story headlined: 'Atrocities: Reporters find no evidence'. The story does not carry a byline. It dismisses witnesses to atrocities who gave evidence in Kezi and quotes the Director of Information Dr John Tsimba as saying:

> There certainly was no evidence of genocide. The two graves in which six people are allegedly buried according to evidence of a half-serious man purporting to be a father of one of the dead, certainly cannot be equated to genocide of 30000 people (11 May 1984).

The circumstances surrounding the story are that on 10 May 1984, Peter Godwin of the *Sunday Times* (UK) (who had written about the atrocities before) and other journalists numbering about 50 were led by Dr Tsimba and Commander of the Army General Rex Nhongo (Solomon Mujuru) to villagers in Kezi. The former rounded up villagers and asked them to tell their stories of Gukurahundi. The villagers bravely did so but Dr Tsimba then enquired why they had not shown the evidence to Enos Nkala (the then Minister of National Affairs between 1983 and 1985) who had visited the area before. This was because a lot of evidence such as mass graves were not those that could have been identified by the villagers but ones that had been dug the night before so as to show the international media that there were no atrocities. The villagers could not have said anything to Nkala, a senior member of Mugabe's administration, who was known to be vindictive and to openly support the Fifth Brigade.[8]

It must also be borne in mind that elections were to be held a year later in 1985 and therefore all efforts were directed at discrediting PF-ZAPU and at the same time dealing with its supporters through the Fifth Brigade. To this end after 'successfully' stage managing a fact-finding mission, *The Chronicle* was back again on the 19 May 1984 with the headline: 'PM warns PF-ZAPU of war to the finish:

---

8 According to CCJPZ and LRF(1997), Nkala was instrumental in the genocide. The report cites him warning PF-ZAPU supporters that ZANU-PF would deliver a few blows to them.

Forces to flush out dissidents'.

Mugabe then betrays his hatred for PF-ZAPU, as quoted by *The Chronicle*:

> PF-ZAPU [has] started something and I want to assure you we are going to see this thing through to the bitter end. I shall give power to the police and the security forces to mount a manhunt not only in houses but also in bushes, anthills and trees. Anybody here who belongs to PF-ZAPU will have to answer for it (*Chronicle* 19 May 1984).

In apparent reference to the Ndebele ethnic composition of PF-ZAPU and therefore dissidents, Mugabe said:

> They started to murder people and brought spears in Zimbabwe. There is no one we fear. From today the direction we will take will bear heavily on PF-ZAPU. PF-ZAPU has opened a new chapter. There is going to be a new road that we are going to walk and PF-ZAPU must be prepared for a very tough exceedingly tough road (19 May 1984).

Reminiscent of the Rwandan media during the genocide of 1994 that encouraged Hutus to slaughter the minority Tutsi *The Chronicle* of 24 June 1984 quoted the Midlands governor Benson Ndemera inciting ZANU-PF supporters to fight. He said:

> ... If you are provoked you have the right to defend yourself. And should this happen you must sting like a black mamba which once it has struck there is no cure for the bite.

The result of such reckless statements was massive demonstrations against PF-ZAPU where their supporters were killed. One sees here *The Chronicle* justifying the brutality meted on fellow citizens and also failing to condemn these riots. On the 19 June 1984, the paper had unashamedly written:

> Thousands of Zimbabweans yesterday demonstrated calling for the immediate arrest of PF-ZAPU leader Dr Joshua Nkomo and the closure of all PF-ZAPU offices in the Midlands province. Police watched as people were beaten and cars set on fire. "The mob was too big I'm sure they (police) could not stop it," said another witness who asked not to be named (*Chronicle* 19 June 1984).

What is striking about the above quote is the reference to the unnamed source vehemently defending law enforcement's failure to control a mob. What this story intended to do was to scare any PF-ZAPU supporter into submission so that dictatorship could thrive. There was no PF-ZAPU supporter who could openly declare his or her allegiance to the party because they would be beaten, their cars and houses would be set on fire and the police would stand by because the mob would be 'too big'. Also to be noted is the use of the word 'Zimbabweans' instead of the residents of Kwekwe or the Midlands. The impression created here is that Zimbabweans as a whole are against Nkomo, PF-ZAPU and dissidents and therefore any action against these three is justified as it for the public good even if people are killed.

Two days later, *The Chronicle* under a story headlined: 'Deaths reported in anti-PF-ZAPU violence – 141 injured in Kwekwe clashes' stated:

> Anti-minority party violence in the last week has claimed the lives of two people and another 35 are in hospital as a result, a Government statement said in Harare last night. The one sentence statement gave no clue as to where the two deaths occurred. (*Chronicle* 21 June 1984).

The story went on to say that in the suburbs of Amaveni and Imbizo in Kwekwe, houses were burnt and police said there was nothing they could do. The paper did not condemn the riots, or the failure by the police to protect PF-ZAPU supporters because to *The Chronicle* these were 'dissidents' who were supposed to be 'wiped out'. It is no wonder that the following day *The Chronicle* commented:

> The strengthening of the ZRP position, perhaps with army units must be considered in a bid to bring this chaotic situation, **which even the dissidents themselves have been unable to achieve so far** (my emphasis) under control. (*Chronicle* 22 June 1984).

What this suggests is that even *The Chronicle* knew that dissidents were not doing much damage but they never bothered to publish this side of the story. Instead, what followed were a series of headlines meant to further discredit PF-ZAPU. The media's function according to the propaganda model (Herman & Chomsky 1988) is to reduce the subordinate population's ability to think, thereby inducing group apathy. Thus the state-owned *Chronicle*, the only daily paper circulating in Matabeleland, established a framework of news through select use of use topics and by emphasising the wrongs done by PF-ZAPU, all of which served the interests of the dominant elite (ZANU-PF) in society.

What is apparent with regard to *The Chronicle* is that the paper consistently praised Gukurahundi in and subtly supported ZANU-PF government's efforts of creating a one-party state. Instead of criticising violence, the paper published stories that incited violence, and attributed state-sponsored violence to the dissidents. It is clear that *The Chronicle* worked hand in hand with the state apparatus through the police, CIO, army and youth brigades. While the latter were beating up and killing people *The Chronicle* was massaging people's minds. The *Chronicle* should be seen as an extension of the state's ideological apparatus. The issue of 22 June 1984 provides just another example of this in its headline: 'PF-ZAPU is a dead donkey' where

Callistus Ndlovu is quoted as saying:

> The government sent the army to this place [Plumtree] to try and salvage you people from dissident slavery. It is now up to you to completely free yourselves from this slavery by joining the party [ZANU-PF] that has a future for everybody in Zimbabwe.

Schlesinger (1993) observes that the media can have the power to help preserve a cultural space or collective identity. His view is supported by Fowler (1991) who argues that the media plays a critical role in creating and sustaining a common culture, which in this case was a culture of supporting ZANU-PF. It is our argument that The *Chronicle* consistently attempted to create a collective identity in which everyone became a loyal member of ZANU-PF.

Conclusion

Against this background it is sufficient to say that newspaper discourses (text, pictures, and cartoons) do not offer neutral descriptions of the world but they actively seek to shape the world toward a certain viewpoint and strive to hide contradictions. Teasing out the discourse on Gukurahundi using The *Chronicle* as an example one finds that the paper assumes the position of the ZANU-PF government against the people of Matabeleland who happened to be Ndebele and supported PF-ZAPU. Therefore, our central contention is that The *Chronicle* facilitated and fomented the atrocities and that the international media essentially helped The *Chronicle* by ignoring the complexities of the story. Assuming a hegemonic role The *Chronicle* tried to naturalise the beatings and murder of the Ndebele people.

8

Making sense of that 'moment of madness': Virtual discussion of Gukurahundi on social media in Zimbabwe

Gibson Ncube and Yemurai Chikwangura-Gwatirisa

Introduction

In this chapter, we grapple with the contentious issue in Zimbabwe's post-independent history that is the Gukurahundi genocide. Gukurahundi has come to refer to the whole tumultuous period between 1983 and 1987 during which the Fifth Brigade killed an estimated 20,000 civilians and left many more maimed, physically, and psychologically, in the provinces of Matabeleland and the Midlands (CCJPZ and LRF 1997). Coltart (2016:139) describes the ruthless brutality that characterised the operations of the Fifth Brigade as they sought to deal with 'unruly dissidents':

> From late January to mid-March 1983, the Fifth Brigade murdered and tortured thousands of civilians, burnt hundreds of villages, and raped and pillaged entire communities. There were horrific public executions, people were lined up and shot in cold blood; on many occasions soldiers would arrive at villages with lists of people affiliated to ZAPU and those found would be assassinated in front of their families. On other occasions, entire families were herded into grass-roofed huts, which were then set alight. Pregnant women were bayonetted, killing the babies in their wombs. Young Ndebele men between the ages of 16 and 40 were particularly vulnerable and were frequently targeted and shot in cold blood.

What Coltart highlights above is not just the brutality of this highly trained force, but also the way in which tribe and ethnicity underpinned its bloody operations targeting unarmed civilians. The people who were terrorised, maimed, and killed were largely those who were Ndebele. These people were considered to be supporters of not just PF-ZAPU but also of the dissidents, disaffected ex-combatants, who were undermining the government of Mugabe.[1] Many would argue that the reasons of the dissidents were justifiable even if their actions were not.

Interestingly, 'Gukurahundi' is a Shona word that means 'the storm of the summer that sweeps away the chaff' (Sithole and Makumbe 1997:133). We argue that the violence of the Fifth Brigade was in fact the operationalisation of the trope of dirt. The chaff, a synecdoche of rubbish, referred to the inhabitants of Midlands and Matabeleland who, through their support of Mugabe's arch-rival Joshua Nkomo, were a threat to the rule of Mugabe. Ncube (2018:48) explains in this regard that:

> In essence, Gukurahundi was a form of ethnic cleansing whose aim was to subdue any form of dissidence emanating from the Matabeleland and Midlands regions. It is worth pointing out that an exercise that sought to crush dissenting voices, through the cleansing of Matabeleland and Midlands landscape, ended up being an ethnic cleansing in which Ndebeles were either tortured, maimed or killed.

Writer and academic Tshuma (2018a) refers to the Gukurahundi genocide as Zimbabwe's 'original sin'. Labelling it in this way suggests that, like the sin of Adam and Eve, it was the first sin whose effects can still be felt today. Gukurahundi, as we will demonstrate in this chapter, continues to haunt Zimbabwe's national psyche. The genocide remains a spectre whose reappearance is persistent. In Derrida's (1993) theorisation, a spectre leaves a trace, and this refers to a mark that represents a past 'something' that no longer exists in the present moment. Although Gukurahundi took place over five years, close to four decades ago, it remains a challenging issue, especially for the people of Matabeleland and the Midlands provinces. Gukurahundi is a challenge because openly discussing the genocide has been virtually criminalised with the state preferring to adopt a policy of collective amnesia (Ncube 2022). Artists

---

1   Alexander (1998) posits that the role of dissidents in Gukurahundi is often neglected or downplayed. Dissidents, however, played a central role in how the genocide started, unfolded and was framed. At independence, there was animosity between the main political parties: ZANU-PF and PF-ZAPU. Robert Mugabe accused the latter of sabotaging the stability of the country and in January 1981, he demoted Joshua Nkomo from the Ministry of Home Affairs to the Ministry of Public Affairs and then to a ministry without portfolio. Thereafter, all PF-ZAPU aligned ministers were fired from the cabinet. These political wrangles spilled out into the army where ethnic tensions affected the demobilisation process. In 1982, two senior army generals, Dumiso Dabengwa and Lookout Masuku, were accused of keeping an arms cache. Some former ZIPRA combatants reacted by returning to the bush and operating as dissidents. Mugabe deployed the Fifth Brigade in January 1983 to ostensibly quell the dissidents who were allegedly destabilising peace in south-western Zimbabwe and also disrupting the reign of the ZANU PF regime.

who have tried to represent Gukurahundi in their work have been arrested and their works of art have been censured and banned. Attempts at erecting memorials and plaques have also been met with resistance with numerous such plaques destroyed by unknown assailants (Moore 2009).

Upon the attainment of independence and in the aftermath of the inaugural elections which were won by the Zimbabwe African National Union–Patriotic Front (ZANU-PF), we argue that there was an immediate attempt to forge a one-party state. Engaging with comprehensive scholarship on Zimbabwe's history, Mpofu (2021:41) explains that:

> Before and after Zimbabwe's independence from Rhodesia a 'one-party state psychology' possessed Mugabe and ZANU-PF turning the leader and the party into vigorous proponents of a one-man rule and one-party political regime in Zimbabwe where the political opposition became unwanted. Nkomo and ZAPU, under that tyrannical one man and one-party political climate, came to be constructed as enemies and other undesirable objects that are legitimate candidates for elimination.

Such an endeavour was to be operationalised through the elimination of the Patriotic Front- Zimbabwe African People's Union (PF-ZAPU) as a viable political opposition. Six months into his first tenure as leader of post-independent Zimbabwe, Robert Mugabe 'entered into an agreement with the North Koreans to train a praetorian guard – this became the Fifth Brigade, given the name 'Gukurahundi' by Mugabe himself' (Eppel 2008:10).

The focus of our argument in this chapter is the question of how Gukurahundi has been defined and interpreted in Zimbabwe's social media platforms, with particular focus on Twitter. Of specific interest is the way the governments of Mugabe and now of Emmerson Mnangagwa have sought to expunge all forms of discourse about this period of Zimbabwe's recent history which Mugabe acknowledged only as a 'moment of madness' (Ellis 2006:40). We are interested in the role that social media, especially Twitter, has played in offering counter spaces for the free discussion of these genocidal years. We grapple with the discursive potentiality of social media as well as its limits. Of specific interest to us are the reasons behind the burgeoning of online discussions about Gukurahundi since the ascension to power of Emmerson Mnangagwa in November 2017. Is it that the 'new dispensation' created an enabling environment or was such discussion necessitated by the fact that Mnangagwa, one of the main architects of the genocide (Tendi 2020:200), had ascended to the presidency? Or could it be that the rapid development of information and communication technologies has meant that the government has to some extent lost its ability to shape the narratives about Gukurahundi? Social media platforms, as we will argue, operate beyond the power of the state, which normally has a grip on the public sphere.² These are some of the questions that this chapter sets out to grapple with in considering the multifaceted meanings and implications of the evocation and discussion of the genocide in diverse online spaces, especially Twitter.

In Zimbabwe, social media has played an important role in destabilising the state's stranglehold on the mainstream media and also on who is able to access information. In what they termed the 'Propaganda Model', Herman and Chomsky (1988:5) posit that 'In countries where the levers of power are in the hands of a state bureaucracy, the monopolistic control over the media, often supplemented by official censorship, makes it clear that the media serve the ends of a dominant elite.' They go on to underscore that:

> A propaganda model focuses on this inequality of wealth and power and its multilevel effects on mass-media interests and choices. It traces the routes by which money and power are able to filter out the news fit to print, marginalise dissent, and allow the government and dominant private interests to get their messages across to the public (ibid.).

These ideas highlight how those with power, both real and symbolic, have the capacity to shape the kinds of narratives that can be articulated in the public sphere. For a long time, the state in Zimbabwe had a control of the mainstream print and electronic media. The advent of social media platforms such as Facebook and WhatsApp revolutionised not only how citizens could access information but more importantly the kinds of narratives that could be produced and shared. Siziba and Ncube (2015:518) explain in this regard that 'virtual spaces offer alternative platforms away from the strictures of main-stream media which has remained by and large state-controlled.' Social media has thus opened new avenues of expression for citizens so that they are able to discuss topical issues without the fear of censure and retribution. This, of course, does not mean that the state has not been able to stamp its authority and govern virtual spaces. Indeed, some people have been arrested and charged with various criminal offenses for what they have shared or said on social media.³ What we underscore rather, is that the certain level of

---

2   The situation is however complex. The state has generally had control over broadcasting as well as several newspapers. However, it has allowed independent media, especially newspapers, and a few community radio stations. The internet and social media platforms coupled with satellite dishes have ensured that citizens have access to alternative sources of information and news. Despite such a situation, the state has continuously intimidated journalists who offer counter-state narratives. This has inadvertently led journalists to self-censor so as not to be arrested and intimidated by state security agents.

3   High-profile arrests include Evan Mawarire who was arrested for subverting a constitutionally elected government because of the peaceful online protest he led under the hashtag #ThisFlag. Also, independent journalist, Hopewell Chin'ono, has over the past few years been arrested several times for utterances he has made online. (see Mugari 2020)

anonymity which is afforded by social media spaces has been important in forging new democratisation practices in Zimbabwe and other countries the world over.

Questions of our positionalities

As researchers, our different backgrounds have had an impact on how we research Gukurahundi. Rose (1997) explains that it is important to be cognisant of 'the role of the (multiple) 'self', showing how a researcher's positionality (in terms of race, nationality, age, gender, social and economic status, sexuality) may influence the 'data' collected and thus information that becomes coded as 'knowledge'.' It is therefore important to highlight the different forms of privilege, in the expansive sense of the term, which have an impact on how research is conducted. Although the concept of positionality was initially associated with feminist ideology to challenge gender inequalities and centre the voices of women, it has more recently been used to also unmask, flag and highlight different forms of social inequality beyond gender. We are interested in making sense of the Gukurahundi genocide which is largely marginalised in imagining Zimbabwe.

The two authors of this chapter are both born frees in that we were born after Zimbabwe's attainment of independence in 1980. The first author is Ndebele and his rural home is in Tsholotsho, in Matabeleland North province. The second author is Shona and originates from Chitungwiza, in Mashonaland province. Our backgrounds are important to the ways in which they represent the necessity of dialogue between two different ethnic groups when considering Gukurahundi, its aftermath and afterlives.

Although the first author was barely three years old when Gukurahundi began, he remembers quite vividly the army trucks conducting patrols in the neighbourhood of Queens Park East where he grew up, and how, as children, they knew that an army truck signalled danger and instilled fear. Children would quickly run home at the sight of the army trucks. As the first author grew up, Gukurahundi was never spoken about. It was only as a teenager and young adult that he was able to have discussions with older family members about what Gukurahundi meant and what people experienced. Relatives from the rural areas had particularly gruelling stories to tell, and in this way, the author has inherited in a very intimate manner the ways in which the experiences of traumatic events can be transmitted from one generation to another (Hirsch 1992:18).

The second author was born towards the end of Gukurahundi but also grew up hearing about it from her father whose brother lived in Bulawayo during the period of the genocide. One story that she remembers is that their father's brother and his family had to leave Matabeleland for Chitungwiza. Although her uncle could speak Shona and Ndebele as well, he did not feel safe in Matabeleland at that time. In the

1990s, although it was some time after the genocide, the festering tensions made it difficult for the second author to visit her family in Bulawayo.

We refer to our positionality because it has an impact on the way in which we approach the question of Gukurahundi, and we are cognisant of the kinds of 'conceptual baggage' (Kirby and McKenna 1989) that we bring to the topic. As a Ndebele who lost relatives during the genocide, the first author could be viewed to be emotional in his consideration of the genocide and its diverse effects. On the other hand, the second author must grapple with her 'Shonaness' in thinking of the genocide. Although our positionalities might be considered antithetical, we find that our cultural and ethnic backgrounds subject a measure of objectivity through the triangulation of our different cultural lenses. We occupy an ideal and productive position between the two ethnic groups to explore the delicate and sensitive issue of Gukurahundi. Through triangulation of our positionalities we are simultaneously not too close to have oversights and not too distant to have a distorted view of the question of Gukurahundi. Our diverse forms of post-memory allow us to think of the period in ways that refuse to reproduce the antagonism which often characterises inter-tribal discussions of Gukurahundi.

Historical contextualisation of Gukurahundi

From the early 1960s, the black majority of Zimbabwe took part in a protracted armed struggle against the white minority Rhodesian regime. Black Zimbabweans were united in their fight against their common enemy and were joyous when the war ended with their victory and independence in 1980. However, some felt that despite the achievement of black majority rule, the war had exacerbated tribal and ethnic divisions.

During the war of liberation, two major forces had fought against white rule: the Zimbabwe African National Liberation Army (ZANLA), the armed wing of ZANU; and the Zimbabwe People's Revolutionary Army (ZIPRA), the armed wing of ZAPU. Fidelis Mukonori (2017) argues that the two political parties, ZANU and ZAPU, became increasingly divided by the training methods that their soldiers received during the armed struggle. ZANLA employed a guerrilla-style insurgency and were Chinese trained, whilst ZIPRA were a conventional army with Russian training. ZANLA recruited mostly Shona and ZIPRA recruited mostly Ndebele people. As Ncube and Siziba explain:

> The fight for Zimbabwe's independence was led by two military wings which had different ideologies and were primarily composed of the two main ethnic groups in that country: the Ndebele and the Shona (2017b:232).

According to Ndlovu-Gatsheni (2011), the victory of ZANU in the first post-independence elections was 'celebrated as not only a victory of a liberation movement over settler colonialism but also as a victory of Shona political elite over the Ndebele elite'. This victory centred around the creation and imposition of ZANU-PF as the only party in the country. Dissenting voices to this attempt arose in the Matabeleland region. The Entumbane uprisings in 1980 and 1981 were some of the early signs of dissent. The ZANU-PF government was decisive in eliminating these dissenting voices. It has been argued that these dissenting voices began during the liberation struggle and were fuelled by personal differences in the leadership style of PF-ZAPU and ZANU-PF, and then by the integration process of the ZIPRA, ZANLA and Rhodesian forces into the Zimbabwe National Army (ZNA) after the attainment of independence (see Tendi 2020). After independence, former ZIPRA soldiers were often subjected to harassment, torture, denial of promotion, and many were unlawfully dismissed from being soldiers (CCJPZ and LRF 1997:54).

The North Korean trained Fifth Brigade went into the rural areas of Matabeleland and the Midlands in a bid to eliminate all dissenting elements. An estimated 20,000 people lost their lives during this operation, which turned out to be more of an ethnic cleansing exercise than a political one. This period, as affirmed by Fontein, 'remains a massive scar on Zimbabwe's post-colonial milieu, and hugely a sensitive topic' (2010:429). What is also worth pointing out is that Mugabe and successive ZANU-PF governments have refused to deal decisively with Gukurahundi and its aftermath. Although Mugabe instituted the Dumbuchena and Chihambakwe commissions of inquiry – the former looking into what happened at Entumbane in 1980-81 and the latter examining Gukurahundi 1983-85, neither report was made public and both are said to have been lost. This is just another example of how an open discussion of Gukurahundi has been undermined and even criminalised (Maedza 2019). Now, we will look at the potential of online spaces in creating counter spaces and discourses about Gukurahundi.

Genocidal trauma and the limits of open discussion of such trauma: Theoretical and methodological issues

Antze and Lambek (1996:xii) explain that 'memory worth talking about – worth remembering – is memory of trauma'. They further develop the idea that 'memory becomes a 'site', a monument visited, rather than a context, a landscape inhabited. The ruins of memory are subject to restoration, and we all become alienated tourists of our pasts' (ibid.:xiii). These observations are important in articulating the way past traumatic experiences are handled. Countries that have experienced widespread collective traumatic events such as wars and/or genocides have dealt with these experiences in different ways. Upon the demise of apartheid in South Africa, a Truth and Reconciliation Commission (TRC) was mandated to investigate and document 'gross human rights violations committed within and outside South Africa during the period 1960-94' (TRC 1998:24). The Commission had to 'compile as complete a picture as possible of these events and violations' and to attempt 'to reflect fairly and fully the motives and perspectives of both the alleged perpetrators of gross human rights violations and of their victims' (ibid.). Although this Commission has been criticised for the way in which it carried out its processes, it afforded post-apartheid South Africa a necessary self-reflexive moment to rethink the past and forge ahead with the construction of a democratic, multi-ethnic, 'rainbow nation'.

In Rwanda, after the 1992 genocide that left an estimated 800,000 people dead in a space of 100 days, Gacaca Community Courts were established. Ng et al. explain what these courts set out to achieve:

> Following the genocide, many survivors gave written and oral accounts of their genocide experiences. Genocide testimonies are often seen as a means of bearing witness to the realities of mass violence, with the goal of education, advocacy, and justice, and often the hope that the experiences of genocide would become part of collective knowledge and contribute to society's acknowledgment of survivors' suffering and survival. Although testimonies are often seen primarily as a way to preserve history and help societies and communities, it is possible that their content could be used to provide insight into the ways that survivors conceptualise their genocide experience (2015: 304).

What they highlight above is the need for dealing collectively and decisively with traumatic past experiences especially when mass violence is involved. They argue, for example, that genocide testimonies make it possible not just to archive such ordeals but also to acknowledge the reality of these lived experiences.

On the other hand, Mugabe argued that attempts to revisit Gukurahundi would threaten the cohesion of Zimbabwe: 'If we dig up the country's history in this way, we wreck the nation and tear up our people apart into factions' (Wetherell 1997:21). In its report on the Gukurahundi massacres, the CCJPZ contradicts this idea:

> Those who would rather the events of the 1980s remain shrouded in secrecy will claim that discussing them will reopen old wounds. However, it was clear during the interviewing procedure that, for thousands of people, these wounds have never healed: people still suffer today, physically, psychologically, and practically, as a result if what they experienced in the 1980s. Far from 'reopening' old wounds, the victims being allowed to speak out and having their stories validated by a non-judgmental audience has begun what is hoped will be a healing process (CCJPZ and LRF 1997:16).

Khumalo (2018:2) attests that efforts by the state to ensure that Gukurahundi remains an unaccountable memory speaks to a form of silencing that is itself an 'act of considering the Gukurahundi era a closed chapter, whose memorialisation and documentation are viewed as threatening unity and peace'. President Mnangagwa has stated that 'we should look into the future. The thrust should not be for us, in this new dispensation, to go and engage with the past'.[4] Coltart, in reaction to these words by the President, explains that 'these were not excesses but crimes against humanity in which Mnangagwa played a critical role. Thirty-four years on, Mnangagwa has a crucial role to heal this festering wound. He must acknowledge the atrocities, give an unequivocal apology and reorder the budget to arrange for communal reparation to be made to the affected parties. Any attempt by him to divert responsibility will simply anger victims more'.[5]

Ncube and Siziba (2017b:232) point out that 'in spite of the number of lives that were lost and the devastating trauma that this period entailed, the state has resisted any form of dialogue or engagement with citizens about Gukurahundi'. Moreover, all forms of artistic representation of Gukurahundi have been systematically stifled. For example, Owen Maseko's art exhibition, 'Sibathontisele' (which means 'let's drip on them'), was banned and the artist was charged for undermining the authority of the President under the Public Order and Security Act. In 2018, following the release of his documentary, 'Gukurahundi Genocide: 36 years later', Zenzele Ndebele was questioned over the documentary. He also received death threats from unknown people. Be that as it may, there have been a few novels that have explored the subject; for example, Yvonne Vera's *The Stone Virgins* (2002), Christopher Mlalazi's *Running with Mother* (2012), Novuyo Rosa Tshuma's *House of Stone* (2018b) and *Glory* by NoViolet Bulawayo (2022) have all offered diverse representations of Gukurahundi. These works have also been the subject of numerous academic studies (see Mangena 2019) and have elicited heated discussions on online spaces. We contend that literature has remained relatively uncensored because, as Nyamfukudza (2005:23) stated, Zimbabwe does not have a robust culture of reading, yet alone critical reading, to such an extent that 'the best way to hide information in Zimbabwe is to publish it in a book'.

What we have shown in this section is that any discussion of Gukurahundi in Zimbabwe remains as material text-under-erasure. This means that there are limited spaces in and through which it is possible to talk openly and freely about the traumatic genocide. We pause here to ask if the silence that has been created around Gukurahundi is in fact a form of speech. Charles Mungoshi explored a similar conundrum in his aptly entitled collection of short-stories *Kunyarara Hakusi Kutaura?* (1983) (Could silence be a form of speaking?), but that is not the pith of our deliberations.

---

4 '"Forget about Gukurahundi," says Mnangagwa', *Bulawayo24*, 24 January 2018.
5 Ibid.

If discussing Gukurahundi remains difficult, if not impossible, in the traditional public sphere, it is necessary to find other spaces and other temporalities in which to speak about these violations. In the next sections, we consider the vast potential of social media and other virtual platforms in creating spaces where Gukurahundi can be discussed without the interference of the state, which has tended to thwart or silence dialogue or debate about Gukurahundi because it runs counter to their attempt to foster the myth of national unity. We ask if the latter can in fact be founded on silencing narratives, experiences and ways of thinking.

For the purposes of this study, we focus on the discussion of Gukurahundi on Twitter. We have specifically chosen to concentrate on Twitter because of the ease of engaging in discussions on this micro-blogging social media platform. We made use of different applications to go through Tweets posted that referenced Gukurahundi, one way or the other. Tweet Binder was able to sift through tweets that contained Gukurahundi as key word and could sense the tonality of the tweets and then group them into three categories: neutral, negative, and positive. We used Tweet Binder in conjunction with the Application Programming Interface (API) for Twitter. The API was able to gather tweets and retweets as well as replies to tweets. The API was particularly useful to identify specific handles (or user-names) of people who post tweets. The API could also identify important information such as date and time when a tweet was posted including the geographical location from where the tweet was posted.

For the purposes of this study, we randomly selected tweets which were in the top trends: #Gukurahundi, #Asakhe and #SecondRepublic. Our analysis of the selected tweets was within the ambit of the 'Guidelines for use of tweets in broadcast or other offline media' which prescribe that it is allowed to republish tweets only if the said tweets remain unaltered. Through and in accordance with this guideline, we could ethically engage with the selected tweets in a way that did not infringe on the intellectual property of those who posted the tweets.

Discussing and making sense of Gukurahundi on Twitter

Except for some literary texts previously mentioned in this chapter, space to discuss the Gukurahundi atrocities has been largely absent. However, many survivors still feel the effects of the trauma that they experienced. The documentaries produced by Zenzele Ndebele, for example, provide empirical data in which survivors of the genocide describe their experiences first hand and also speak of the traumas that they face on a daily basis (see Rwafa 2012, Ndlovu and Tshuma 2021). That they are unable to find an avenue for talking about their ordeals, inhibits the process of catharsis. Meantime, the state has compelled the victims to forgive and forget, to let sleeping dogs lie or let bygones be bygones (Murambadoro 2015). Several

Ndebele proverbs reflect on the ease of forgetting. For example, '*isihlahla asikhohlwa kodwa ihloka liyakhohlwa*' (the tree does not forget but the axe forgets), or '*umenzi uyakhohlwa, umenziwa kakhohlwa*' (the perpetrator forgets while the victim does not forget). Wrongdoing can be easily forgotten but victims must nurse the injuries, physical or mental.

The advent of social media has created dialogical spaces where citizens are able to discuss diverse issues of concern to them. As stated above, Mnangagwa's succession has led to an increase in the discussion of Gukurahundi, which some have interpreted as a positive development. Tweet Binder showed a spike in the use of the term around the time that Mnangagwa took over as president of Zimbabwe. Below are two reports created by Tweet Binder which show the stark difference in the number of tweets which use the key term 'Gukurahundi'.

Figure 1: Tweet activity during the twilight of Robert Mugabe's tenure

TWEET ACTIVITY STATS (JANUARY 2015)

	TOTAL TWEETS	POTENTIAL IMPACTS	CONTRIBUTORS	LINKS/PICS	RETWEETS
NEUTRAL	20	31,802	12	2	14
POSITIVE	13	22,659	8	3	18
NEGATIVE	33	60,550	54	3	11

Figure 2: Tweet activity during the dawn of Emmerson Mnangagwa's tenure

TWEET ACTIVITY STATS (JANUARY 2018)

	TOTAL TWEETS	POTENTIAL IMPACTS	CONTRIBUTORS	LINKS/PICS	RETWEETS
NEUTRAL	110	351,782	138	12	61
POSITIVE	20	50,409	19	2	12
NEGATIVE	55	603,320	60	9	14

The two figures above show that the number of tweets that were neutral, positive, and negative on Gukurahundi rose from a total of 66 in January 2015 to a total of 185 in January 2018. Despite this spike which coincided with Mnangagwa's ascension to power, we posit three arguments that counter the idea that the 'Second Republic' has been more permissive of the discussion of Gukurahundi. Firstly, there has been increased internet penetration, through smartphones, since the early 2000s. Secondly, social media platforms such as Facebook and Twitter allow people to create fictitious personae that protect their identities and so allow them greater freedom of expression. Thirdly, Ncube (2022:141) argues that the increase in the Gukurahundi discussion has been as a result of the fact that Mnangagwa 'is considered to be one of the chief architects of Gukurahundi, given that he was Minister of State Security' during the genocide. Similarly, the 'death of Perrence Shiri in July 2020 also saw Gukurahundi trending on social media platforms, because he was the commander of the praetorian army that perpetrated the atrocities in Matabeleland and the Midlands' (ibid.).

It should be emphasised that social media can offer anonymity and safety to interlocutors which is not necessarily the case in traditional media. On Twitter, numerous accounts have been set up that are devoted to creating Gukurahundi counter narratives. These include accounts such as 'Genocide Against the Ndebele Memorial Centre', 'Gukurahundi Genocide' and 'Gukurahundi Genocide Survivors'. In addition, individuals such as journalist Zenzele Ndebele, lawyer Siphosami Malunga and human rights activist Thandekile Moyo have been important interlocutors. Ndlovu (2018a:304) emphasises the importance of social media platforms:

> Through interactive facilities such as YouTube, new forms of witnessing are emerging as Gukurahundi survivors are using new technologies to preserve and disseminate the knowledge of the traumatic past events. Given the repressive political environment in Zimbabwe, new media are playing a key role in widening the democratic space, promoting freedom of expression, and preserving and circulating new witness accounts.

Siziba and Ncube (2015:519) affirm that given a situation in which there is a constriction of the public sphere in Zimbabwe through oppressive pieces of legislation such as the Public Order and Security Act as well as the Access to Information and Protection of Privacy Act, social media has allowed citizens to move closer to the ideal of public responsibility in a global world and the youth, in particular, have become proactive with regard to sociocultural and political issues. Clearly, the state can no longer influence the personal or collective memories of its citizens, nor can it prohibit public discussions. Social media has enabled the mobilisation of resentments and aggressions arising from the recall of 'old' injuries that have been repressed for decades. Recollection is vital for any society so as not to repeat the same mistakes and allow for a future without violence, killings, rapes, and bitterness.

Commenting on the role of social media, Coltart explains through a message on Twitter:

Social media has reconceptualised the boundaries of what is known, what should be known and what should remain unknown. It is an important prism through which to produce, curate and archive knowledge and knowledge systems.

As we have stated several times, because President Mnangagwa, current Vice President Chiwengwa and the late Perrence Shiri were profoundly implicated in the administration of the massacres, their current leadership roles have provoked increased debate of Gukurahundi. Gwekwerere and Mpondi (2018:12) argue that: 'Mnangagwa's wilful forgetting of this experience constitutes an attempt at historical erasure. It can also be interpreted as indicative of his party's arrogance in the face of the pain and injury of others'. According to Meier (2010), the ability to forget should be encouraged as it can be viewed as a virtue considering that remembering often always brings back unpleasant memories, a desire for retribution and a sense of bitterness. In our view, however, the notion of forgetting is one that would be pushed by the perpetrator of violence, especially one still in power, as is the case in Zimbabwe. There has always been, for the aggrieved, a need to forge spaces to speak, remember and recover historical truths. This is an issue which was raised once again within the framework of the Motlanthe Commission of Inquiry into the killings of citizens after the July 2018 elections.

What Gukurahundi and the 2018 killings have in common is the way in which they highlight how power is exercised, which the ruling party has constantly used to curtail alternative voices and discourses. The then MDC Alliance leader, Nelson Chamisa and his deputy Tendai Biti when called to give an account of what transpired on 1 August 2018, began by referring back to Gukurahundi and numerous other state-sponsored atrocities. Gukurahundi will constantly be a reference point in understanding how the Zimbabwean state makes use of extreme violence against its own citizens.

Two noteworthy interlocutors to the Gukurahundi debate on Twitter were Novuyo Rosa Tshuma (@NovuyoRTshuma) whose novel *House of Stone* centres on Gukurahundi, and Zenzele Ndebele (@zenzele). These two have made use of their Twitter platforms to bring to the fore discourses on Gukurahundi, thus breaking the scandalous silence that has prevailed for four decades. In an interview with Chikwava (2018:48), Tshuma explains:

> Well, we can ask ourselves if forgetting the past has created national unity. Has it? Has keeping quiet about Gukurahundi fostered unity in Zimbabwe? No. It has instead contributed to creating the authoritarian and tyrannical culture that became prominent, especially over the past two decades. Had we faced our past about Gukurahundi a long time ago, would this authoritarian culture, this culture of dealing violently with any non-Zanu (PF) supporters, of deeming others non-Zimbabweans and expelling them from the Zimbabwean imagination, have bloomed? That is one way of understanding the past's relationship to the present. This goes to matters of the nation's spirit, to its legacy, which goes beyond the material – to the spiritual, the emotional, the philosophical, the psychological, the cultural; all those elements that make us more than just our bodies – that make us human beings.

For Tshuma, it is essential to open the discussion because expelling such memories from the national psyche speaks to the degradation of the nation's very spirit and indeed legacy. Using her novel as the vector, Tshuma is engaged in an enterprise of *desilencing* the past and moving from the periphery to the mainstream, conversations that need to be foregrounded about 'Zimbabwe's original or first sin'.

Ndebele uses his Twitter platform as a formidable space to curate, document and archive different narratives including work that he has done and continues to do as a journalist. His tweets end with the hashtag #Asakhe which is Ndebele for 'let us build'. In essence, he is building knowledge about and narratives of Gukurahundi through engagement with different interlocutors on the social media platforms. For example, on 24 April 2018, he tweeted as below:

Naturally, this tweet gave rise to a variety of different responses. But that people can engage in a civil manner over a very contentious issue shows that social media can offer a safe mediating space. Such engagements make it possible to gather information about how Zimbabweans feel about Gukurahundi and how they strive (or not) to make sense of it especially within a polarised and polarising contemporary moment.

What is particularly challenging in the discussions about Gukurahundi on social media is the presence of interlocutors who deny Gukurahundi and its afterlives.

It has been suggested that such interlocutors are ghost accounts that are run by the state in effort to frame a situation that justifies the excesses of Gukurahundi. Whilst social media offers a space for victims and their families to vent their anger and frustration, it also provides a space for perpetrators and their sympathisers to express their ideas in which they interpret Gukurahundi as a necessary evil.

One last point that we want to discuss is the fact that the people who use social media space are ordinarily young people who did not personally experience Gukurahundi. However, the genocide and its afterlives now form a part of their intimate and daily lived experiences – the trauma of the genocide has been transmitted to them. Time will tell what this young generation will be able to achieve through social media and will reveal if this can provide an effective mediating space that will allow for the issue to be discussed in a constructive way in which the aggrieved find peace and in which the perpetrators are also able to request forgiveness.

Conclusion

In this chapter, we have shown that social media offers an important mediating space particularly when such spaces are not available in the traditional public sphere. We have demonstrated that more work needs to be done to examine the full extent and reach of this medium in mediating large-scale traumatic experiences such as the Gukurahundi genocide. Although cognizant of the rich and textured conversations that have taken place and are taking place online, we pause to conclude with a series of questions: (a) will these diverse and free conversations ever have the capacity to transcend the virtuality of these online spaces? (b) Will a day and time come when these conversations can be held in a civil manner in the public sphere? (c) Can such conversations be honestly conducted in spaces where there is no recourse to masked or anonymous online identities? (d) If this is not possible, what needs to be done to create such safe discursive spaces in contemporary Zimbabwe?

9

Gukurahundi Atrocities and Accountability Challenges in Zimbabwe: A Case For International Justice[1]

Siphosami Malunga

1. Introduction

Between 1983 and 1987, the Fifth Brigade of the Zimbabwe National Army (ZNA) committed heinous atrocities against civilians in Matabeleland and Midlands. An estimated 20,000 civilians were killed, thousands enforcedly disappeared, raped and their homes and properties destroyed. This chapter examines the atrocities committed by the Fifth Brigade and other security agencies in Zimbabwe (commonly known as Gukurahundi atrocities), between 1983 and 1987 from the perspective of international criminal law (ICL). The question of accountability for these atrocities has remained unresolved, with perpetrators continuing to exercise impunity. In response to complaints from religious leaders, diplomats and human rights organisations, Prime Minister Mugabe established the Zimbabwe Commission of Inquiry into the Matabeleland disturbances to investigate alleged massacres of civilians by the Fifth Brigade, which had been deployed to Matabeleland North in January 1983. The report is commonly known as the Chihambakwe Commission of Inquiry after its Chairperson, Simplicius Chihambakwe. The government, however, refused to publish the commission's findings and make the report public (Yap 2001).

Much of the evidence of the atrocities came from the victims themselves and many witnesses, doctors, church officials, lawyers and court judgements. The atrocities were documented at the time by human rights and media organisations. The two authoritative human rights reports of atrocities at the time are: *Zimbabwe, Wages of War* (Berkeley and Schrage 1986) and *Breaking the Silence; Building True*

---

[1] This chapter is part of the author's doctoral thesis submitted to the University of Witwatersrand.

Peace (CCJPZ and LRF 1997). The former is based on two visits to Zimbabwe by representatives of the Lawyers Committee for Human Rights whose representatives met with numerous victims and their relatives. They also spoke to church leaders, political party leaders, lawyers, journalists, academics, human rights workers and government officials including the Minister of Justice, Minister of State Security in the Prime Minister's Office, the Chief Justice, the Chairman of the Detainee Review Tribunal Simplisius Chihambakwe.

Over the years, many victims have also come forward to tell their stories of the atrocities committed against them (Habakkuk Trust 2020). Nonetheless, the Zimbabwean government has refused to formally acknowledge that it committed atrocities in Matabeleland (Alexander 2021). However, on several occasions, the government has – without accepting responsibility – alluded to the need to address the consequences of Gukurahundi including the question of compensation for its victims.[2] In 1999, Mugabe called Gukurahundi a 'moment of madness' (Maedza 2019).[3] Moreover, in 2013, the Zimbabwean government established the National Peace and Reconciliation Commission (NPRC) but failed to operationalise it and the NPRC Act was only passed in 2018. Since taking over as President, Mnangagwa, himself implicated, has made numerous promises to work with civil society and chiefs to resolve Gukurahundi by allowing public debate, exhumations, and the issuance of death and birth certificates to descendants of victims among other promises.[4] There have, however, been no meaningful efforts to implement these promises, including the latest plan for chiefs to resolve Gukurahundi atrocities.[5]

2. An overview of Gukurahundi atrocities

Within six weeks of deployment to Matabeleland North in late January 1983, the Fifth Brigade had murdered over 2,000 civilians, hundreds of homesteads had been burnt, and thousands of civilians had been beaten (CCJPZ and LRF 1997). It would torture, detain and kill thousands more in the months that followed and thousands more when redeployed to Matabeleland South in February 1984 (ibid.). The CCJPZ estimates that between 3,500 and 4,000 people were killed in only two districts that it accessed (ibid.). It also reports that almost 2,000 villagers had been killed within weeks of Gukurahundi arriving in Tsholotsho (ibid.). Given that Gukurahundi took place over a period of four years and that the Fifth Brigade abducted and

---

2 'No Compensation for Gukurahundi Victims', *The Chronicle*, 7 June 2012.
3 'New documents claim to prove Mugabe ordered Gukurahundi killings', *The Guardian*, 19 May 2015.
4 'Zimbabwe Govt to Give Gukurahundi Victims Birth, Death Certificates and Medical Care', *Voice of America*, 10 April 2019.
5 'Mnangagwa, chiefs resolve to deal with Gukurahundi exhumations on a case by case basis', *CITE News 21* August 2021.

disappeared thousands of its victims and imposed a curfew and a food embargo which caused mass starvation, the death toll could well be beyond 20,000 (ibid.). The atrocities committed by the Gukurahundi have been classified as internatioal crimes of genocide, crimes against humanity and war crimes (Malunga 2021). This chapter, however, draws on examples from each of the Matabeleland provinces and the Midlands to illustrate the genocide by the Fifth Brigade.

The most serious of Gukurahundi crimes is mass murder (ibid.: 48). Villagers would be rounded up into groups and publicly executed. There were many such public executions, though some were also carried out in secrecy. The Fifth Brigade also organised systematic public beatings and torture (ibid.; Berkeley and Schrage 1986). It also committed mass rapes, the burning of hundreds of homesteads and villages, and the destruction of property and livestock (ibid.). This chapter will illustrate select non-exhaustive examples of atrocities considered especially heinous.

2.1 Atrocities in Matabeleland North

The Siwale River Massacre

One of the most monstrous of Gukurahundi crimes is the Siwale River Massacre in Lupane, in which 62 civilians were shot in cold blood on the banks of the river on 5 March 1983 after being severely beaten. Fifty-five (55) died, whilst seven survived by pretending to be dead (ibid.: 48). The following account from a surviving victim and witness of the massacre is illustrative (ibid.):

> On 5 March 1983, four people were taken from our home. The youngest was myself, then a girl of fifteen. The 5 Brigade took us – there were more than a hundred of them. [T]hey woke us up and accused […] us – me and my three brothers – of being dissidents. They then marched us at gunpoint for about three hours until we reached a camp.
>
> [T]hey took us to a building where there were finally 62 people. Then they took us out one by one and beat us. They beat me with a thick stick eighteen inches long all over the body. We were beaten until about 3am.
>
> Then the 5 Brigade marched us to the Siwale River, a few hundred meters away. All 62 of us were lined up and shot by the 5 Brigade. One of my brothers was killed instantly, from a bullet through his stomach. By some chance, 7 of us survived with gunshot wounds. I was shot in the left thigh. The 5 Brigade finished off some of the others who survived, but my two brothers and I pretended to be dead.
>
> After some time, we managed to get home. The 5 Brigade came looking for survivors of this incident at home – they found my brother R who was badly injured, but they left him. My brother had a gunshot wound in the chest and arm, and later had to have his arm amputated first at the elbow and then later at the shoulder. [He] had to have his foot amputated because of a bullet wound.

Other atrocities in Tsholotsho

In January 1983, the Fifth Brigade killed 25 people in Pelandaba village and tortured a further 50 (ibid.: 87). In the same month, they killed 24 people in Mbiriya and Nxuma villages (ibid.: 159-60). Similarly, in February, they killed 50 people at Egceni and another twelve from Soloboni village, some were bayoneted and beaten to death (ibid. p. 88). Also, in the same month the Fifth Brigade burned down 30 homesteads in Sandawana village and killed at least one person (ibid.: 160). In a separate incident on 28 February, Fifth Brigade soldiers rounded up villagers and put two men, seven women with two babies and three children in a hut and set it alight. Twelve people ran out and six were shot and killed, including a baby and a young girl. Nine people were killed (ibid.: 87). In February, villagers were forced to witness the burning to death of 26 villagers –including women and children, in three huts in Dlamini village. In one incident, 22 women were killed. There was only one survivor (ibid.).

2.2 Atrocities in Matabeleland South

Bhalagwe Detention Camp

One year after its initial deployment to Matabeleland North, on 2 February 1984, the Fifth Brigade was redeployed to Matabeleland South (ibid.: 119-24). In addition to mass beatings, torture, rape and burning of villages, a curfew, a food embargo and deliberate starvation of villagers in the context of a severe drought, it established a mass detention camp at Bhalagwe in Matobo District. The excerpt below is drawn from accounts by surviving victims (CCJPZ and LRF 1997):

> Conditions were brutal. Sheds of six by twelve metres were [each] packed with 136 people who were given no bedding and fed once every two days. One small jam tin of water was provided per day for inmates living in temperatures of over 30 degrees and subjected to multiple forms of physical abuse. When not confined to their sheds or undergoing torture, prisoners were made to do hard labour.
>
> Electric shocks, simulated drownings and beatings were used by the CIO in its attempts to extract confessions of dissident support or activity, while Fifth Brigade experimented with a wide variety of tortures... Much of the cruelty had a sexual angle to it. Men were forced to attempt sex with donkeys and beaten when they failed to attain erections. A female member of the CIO, who became particularly notorious at Bhalagwe for her 'cruel, ruthless, savage, inhuman' behaviour, would stand astride her victims, asking them what they saw; if too embarrassed to say, they would be 'severely beaten for lying', but if they provided an answer they would receive the same treatment for failing to become aroused and thus 'saying she was not a woman.' They laughed and seemed to enjoy people groaning in pain to death [and] women failing to walk after their private parts

were poked with sharp objects' Most women were kept for a few days, but some were taken as sex slaves by Fifth Brigade and spent a much longer period in the camp. A woman abducted from her home at night described the ordeal she and others suffered at Bhalagwe: "We were beaten daily by the CIO. We were made wives for the officers (girls and young married women). From the forced sex, I am suffering from the disorder of my reproductive organs…I miscarry anytime I am pregnant. I have no children.

2.3. *Enforced Disappearances in Matabeleland and Midlands*

A most prevalent Gukurahundi crime was the abduction and disappearance of civilians- who are presumed to have been subsequently killed (ibid.: 64).

> Throughout 1983, but particularly after March 1983, there was an increase in disappearances: Fifth Brigade and CIO removed men from buses, trains, or from their homes, and they were never seen again. Such people were often taken because their names were on a list showing them to be either ex-ZIPRA, or some kind of ZAPU [Zimbabwe African People's Union] official. Others who were taken had failed to produce their identity cards when pulled from a bus or train by Fifth Brigade. Some who were killed or detained were merely young men who were considered to be of "dissident age."

There was also a sharp rise in politically motivated abductions targeting ZAPU officials ahead of the elections in 1985. In Tsholotsho alone, over 120 civilians were abducted in February 1985 (ibid.). Among the well-documented cases of enforced disappearances is that of eleven men who were abducted from Silobela in the Midlands on 30 January 1985 (ibid.). The Central Intelligence Organisation (CIO) abducted another nine men from the same area in August 1985. According to Berkeley and Schrage (1986), the wife of one of the nine victims, Mr B, a ZAPU Branch Vice-Chairman (aged 70) abducted on 30 January 1985 reported:

> They came in the middle of the night. The gunmen asked me to cook for them. Then they asked [my husband] to accompany them to a meeting in Nkayi. When he refused, they forced him to come with them. They dragged him out of the hut. That is the last I saw of him. I saw the lights of the vehicles. We stood in the yard expecting to hear gunshots. From the distance, we heard someone cry in pain, but just briefly. Sometime after the incident, there was the sound of a car. [The following day], my son followed the foot tracks, until he came to a spot where there were some car marks and a lot of footprints.

Berkeley and Schrage (1986 p. 64), also highlight that another wife of one of the eleven Silobela abductees, a former ZAPU Branch Chairman from Silobela stated that:

> They came around midnight when we were asleep. The gunmen were many, maybe 10, all armed. Some of the guns were similar to the guns the Rhodesian army had during the war. They spoke Shona mainly and some broken Sindebele. My husband was dragged away. When they had gone, I took my children and stood in the yard, waiting and expecting to hear a gunshot, because I thought they would kill him. We waited there almost an hour. Then we heard the sound of a car in the direction they had gone. There we saw cars pass by on the road. They were *jipis*. Land Rovers. It was dark, and we could not see their colour, but they were certainly government trucks. The police never came to my house to investigate. My husband had eleven children.

All the abductees mentioned above were never seen again. The Silobela eleven were subsequently declared 'Missing, Presumed Dead' by the courts (CCJPZ and LRF 1997: 107). Despite numerous pleas from the widows and relatives of the disappeared men, the government has refused to acknowledge or apologise, leaving the families in a permanent state of limbo and psychological anguish (Berkeley and Schrage 1986 p.64).

2.4 Systematic and mass rape

Yet another notorious and sadistic crime of Gukurahundi was the rape of women and young girls. It features in almost every instance where the Brigade committed crimes against villagers. The following non-exhaustive examples below are illustrative.

CCJPZ and LRF (1997) document rape by the Fifth Brigade in a village at Bhanti Kraal, Nanda Area and Nemane School in 1983. Similarly, in 1983 and 1984 the Fifth Brigade raped women and girls in Gariya village, Sipongweni village, Mahlaba Village, Tshipisane Village, Sipepa area about 10km west of Gwayi Mission, Beula Area in Matobo, Sun Yat Sen camp and Antelope Mine, Matobo. In March 1983, at Kapane, about 20km west of Gwayi Mission, th Fifth Brigade took away about 50 girls and repeatedly raped them over the several months until it left the area. Some of the girls fell pregnant due to the rapes and left school (ibid.: 105). In Korodziba village, the Fifth Brigade tortured and raped 20-30 schoolgirls under sixteen years old and then ordered them to have sex with some boys while the soldiers watched (ibid.: 156). In May 1983, the Fifth Brigade raped ten schoolgirls daily after school at Emkanyeni Village near Dhlamini Rest Camp (ibid.: 99). In November 1982, the ZNA raped several (eight) girls for several days in Neshango Line next to Ningombeneshango Airstrip before leaving by helicopter. On 3 February 1983, the Fifth Brigade shot two young pregnant girls (raped in November) bayonetted their stomachs open to reveal the still moving foetuses (ibid.: 85).

In view of the gravity, scale and the high-level of perpetrators that committed Gukurahundi atrocities, it is evident that they constitute international crimes of genocide, crimes against humanity (CAH) and war crimes (Killander and Nyathi 2015; Malunga 2021). Amongst other crimes, the Siwale Massacre qualifies as the crime against humanity of extermination and the genocidal crime of killing members of an ethnic group or the war crime of killing civilians. The systematic and mass rape committed by the Fifth Brigade in Matabeleland and Midlands constitutes a widespread and systematic attack on the civilian population which is an integral element establishing CAH, as elaborated by the Criminal Tribunal to Rwanda (ICTR) in *Prosecutor v Jean Paul Akayesu*, ICTR-96-4-A, Trial Chamber Judgement of 2 September 1998 (*Akayesu* Trial Chamber) and the ICTY in *Prosecutor v. Kunarac et al.*, IT-96-23-A (*Kunarac et al* Trial Chamber) and *Prosecutor v. Anto Furundžija*, IT-95-17-1, Trial Chamber Judgment of 10 December 1998, para 185 (*Furundžija* Trial Chamber). Additionally, the systematic rape constitutes genocide in that it was part of a plan to destroy in part or in whole the Ndebele population by preventing its will and ability to procreate akin to the genocidal rape of the Tutsis in Rwanda which took place a decade later (Malunga 2022). The Bhalagwe detentions qualify as the crime against humanity of severe imprisonment and arbitrary detention whilst many other crimes qualify as torture (Malunga 2021). The following section will examine the challenges to achieving accountability in Zimbabwe.

3. Challenges to National accountability

Ordinarily, crimes are often investigated, prosecuted and punished within the domestic jurisdictions where they occur (Ryngaert 2008). Many countries, including Zimbabwe, have criminal justice systems responsible for investigating, prosecuting and punishing crimes. Yet most crimes committed by the Fifth Brigade have not been investigated, prosecuted or punished. There are, however, some exceptions which include the prosecution and conviction of Robert Masikini, a CIO officer for killing an inmate in his custody and the prosecution of 75 members of security service including four Fifth Brigade soldiers for killing civilians in Matabeleland. In all these cases the perpetrators were pardoned via amnesty by the then Prime Minister Mugabe. It is therefore important to examine challenges to ensuring accountability for the Gukurahundi crimes that make it necessary for international justice system to be sought. Zimbabwe's response to Gukurahundi atrocities has been characterised by failure, inability and unwillingness to investigate, prosecute and punish the crimes.

3.1 National capacity to investigate, prosecute and punish grave crimes

Gukurahundi crimes are distinguishable from ordinary crimes because of their gravity, scale and distinction of the perpetrators which include individuals who hold leadership positions in Zimbabwe's government, military and security sector. Additionally, Gukurahundi crimes are distinguishable from ordinary crimes by their level of organisation (Heller 2017; Einarsen 2012). These features are critical elements of international crimes. Whilst much of the conduct of the Fifth Brigade constitutes crimes under the Zimbabwean criminal law, their gravity, scale and levels of organisation are unprecedented. Investigations of international crimes are complex and require specialised skills and capacities. The Zimbabwean criminal justice system has no experience of investigating and prosecuting such grave crimes. Historically, *ad hoc* or specialised hybrid tribunals with skilled or expert investigators have been established for this purpose. In addition, even where the State is willing and able to prosecute, highly qualified international criminal prosecutors are required to prosecute the cases once investigated (Perriello and Marieke 2006). Lastly, the adjudication of the cases requires minimum levels of understanding or knowledge of ICL by the judges that adjudicate these cases (ibid.). Developing the capacity to investigate, prosecute and punish atrocities requires the requisite allocation of resources. Although these models may not apply and not be recommended for Zimbabwe, the ICTR and ICTY had budgets of over $200 million and $116 million respectively when they were fully operational. In 2008 the Special Court in Sierra Leone (SCSL) had an annual budget of $36 million in 2008 and $75 million for the first three years of its operation in 2002 and spent $300 million in ten years of operation.[6] While it is by no means suggested that the cost of pursuing international justice and accountability for Gukurahundi through the Zimbabwean criminal justice or international system or would be that high, it is evident that the process would require significant financial and technical support. The next section will examine the limitations of national accountability mechanisms.

3.2 Limitations of national accountability mechanisms

Apart from the capacity challenges addressed above, other significant political, legal, and other obstacles limit or stand in the way of national accountability for Gukurahundi. These obstacles make it impossible to pursue justice. Each will be briefly addressed in turn below.

Implications of the 1988 Amnesty

Following the signing of the Unity Accord in December 1987, then Prime Minister Mugabe announced an amnesty for all dissidents on 18 April 1988 which was promulgated as Clemency Order No. 1 of 1988 on 28 April 1988. It provided a full pardon for any crimes – including murder, rape and robbery – committed by any dissidents who reported to the police between 19 April and 31 May 1988. In June

---

6 'The Special Court for Sierra Leone rests-for good', *Africa Renewal*, April 2014.

1988, the amnesty was extended to include all members of the security forces who had committed human rights violations: all army personnel serving prison sentences for crimes committed in the 1980s were released from prison (CCJPZ and LRF 1997: 73). The implication of the amnesty was to completely indemnify the Fifth Brigade and dissidents for all the crimes they committed.

Seventy-five (75) members of the security forces who had been charged or convicted of offences relating to human rights abuses were released including, as stated above, a CIO official, Robert Masikini, convicted a week earlier of the cold-blooded murder of a political detainee in his custody. Four Fifth Brigade soldiers convicted of the abduction and murder of two men and two women –also subjected to degrading sexual abuse- in Matabeleland in 1983 were also released as part of the amnesty (Carver 1989). The legality of this amnesty is nonetheless challengeable.

An amnesty granted to individuals accused/convicted of committing grave international crimes such as genocide, CAH and war crimes is invalid under customary international law. In Furundžija Trial Chamber para 155, the ICTY held that amnesties in relation to torture were invalid under international law and that beneficiaries of such amnesty would be held liable for torture by foreign courts. Some national courts have found amnesties conferred to perpetrators of serious human rights violations to be in violation of international law and the duty to prosecute serious international crimes (Bakker 2005). Despite amnesties being a central feature of peace agreements, in Prosecutor v Kallon et al, SCSL-2004-15/16-AR72(E) Appeals Chamber Decision of 13 March 2004, para 82 (Lome Amnesty Case), the SCSL found that there is a 'crystallising international norm that a government cannot grant amnesty for serious violations of crimes under international law.' The SCSL also found that although states have the sovereign right to confer amnesties, such right does not limit the right of other countries to exercise universal jurisdiction over international crimes. The amnesty conferred by the Lomé Peace Agreement was found by the SCSL as not applicable or binding on other states, especially on international or hybrid tribunals tasked with pursuing international justice (Meisenberg 2004). Notably, Article 10 of the Statute of the SCSL precludes amnesties for crimes within its jurisdiction. International scholars have also argued for the growing presumption against amnesties (Gavron 2002). ICRC states that under customary international humanitarian law, individuals suspected, accused or sentenced to war crimes are excluded from amnesty granted by Article 6(5) of Additional Protocol II of 1977.

The legality of the 1988 Amnesty is questionable. Although amnesties feature commonly in domestic or national legal systems, their applicability to international crimes is unsettled, and there is a growing trend and practice towards restricting their applicability. An amnesty granted to individuals accused or convicted of committing grave international crimes such as genocide, CAH and war crimes is invalid under customary international law (Cassese 2003: 315).

Political incumbency and impunity

The main obstacle to accountability for Gukurahundi atrocities over the past 40 years is that the government and military officials who planned and executed the atrocities have remained in power and, therefore, in control of all the political, legal and justice institutions that would ordinarily hold them accountable. Robert Mugabe, Prime Minister during Gukurahundi campaign continued to govern Zimbabwe until 2017 when he was ousted in a military coup. He was replaced as president by Emmerson Mnangagwa, Minister of State Security in the Prime Minister's Office during Gukurahundi atrocities and a leading figure in Gukurahundi campaign. Sydney Sekeramayi, Minister of State (Defence) during Gukurahundi atrocities and a key architect and player, also remained in government as Minister until Mugabe's removal in the coup in 2017.[7] The leading military players have not only retained their positions but have been promoted over the years. Before his death in 2020, former Colonel Perence Shiri, Commander of the Fifth Brigade, was promoted to Air Marshall and head of the Zimbabwe Air Force. After the coup in 2017, he was appointed as Minister of Agriculture.[8] Similarly, former Colonel Edmore Chimonyo, who replaced Perence Shiri as Commander of the Fifth Brigade, would ultimately be promoted to General and Commander of the ZNA.[9] The former Brigadier of 1 Brigade, which provided logistical and operational support to the Fifth Brigade, Dominic Chinenge, later Constantine Chiwenga would be promoted to Commander of the Zimbabwe Defence Forces and after the 2017 coup to Vice President of Zimbabwe.[10] Coupled with the 1988 Amnesty, political and military power and control have helped shield perpetrators from accountability (Sachikonye 2011; Dorman 2016; Alexander and McGregor 2013).

3.3 Challenges in the Zimbabwean legal framework

The challenges to investigating, prosecuting and punishing perpetrators of international crimes under the Zimbabwean criminal legal system go beyond the 1988 Amnesty discussed above and extend to structural shortcomings in the legal framework. The criminal law of Zimbabwe is governed by the Zimbabwean Criminal Law (Codification and Reform) Act [Chapter 9:23] of 2004 (Criminal Code). It can be argued that the Criminal Code is not in line with Zimbabwe's Constitution as

---

7 'ED, Chiwenga and Sekeramayi Cornered Over Gukurahundi', *Newsday*, 23 August 2021.
8 'Zimbabwean Agriculture Minister Shiri Has Died, Government Says', *Bloomberg*, 29 July 2020.
9 'Chimonyo: Gukurahundi follows him to the grave,' *The Zimbabwe Independent*, 12 July 2021; 'Victims Sad Chimonyo died without facing Gukurahundi Justice', New Zimbabwean, 9 July 2021.
10 'Zimbabwe Coup General Appointed Vice President', *Deutsche Welle*, 27 December 2017.

it fails to criminalise and punish gross violations of human rights enshrined under Sections 48- 53 of the Constitution.

Scope of crimes in Zimbabwe Criminal Code

The Criminal Code does not contain provisions prohibiting CAH and war crimes. Since June 2000, however, the crime of Genocide has been prohibited by the Genocide Act [Chapter 9:20] of 2000 (Genocide Act). Much of the conduct of Gukurahundi, including murder, kidnapping, and torture, constitute crimes in Zimbabwe.

Section 47 of the Criminal Code defines murder. It does not, however, provide for the equivalent international crime of mass murder or extermination – one of the main crimes committed by the Fifth Brigade. Section 4 of the Genocide Act provides for the crime of genocide and adequately uses the definitions in the Genocide Convention. The downside of the Genocide Act is the requirement that the Attorney General approves any prosecution for this offence as stipulated under Section 5 of the Act. The Criminal Code does not provide for the crime of torture. Instead, Section 88 provides for crimes against bodily injury.

Section 93 of the Criminal Code provides for the crime of kidnapping or unlawful detention alternatively known as abduction. The crime of kidnapping ostensibly encompasses the international crime of unlawful imprisonment and severe deprivation of liberty but lacks the detailed specification contained in the international crime. The crime of abduction under the Criminal Code however does not encompass enforced disappearance, one of the most prevalent crimes of Gukurahundi. This lacuna in the Criminal Code would create a massive challenge in holding perpetrators of disappearances accountable. However, since some victims of enforced disappearances have been declared 'missing presumed dead' by Zimbabwean courts, perpetrators may be prosecuted for this crime as murder.

Scope of Criminal Responsibility

Sections 9 and 10 of the Criminal Code contain extensive provisions on criminal liability for criminal conduct including acts of commission and omission. The provisions of the Criminal Code on criminal liability seek to address many conceivable forms of criminal responsibility arising from acts and omissions. However, the provisions related to omissions are exceedingly narrow and do not envisage superior or command responsibility required to address international crimes effectively. The provisions do not also envisage collective or system criminality that characterises international crimes.

Statute of limitations

The prescription of criminal offences is provided for in the Zimbabwean Criminal

Procedure and Evidence Act [Chapter 9:07] of 2016. Section 111 of the Act provides that any lapse of time offences shall not bar the 'right of prosecution for murder'. This provision means that in the absence of the 1988 Amnesty, murder by Gukurahundi would be prosecutable in perpetuity. All other crimes prescribe after twenty years under Section 111 of the Act. This provision implies that apart from murder, no other Gukurahundi crime is prosecutable under Zimbabwean law because over twenty years have elapsed since the commission of the offences.

Based on international customary law, there is no statute of limitations for international crimes under ICL. The Convention on the Non-Applicability of Statutory Limitations to War Crimes and Crimes Against Humanity provides that no statutory limitation shall apply to war crimes, CAH, apartheid, and genocide irrespective of the date of their commission. The restriction of the *nullum crime sine lege* principle constitutes a key attribute of international crimes and has been reaffirmed by the jurisprudence of the ad hoc international criminal tribunals including in *Prosecutor v. Zejnil Delalic et al*, IT-96-21-T, Trial Chamber, para 817. In dismissing the application of the principle in the International Military Tribunal (Nuremberg) Judgement of 1 October 1946, Judge Roling stated that:

> … the prohibition of *ex post facto* law is an expression of political wisdom, not necessarily applicable in present international relations. This maxim of liberty may, if circumstances necessitate it, be disregarded even by powers victorious in a war fought for freedom.

4. Prospects for international justice

4.1 Non-applicability of the International Criminal Court (ICC)

Zimbabwe signed the Statute of the ICC in 1998, but it has not ratified it. The ICC has jurisdiction over nationals of State parties or international crimes of genocide, CAH and war crimes that occur in the territory of State parties (Rome Statute 1998). In addition, the temporal jurisdiction is restricted to crimes that occurred after the Statute of the ICC came into force on 1 July 2002. Jurisdiction of the ICC can also be established via UN Security Council (UNSC) referral in terms of Chapter VII of the UN Charter, regardless of whether the person investigated is a national of a state party (ibid). The ICC does not provide any viable option for accountability for Gukurahundi atrocities. First, Zimbabwe is not a state party to the Rome Statute, having signed but not ratified the treaty. Additionally, the atrocities occurred between 1983 and 1987 i.e. before the court was established.

4.2. Opportunities and limitations of universal jurisdiction

Universal jurisdiction empowers the domestic judicial systems to investigate and prosecute certain crimes, even if they were not committed on a state's territory, by one of its nationals, or against one of its nationals. International crimes are universal and thus fall within the purview of universal jurisdiction (Einarsen 2012; Bassiouni 2008: 142). Universal jurisdiction is distinct from the jurisdiction of the ICC and relates to the ability of national courts of states to exercise jurisdiction over extra-territorial crimes and non-nationals (Dube, 2015).

Universal jurisdiction, despite its limitations discussed below, sometimes offers the last and only hope for justice for victims in states where national authorities are not willing or able to prosecute such crimes (Paulet 2019). It also contributes directly to the fight against impunity for international crimes, strengthening the rule of international law and reducing the existence of safe havens for international criminals (ibid.).

Some countries, like South Africa, have enacted legislation such as the ICC Act of 2002 which empowers the country to exercise universal jurisdiction over perpetrators of international crimes. In *National Police Commissioner of the South African Police Service v Southern African Human Rights Litigation Centre Trust* (CCT 02/14) [2014] (*Torture Docket case*), the South African Constitutional Court has held that South African authorities – the South African Police Service and National Prosecution Authority – have a duty to investigate and prosecute international crimes allegedly committed in Zimbabwe. This decision provides a significant opening for the exercise of universal jurisdiction. However, despite this decision, South Africa has yet to exercise this duty. It is also pertinent to highlight the shortcomings of universal jurisdiction such as the diplomatic standoffs associated with triggering it as well as perpetrators avoiding countries willing to initiate prosecution under universal jurisdiction.

Another significant limitation to universal jurisdiction is the recognition of personal immunities from civil and criminal jurisdiction for state officials and heads of state. However, the case is unclear in relation to functional immunity. It is necessary to distinguish between functional immunity and personal immunity for international crimes. The former relates to immunity granted to heads of state and state officials acting on behalf of the State in the course of their duties, whereas the latter relates to immunity granted to heads of state or state officials for personal acts. The immunity extends to both civil and criminal jurisdictions. Whether exceptions to functional immunity exist under customary international law for international crimes has been a subject of intense debate among scholars (Stahn 2019: 251; Ryngaert 2008; Zappalà 2001).

The exception to functional immunity regarding international crimes was first addressed by the Nuremberg Tribunal, which held that 'he who violates the laws of war cannot obtain immunity while acting in pursuance of the authority of the

State, if the state in authorising his action moves outside its competence under international law.' This principle was reaffirmed by the minority judgement of the *Arrest Warrant* case. Judges Higgins, Kooijmans and Buergenthal held that 'serious international crimes cannot be regarded as official acts because they are neither normal State functions nor functions that a State alone (in contrast to an individual) can perform.'

Zappalà makes compelling arguments that there are exceptions to functional immunity. He argues that certain international crimes cannot be considered as performance of official duties, and as such, both the State and the individual are considered culpable (ibid.: 601). This reasoning was affirmed by the United Kingdom House of Lords in *R v. Bow Street Metropolitan Stipendiary Magistrate, ex parte Pinochet Ugarte* [2000] 1 AC 61 and by the German Federal Court of Justice which held that State practice shows that there is immunity except for international crimes, namely genocide, war crimes and CAH (ibid.).

Exceptions to functional immunity regarding international crimes are provided under Article IV of the Genocide Convention, Article 7 of the Statute of the ICTY, Article 6 of the Statute of the ICTR and Article 27 of the Rome Statute. The inclusion of the exception to functional immunity in all the aforementioned statutes and conventions may suggest a progression towards the formation of custom, as such instruments are taken into account in analysing if a norm has crystallised into customary international law (ibid.). Furthermore, it seems the International Law Commission (ILC) has constantly taken a position that there are exceptions to functional immunity in relation to international crimes (ILC 1996; ILC 2017). Notably, the Nuremberg Principles, which the UN General Assembly unanimously approved, contained exceptions to functional immunity with regard to international crimes (Zappalà 2001, p. 601).

However, in the *Arrest Warrant Case,* the International Court of Justice (ICJ) held that an arrest warrant issued by Belgian authorities against the Minister of Foreign Affairs of Congo, Abdoulaye Yeroda Ndombasi, violated international law because he was entitled to diplomatic immunity. The ICC Pre-Trial Chamber reaffirmed this reasoning in *Prosecutor v. Al-Bashir*, ICC-02/05-01/09, Pre-Trial Chamber Decision of 6 July 2017, para 68 (*Al-Bashir*), which held that it was 'unable to identify a rule in customary international law that would exclude immunity for Heads of State when their arrest is sought for international crimes by another State, even when the arrest is sought on behalf of an international court, including, specifically, this Court.' This view was also shared by the District Court of the Hague, which held that functional immunity extends to all international crimes without exception (Ryngaert 2020).

The South African High Court held in *Southern Africa Litigation Centre v Minister of Justice and Constitutional Development and Others* (27740/2015) [2015], para

28.8 (*Al Bashir* case), that ordinarily heads of state enjoy immunity under customary international law but that this immunity is excluded or waived in relation to crimes and obligations under the Rome Statute and waived by the UNSC. The *Syria Torture Case* is one of the most recent example of the successful use of universal jurisdiction to combat impunity. The German Courts successfully prosecuted and convicted a Syrian Colonel, Anwar Raslan, for CAH involving up to 4,000 victims for atrocities committed in a Syrian jail. In the *Torture Docket* case, the South African Constitutional Court held that 'the universal jurisdiction to investigate international crimes is not absolute. It is subject to at least two limitations [first] the principle of subsidiarity– namely there must be a substantial and true connection between the subject matter and the source of the jurisdiction and [secondly] the principle of non-intervention in the affairs of another country must be observed; investigating international crimes committed abroad is permissible only if the country with jurisdiction is unwilling or unable to prosecute and only if the investigation is confined to the territory of the investigating state.' It is evident that political considerations often stand in the way of the exercise of universal jurisdiction. Despite its limitations, universal jurisdiction remains one of the few viable options to address Gukurahundi atrocities. Based on this reasoning, countries seeking to apply such universal jurisdiction would first have to satisfy themselves that Zimbabwe is unwilling or unable to investigate and prosecute the aforementioned atrocities.

4.3. The international duty to investigate, prosecute and punish international crimes

There is an international obligation to investigate, prosecute and punish known perpetrators (Orentlicher, 1991; Roht-Arriaza 1990). This obligation persists long after the commission of an international crime (ibid.). In the case of continuing crimes, the obligation is to prevent the further commission of international crimes (ibid.).

The fulfilment of this duty has culminated in the prosecution of the Khmer Rouge in Cambodia, the former President of Chad, Hissene Habre, former President of Liberia Charles Taylor in Sierra Leone, and militia leaders in East Timor (Reiger and Wierda 2006). The unprecedented ICC prosecution of Kenyan President Uhuru Kenyatta and Vice President William Ruto and Ivorian President Laurent Gbagbo for election-related violence has also broken new ground in ICL despite being unsuccessful. However, it is unlikely that the Zimbabwean government, comprised of perpetrators of international crimes, will take any steps to investigate, prosecute and punish these crimes (Amnesty International 2022). In light of the impunity discussed above, the next section discusses recommended options to hold known Gukurahundi perpetrators.

4.4 A Hybrid/Mixed Gukurahundi Tribunal?

A conclusion that Gukurahundi atrocities constitute international crimes which attract individual criminal responsibility for Fifth Brigade perpetrators under international law triggers a responsibility to investigate, prosecute and punish both crimes and perpetrators. Notwithstanding the accountability challenges outlined above, the Genocide Act of Zimbabwe contains clear, sufficient and substantive provisions for the prosecution of perpetrators of the Gukurahundi genocide outlined. It is possible to prosecute alleged Gukurahundi perpetrators based on the current law. The Genocide Act contains two significant limitations, namely that only crimes that occurred after its enactment can be prosecuted and that the authorisation of the Attorney General is required to prosecute genocide. The first limitation is challengeable under international law on the grounds that genocide was already a crime under international customary law at the time of the Gukurahundi rendering the nullum crime sine lege principle inapplicable. (Boot 2002, Bineet 2016, Van Schaack 2008) The second limitation is also challengeable on the grounds that the crime of genocide is prohibited by international law and not subject to the decision of the Attorney General. In order to simultaneously implement the Genocide Act and deliver on the international obligation to investigate, prosecute and punish the perpetration of genocide, a Gukurahundi Special Tribunal should be established in Zimbabwe. The tribunal's jurisdiction should be expanded to include CAH and war crimes. The tribunal can take either of two forms: national and fully integrated into the national criminal justice system or hybrid or mixed.

A hybrid tribunal combines national with either regional or international justice (Carroll 2013). They are often the outcome of negotiation between national authorities and the international or regional community, and have been established as a balance or alternative between a fully international or domestic judicial process to hold perpetrators of atrocities accountable (Nouwen 2006). In other words, they provide a bridge that combines national and international elements and offers the required flexibility to respond to complex international crimes within a national context (ibid.). They also provide an opportunity to strengthen the capacity of the national justice system to manage such complex crimes by facilitating collaboration between international and national actors (investigators, prosecutors and judges) in the investigation, prosecution and defence of international crimes.

Hybrid Tribunals often provide a negotiated compromise, one that often allays the concerns of countries reluctant to completely cede sovereignty over the accountability process; and of perpetrators unwilling to face justice in international courts. They also provide an opportunity for victims to participate in proceedings conducted within the country's territory directly and more broadly respond to the needs of victims. Recent examples of hybrid tribunals include the Serious Crimes

Panel in East Timor, the SCSL, the Extraordinary Chamber in Senegal, the Special Tribunal for Lebanon War Crimes Chamber in Bosnia and Herzegovina, and the internationalised panels in Kosovo (Steininger 2018), Extraordinary Chambers in the Courts of Cambodia. Given the limitations of the Zimbabwean national justice system to effectively hold perpetrators of international crimes accountable (as described above), a hybrid tribunal provides a strong alternative. The major constraint to this option in Zimbabwe is that currently perpetrators remain in power and are unlikely to agree to any accountability process whatsoever.

4.5. The International Court of Justice

Besides formal criminal prosecution mechanisms to pursue international justice for atrocities the ICJ has provided an opportunity to address genocide at the international level. In the *Application of the Convention on the Prevention and Punishment of the Crime of Genocide (Bosnia and Herzegovina v. Serbia and Montenegro)*, and more recently *Application of the Convention on the Prevention and Punishment of the Crime of Genocide (The Gambia v. Myanmar)*. Bosnia and Herzegovina and the Gambia invoked the provisions of the Genocide Convention that grant the ICJ with the jurisdiction to determine disputes related to the violation of the Genocide Convention. In both cases the ICJ determined that genocide had indeed occurred and ordered the violating States to take provisional remedial and preventive measures. In *Bosnia and Herzegovina v. Serbia and Montenegro*, the ICJ also found that Serbia had violated its duty to investigate, prosecute and punish the crime of genocide by failing to hand over Ratko Mladić. The ICJ offers some promising prospects in that it allows any State party to the Genocide Convention to petition the court in respect of violations of the convention irrespective of whether the petitioning party is involved or not in the alleged genocidal acts. In that regard, State parties would have been able to bring Zimbabwe before the ICJ had Zimbabwe been a party to the Convention when Gukurahundi atrocities occurred. However, it only signed the Convention in 1991 i.e. well after Gukurahundi atrocities. For this reason, arguably, State parties cannot invoke Zimbabwe's responsibilities under the Convention for acts it committed before it was bound by it. Zimbabwe however remains bound by customary international law because genocide was already prohibited by customary international law at the time of Gukurahundi atrocities (Malunga 2021). In addition to genocide, Zimbabwe is bound by Common Article 3 of the Geneva Convention for war crimes and also by the customary international law prohibition against crimes against humanity (ibid.).

5. Conclusion

This chapter examined the atrocities committed by the Fifth Brigade and other security agencies in Zimbabwe from the perspective of ICL. The victims of Gukurahundi atrocities are yet to access justice. The major challenges faced by the victims and those who want to pursue justice on behalf of the victims have been the Zimbabwe government's failure, inability and unwillingness to investigate, prosecute and punish Gukurahundi atrocities including the granting of 1988 Amnesty which shields political incumbents from accountability. Additionally, the chapter examined existing statute of limitations as well as the challenges in the legal framework. It also interrogated the challenges in achieving justice and accountability for the crimes and argued for international justice for perpetrators by evaluating the prospects for universal jurisdiction. Finally, it evaluated the international duty to investigate, prosecute and punish Gukurahundi perpetrators and explored possible mechanisms for accountability at the international level.

Legal References

International Conventions and Instruments

Convention on the Prevention and Punishment of the Crime of Genocide (1948).
Convention Against Torture and Other Cruel, Inhuman or Degrading Treatment or Punishment (1985).
Convention on the Non-Applicability of Statutory Limitations to War Crimes and Crimes Against Humanity (1968).
Rome Statute of the International Criminal Court (1998).

International Cases

Bosnia and Herzegovina v. Serbia and Montenegro.
Democratic Republic of the Congo v. Belgium
The Gambia v. Myanmar.
Prosecutor v. Al-Bashir, ICC-02/05-01/09
Prosecutor v. Anto Furundžija, IT-95-17-1-T
Prosecutor v. Delalic et al, IT-96-21-T
Prosecutor v. Gbagbo and Blé Goudé, ICC-02/11-01/15.
Prosecutor v Jean Paul Akayesu, ICTR-96-4-A
Prosecutor v Jean Kambanda, ICTR-97-23- A
Prosecutor v. Karadzic, IT-95-5/18-PT
Prosecutor v Kallon et al, SCSL-2004-15-AR72
Prosecutor v. Kenyatta: ICC-01/09-02/11
Prosecutor v. Kunarac et al., IT-96-23-A

Domestic legislation

Constitution of Zimbabwe, 2013.
Criminal Law (Codification and Reform) Act [Chapter 9:23] of 2004.
Criminal Procedure and Evidence Act [Chapter 9:07] of 2016.
Genocide Act [Chapter 9:20] of 2000.
South Africa International Criminal Court Act 27 of 2002.

Domestic Cases

German Federal Court of Justice Judgement of 28 January 2021 – 3 StR 564/19, in *Neue Juristische Wochenschrift* (2021)

National Police Commissioner of the South African Police Service v Southern African Human Rights Litigation Centre Trust (CCT 02/14) [2014] ZACC 30.

R v. Bow Street Metropolitan Stipendiary Magistrate, ex parte Pinochet Ugarte (No.1) [2000] 1 AC 61

Simón Case, Argentine Supreme Court, causa No 17.768 (14 June 2005).

Southern Africa Litigation Centre v Minister of Justice and Constitutional Development and Others (27740/2015) [2015] 402.

10

Unforgettable Memories:
A Survivor's Story[1]

Jameson Moyo

My name is Jameson Moyo, and I am now called JJ. I was born on 5th May, 1961 at St Luke's Hospital in Lupane, and I was named Jeconiah. I come from Mzola 8 in Lupane. My parents were moved there in the fifties when they were forced out of Filabusi (then called Fort Rixon, but which the people called Emakhandeni), as it was being prepared for resettlement by white farmers. My parents had to move on to virgin land that is very sandy, in an area that then had a lot of cattle diseases. Some relatives went to Tsholotsho, and a few went to Nkayi.

We are eight, in our family, four boys and four girls, but we count to ten if I include my late step-brother and sister. By the time I was born my parents were quite settled in Lupane. I grew up herding cattle. I was the eldest boy present in the family. My older step-brother and sister stayed with my grandparents. So I assumed the tasks of the eldest child, and had the experience of manual activities before the right time for me to do so. But I was doing very well in ploughing and my father felt it was not worth allowing me to go to school as I was assisting him and my mother so much.

I was the only child able to do so at that time. I was supposed to go to school when I was six, but I started school when I was seven; and I went to school in March, instead of January, after we had completed ploughing. Only then would my father allow me to go school. We need to be cognisant of the fact that my father and mother never went to school. So, in life, they were competing with those who had

---
[1] As told to Irene Staunton in 2002.

been to school; but they were doing well in cattle ranching and peasant farming, so they felt no pressure to send their children to school. Moreover, the brother whom I followed used to abscond from school and this discouraged them. Nevertheless, our neighbour, Mrs Ndlovu – 'Naka Mellie'[2] – was a mistress[3] and her husband was the headmaster and she knew our family well. So my father and mother were sat down by her and she negotiated that I go to school.

I was the shortest child in class, so I looked very young. There were some boys who were quite big, such that when the educational inspector came, he thought they were too old to be in Sub-A. So he said that some children had to go on the waiting list for the following year because the classroom capacity was too small. So, this manager [suggested] that I should leave. But the mistress advised the man to issue us with some work. She said, 'Amongst these boys that you randomly selected, can you ask this boy (me) to write whatever you want, and these bigger ones to write whatever they want?' We went through that practice, and I did well. Then the mistress shed tears and said, 'You are destroying my class. Without this boy, this class wouldn't be what it is. He is one of the assets in the classroom.' What she was really saying is that when we decide who goes and who remains behind, it shouldn't be according to height. In the end all of us remained at school. Nobody was made to go back home.

When I did my Sub-A, I was in position two. I was helping my parents write letters, because they were not educated. Then, again, the following year my father would not allow me to go to school before we had finished ploughing; and in March, Naka Mellie came to request that I join classes late. So it continued, until my family felt that it was better for them to allow me to attend school.

But I continued herding cattle and working in the fields like any other Matabele boy. I found that when you don't have a brother, is not easy, because we used to be made to fight amongst each other by the bully-boys. I used to defend myself, knowing I had no brother, but at times you would be assaulted for having managed to conquer and that's when I would lose my temper and fight the bully. That's where I had the hard times. [Laughs.] I went up to Grade 7, but then my father wouldn't allow me to continue to secondary level because he said he was a poor man, and couldn't afford it. By then he had around fifteen head of cattle and around twenty goats, but he still called himself a poor man. He felt a lot of challenges. I think it was due to his background. As a result, I dropped out of school in 1974 and remained out until 1977. Then I fought my way back. I went to negotiate with my uncle, who was a headmaster, for him to take me to school. He agreed, but he felt that by now my age was going to affect me when I went to secondary school. So I had to change

---

2   Mother of Mellie.
3   A word often used in Zimbabwe to refer to a female school teacher.

my name and become Jameson Moyo and reduce my age. We cut it by almost five years, from eighteen to thirteen years. I went to reside with my uncle but before we went through the year, the school was burnt down in the intensity of war. (By then my step-brother had left for Zambia for military training. After independence, he remained within the Zimbabwe National Army until his time of death in 1998.)

When the schools were burnt down, I joined the other youths and we participated in the liberation struggle. We would move from one area to the other, whenever the need arose, but we were mainly in Dandanda, by then a no-go area for the Smith regime. There were a lot of ZIPRA forces there and fierce fighting would take place should the soldiers dare to enter that area, which became a recruitment area for ZIPRA.

Then, there was a call-up: most of my colleagues and some relatives were unfortunate because they were rounded up and taken in for training by the Smith regime. I was supposed to fall victim when our cattle were rounded up and taken to the sales. By then people had taken a [political] stand and were no longer taking their cattle for sale and no longer paying any levies. So the government would round up cattle, and take them for sale, and at the sale pens you would be forced to pay the levies that were due, and then given the remainder of the money that, as a result, was very minimal. Two of our biggest oxen were taken, so I and my mother followed them. When we were at the cattle pen, the army came and rounded all the youth up as well as some men who were around 40 to 45.

I was lucky, I got a tip off, three of us did. So we walked for about 60 k's to Dandanda. Then I proceeded to Binga, but my cousin and his friend decided not to do so. They remained behind and in just two or three days they were caught and taken for training. By now, early 1978, my father had already left – running away from call-up – because they wanted to round him up as well. He was more than 50 years old, but some of his age group had already been taken in for army training.

So I caught up with my father in Binga. He had moved there with his cattle. He took the herd and the scotch-cart and went to stay in the bush – quite a few people did that. So I helped him herd cattle and I used to take them for drinking, but the army was still operating in that area, so on some days we dug holes to water the cattle. There was never enough water, so we dug many holes. Then it came to my mind that I couldn't do that forever. One day I would be caught. So I moved into Chibila and I stayed there for the rest of '78. I had joined the other youth. We wanted to cross into Zambia for military training, but it was not easy.

I was still short, though well-built, but they always picked those who were tall, so I was always left behind. One of my cousins, Chorus Masango, managed to cross into Zambia and he trained and returned home [after the war]. But as youth we helped the freedom fighters carry their consignments from one place to the other, and spying here and there. There were many youth from different parts of the country in Chibila and at times the ZIPRAs would take a sizeable number and help them to cross the border. Occasionally, some would be caught by the Smith regime, and some died, but that did not deter us from waiting for the time, which never came, to cross into Zambia for training.

Then the army had a tip-off that there were youth awaiting recruitment in the area, so the district chairman of ZAPU decided to take us to Lusulu to Tsetse Control. We were found employment there. At night we would try to find the guerrillas so that we could be taken across to Zambia, but I did not make it. We would go even to the homestead of the Chief to wait for the ZIPRAs – at times they would come but at times they wouldn't. It was a long wait and in the morning we were supposed to be back at work.

So I remained with Tsetse Control until Independence. In 1980 they screened the youth. The foremen were tasked to identify and employ potential workers, and they decided not to employ me. My colleagues called for my name. I was the youngest, but they loved me. But still the foreman said, 'No, no, no. I cannot take him.' So I jumped on top of a drum and – I was still obsessive about having failed to cross into Zambia because of my height – and I said, 'Now I am the tallest. Can you still not see me?' Then the foreman laughed and said, 'But you don't have an ID,' and I said, 'Here is the new one. I just acquired it.' That's how I got employment in 1980 – re-employment, actually.

I was very happy, but the foreman decided that I should not go out into the bush. He said I was too young and a lorry had been blown up by a landmine. Instead, he said I should cook for him and clean his place, a tent. I did that very well, to the extent that other foremen said that I should cook for them as well, although they had their own boys. So they forced their boys into the forest spraying, that is doing tsetse control.

So I cooked for a year. Then, I went to register at a primary school. I still wanted education and I renewed my contract with my uncle that he should pay for me. My father said he would repay him with cattle, if I didn't get employment or do well at school. But, should I do well, I would pay my uncle back myself. When the contract was sealed, I resigned from my employment. They were not happy. I remember some boys saying that they wanted employment and couldn't find it. And here was somebody who has employment and is resigning. So I told them, 'No, my focus is broader than that,' and I returned to school.

I went back to Nono school in Mzola, where I had done all my primary education. I returned to Grade 7 when it re-opened. Some of the buildings did not have a roof as this had been ripped off when thuggery took place. The grass-thatched houses were burnt down. People just looted whatever remained, after the school was burnt during the war. I wanted to go to secondary school but there were hardly any teachers there; the primary school was better beefed up. So I said, 'Let me bide time.' And I did well. Either I took number one or two, or three.

I was staying with my uncle, his wife was very cruel. She treated me like a slave. I would be given tasks and I would do them very well, I would look after cattle better than the herd boy, but when I arrived home, she would say, 'Are you expecting to eat food? Cooked by whom? With firewood that I have found myself! No ways! Look for your own firewood and your own water.' Then she would take the sadza and use it to brew mahewu – the brew that they make overnight. So I would sleep without food. The following day the same thing would happen.

My uncle was a headmaster, but even he couldn't intervene. It didn't go well with my aunt until one day I collapsed in class due to hunger. Then my cousin and a friend took me to my paternal grandmother. She called my parents and explained my plight to them. Arrangements were made for me to leave school. But I wanted school, so I opted to remain with my uncle and aunt and I moved into Form 1. But things got worse. I could go for three, four days without food. One day I was so hungry that I felt I might fall down. I went to my grandmother. She was drinking her beer. I sat down next to her and drank her beer like nobody would think of. And she said, 'Since when is a child drinking my beer?' I told her that I was hungry. She prepared food for me and that's when I confronted my parents and told them that, even if I die, I will die fighting for school. So they sold a beast – we liked that cow, but they sold it. I had paid for myself in 1981 with the money I had saved in 1980. In fact, my uncle never paid a cent. I even bought my own uniforms, the clothes I was putting on when I was working in his fields, and so forth. I was just sourcing everything for myself. I had a project. I would buy young chickens in Binga and keep them at my parents. Later I would re-sell them, just to keep my money multiplying a bit.

At the end of Form 1, I moved back to my parents. They repaired the bicycle for me because the secondary school was very far from our home as they had moved into Binga: my father had ended up with a homestead there, after he had run away from the call-up. It was really in the bush. My father used the money from the beast to make an advance payment for my Form 2. My uncle never bothered.

Then, when I was in Form 2, on the 8th February 1983 at around ten o'clock … we were practising for athletics, when we saw soldiers everywhere. At the time, with all the disturbances that were taking place,[4] it was said that the ZIPRA forces were trying to overthrow the government. (In fact, I had already met dissidents twice or

---

4   In February 1982, arms caches were found on ZAPU farms. ZANU-PF accused PF-ZAPU of plotting against them, and retribution followed in the period now known as Gukurahundi.

thrice.[5] You see, by then I was staying with my mother's brother because his place was closer to the school. With the tense situation we felt that it was no good for me to cycle long distances because of the curfew.)

We were returning to the classrooms after athletics when we were called back. Actually, the soldiers said they wanted the head boy, head girl and a few boys. So we went to the classrooms, and they remained with these ones. They made the head girl lie down and assaulted her badly. They wanted to know the whereabouts of dissidents, and she said, 'As a female, I know nothing, maybe the head boy knows.' They interpreted this to mean the head boy was a dissident. And they handcuffed him and took him away. We never saw him again – up to today. We were in the classrooms, and we realised things were bad, the Fifth Brigade had caught up with us. They came for us in the classrooms, you know, softly. They told us to run to the football pitch and the netball pitch.

Then they started assaulting us saying that we were not moving as fast as we had been ordered to. When we were seated, the commander of the Fifth Brigade addressed everybody saying they are expecting us to tell them the whereabouts of the dissidents. Nothing else! They wanted dissidents. Should we not co-operate, we would regret not having done so. Nobody could say anything. Nobody knew anything.

Then they started assaulting us from all directions, so that we piled on each other, and the screams … Then they would laugh and allow us to settle again. Then when we were once again seated, they would come again with whips and sticks. And, again, we would pile on top of each other. You can imagine – if you are the one underneath, and everybody is on top of you … And we are talking about a secondary school that had about five hundred students. It was the only secondary school in the area. In 1983 construction was still going on. Everybody from the area was at the school; and also children from the primary school who had been ordered there by the soldiers. We were many that day. The issue was that everybody should tell them the whereabouts of the dissidents.

What transpired is awful because after that first introductory session, the worst was yet to come. We were subdivided into groups of, let's say, about eight. Then they started assaulting us. Two people assaulting one person whilst that person is lying prone. They would first deal with the buttocks and then any part of the body: they wouldn't mind where they beat you. When they were tired, they would pair us and task one person to continue with the beatings, using whips and sticks. It was bad. It was bad. After we had beaten each other, they would then beat the very person

---

5   After the Entumbane clashes in 1980 and 1981, and the discovery of the arms caches, many ex-ZIPRA cadres left the ZNA. Most now claim that this was the only way to stay alive: several hundred became dissidents working in small groups, though with little support and rural people could see no point in further conflict.

tasked to beat the one lying down, so that he inflicts the dreadful pain that they intended. It was bad. Others might have been having their own recipe, but in my group this is what was happening; and in those groups near me, really, I saw them taking the same recipe. At some stage, we were made to fight each other. We would fight while these two soldiers are beating the two who are fighting. They would laugh and enjoy the exercise. This went on from half past ten to around six or half past six: long hours.

The soldiers numbered close to 50 or so, because they were in two groups. I never heard anybody who spoke Ndebele. There were about three police officers whom we knew but they were so frightened, they were not of any help. I was made to understand that even the member who was in charge of that police force, the one that used to patrol the area, was made to lie down and was thoroughly beaten. When they came to the school, they had already beaten him because he was not happy with what they were doing, but he could do nothing.

Later, you would find two or three people fighting one person; instead of one to one, they moved to two or three against the one who appeared to be powerful and overcoming others. And they will be beating these three or four and beating this other one saying, 'You are not doing it the way you were doing it when it was one to one.' So the exercise continued for hours regardless of whether you are female or male. Quite a lot of girls were taken aside, one girl, that I saw, fainted, but I understand that was when they went to the exercise of raping her. A lot of people got injured and no treatment was provided. Actually, they said that no one was supposed to go to the clinic.

Then another group of the Fifth Brigade came in, and they brought in some villagers. One of them was my aunt, whose husband was in the call-up and still had his uniforms but he was not present when the Fifth Brigade arrived, so she was made to carry this uniform to the school and was identified as the wife of a dissident. There was also a cousin, a former ZIPRA cadre, who had come home after the war. He had opted out of the army. But they labelled him a dissident, he and his friend as well. They had been badly beaten when they were brought to the school at around 1 p.m.

We were shown them as dissidents. They were paraded before us because we'd been saying 'We don't know what a dissident look like.' So the soldier said, 'You don't know what a dissident looks like, yet you stay with dissidents! It means you are unfaithful.' They beat them so badly; they would just dash for their mouths with the butt of a gun. They were just a pulp of a human being. You couldn't really distinguish the nose and mouth and eyes, it was just one mess. And they were just bloodied all over, the woman as well – bloodied all over.

Most of our people were also oozing with blood. It was worse with our teachers. The staff at the school was dealt with aside. At times we would be brought together and at times they would be taken aside. They were made to swim in muddy waters; if you failed to have your head submerged, they would just hit you on the skull. It was bad. Female and male alike. They were made to roll in mud and swim, and they were beaten: this was what was taking place on the sides. But, now the [adults] were brought to us and we were together. We were made to queue and everybody in the queue was asked to tell the whereabouts of the dissidents or get a bullet. It was said, should we not, a bullet was going to be drilled into the very first person in front, with a pistol. Unfortunately I was in front of the queue, and then they said, 'You are going to save your colleagues.'

When the commander placed the pistol on my forehead, I remember saying 'The three policemen are our witnesses. Whenever we knocked off school, we would use their vehicle to our place, because it is near their camp: Cewale camp. As a result, whatever they saw is exactly what we witnessed, because we were with them in the evening up to eight o'clock. We would bath with them at the borehole and they were using our soap and towels. So we were close to them. As a result most of us missed meeting with dissidents.'

The soldier screamed, he bellowed, 'Here is a mature politician, can you come for him?' Then he said, *'Chikomana, chikomana!'* calling the soldiers, *'Torai mukomana oyu momamisa uko,'* meaning that his subordinates should remove me from others and deal with me thoroughly. Five men came for me. They took me to the edge of the football pitch, near a fallen tree. Three of them sat there, whilst two were simultaneously beating me on my buttocks. No questions were asked. I was just beaten. I passed out. When I came to my senses, I found one soldier sitting on a log, the others had moved away. A young girl had brought a twenty-litre tin of water, and she was holding that tin – and this person was drinking from the container, and the girl was shivering. Then this man took the tin and poured water on me, and then left with the girl. She was a Form 1 girl. Anyway the soldier took her away, and this is how I survived. I think this girl might have been taken for raping.

I managed to get up but I couldn't walk. It was around six o'clock because the sun had gone down. We were asked to go home, regardless of the curfew, and we went. Most people went home, but I had difficulties. Nearby was a homestead of my mother's distant relative They were informed that I'd been left for dead and they came to wheel me to their homestead in a wheelbarrow. This was the family of Dibha Masango. His wife, Mahlango, made me lie down and tried to make some hot compressions, but it didn't work well as the water was too hot. Then she stopped and made sadza out of mealie-meal, and when she cooked that *isitshwala*, she took a wet cloth and put a sizeable amount of the porridge on it and this is what she used to make the compressions on me. She did this for a long time, until she had covered almost my whole body, because I was just a mess. When I went to pee my urine had a lot of blood and some clots in it. Later she made a bed for me and I slept there. In the morning, she repeated the exercise; this is, I think, part of what saved me.

Then at eight o'clock we were reminded that we were supposed to go to school. Because the Fifth Brigade had said they would kill anyone whom they found at home. So we had no choice but to return for fear of being killed, and getting our parents into a lot of trouble. There was an order that no one should go for treatment at the local clinic. When I turned up at school, almost everybody was there. But no learning took place. We were just seated, discussing our ordeal. People were terrified.

At around nine o'clock some women went to fetch water at a nearby well. They returned running, saying they had heard, amongst those who were shot dead, one a former ZIPRA, who was tied to another person. The other person to whom he was tied [had been] shot in the head but he hadn't died. So he called, in a light voice, 'Come and untie me, I am tied to a dead person but I am not dead.' And then he called for water as well, saying he was thirsty. But the women ran away. Nobody could go to him. They told others, but nobody dared go there. Then the news came that my aunt [had been] shot dead along the way, as the soldiers failed to have her move fast, because she was so badly beaten, she was unable to walk fast, so they decided to shoot her.

We remained at school until around eleven o'clock. Then the soldiers arrived. Some were at the football pitch, some at the netball pitch, and we were called to the football pitch again. I felt I couldn't take it, so I decided to go to the toilet and I remained there until it was dark. I heard my colleagues singing: they were made to sing. The beatings were few on that particular day. But that's when the Fifth Brigade was informed that amongst the two people that they killed, one of them was still alive, and I heard, with my own ears, the sound of a gun, and they killed him. So the relatives were called in to ferry him in a scotch-cart and take both men for burial. That's what happened on that day.

At around seven o'clock, when it was dark, I knew there was curfew, but I started the long walk to my uncle's place. It was very difficult but I tried and I got home quite late. I was moving from one maize field to the other; I would crawl at times, when there was no maize to hide me. I did this until I reached home and then I just got into the house and slept. My cousin, Costern Masango, had informed the parents[6] that I was home and in a bad state. Well, I remained there as it was towards the weekend. Then, on Sunday, when I was just mending up, we went to a neighbour, Mr Ngwenya, to barb him, to cut his hair. It was around half past four, and we said, 'Let's make it fast, otherwise the curfew will get us.' So my cousin, Costern Masango, was doing the barbing, and I went to stand by the road to keep

---

6   Not strictly his parents in the European sense, but in Ndebele culture all the uncles and aunts are in a sense parents and will act *in loco parentis*.

watch and as I stood there, the soldiers crossed, some five hundred metres away.

So we went to another uncle's homestead that was nearby, he did not have grown-up children, only two young ones. We remained there. In the meantime, the soldiers had got hold of the son, Jotham Ngwenya. He had just gone to visit his girlfriend and they found him and the girlfriend and they said he was a curfew-breaker. They tortured him and they told him that they wanted a list of all the youth within the area, particularly those who were active in ZAPU. But again, I was very lucky. I was not from that area, Mzola 52. I was from Mzola 8. So I didn't participate in the youth activities in that area; I participated in Mzola 8, and in Dandanda where we had relatives.

My cousin, Costern, was living in Bulawayo. He only came back home on holidays, so he was never within the youth system; as a result they didn't include him on the list either. So we survived. That night all the youth of that area were rounded up. They actually passed within the yard where we were staying, when they took the youth for torture. They were tortured all night on the other side of the Mzola River.

My sister, who was being married into the Ndlovu family, had just visited her in-laws and they caught up with her on that same night. And she was taken along with her husband, an aunt and many of my friends, one of them my best friend, Titus Moyo. At around four a.m. we heard some gun shots, as if it was a contact. They were shooting dead the youth, who were innocent and unarmed.

All in all, the youth who were killed on that day were thirteen. The fourteenth one managed to come out alive. Actually, they shot him on the arm. The fifteenth one was my uncle, Mr Nkomo: he was made to hold a woman who couldn't even stand up, so that they shoot both of them at once. When they shot at them, he fell down at the crack of the gun with this woman. He was not shot himself, but badly beaten. One boy came out alive but he was badly beaten as well as badly shot, to the extent that really he was just a bunch of broken bones.

In the morning, a Monday, we were bathing and preparing to go to school, as we had no choice. I had just washed one leg when the young brother of Titus arrived at my uncle Moses Masango's homestead. He was crying. He told us, 'When you heard the guns, all the youth were killed.' He has been sent to tell the villagers that by ten o'clock they should have buried all those bodies. Should they not do so, the whole village would be killed. So when the relatives went to the place, they found two people who were still alive, so they took these people to their families, one was ferried in a wheelbarrow, one was put in a scotch-cart and taken to his homestead. The other one, who had a broken arm, was Richard Nyoni, he is still alive as I narrate this story, and he has one arm.

The villagers buried most of these dead youth at their homesteads. But when they were about to bury the last four they realised that they couldn't make it before ten. So they dug one pit and put these four into a shallow grave. It was mainly the women who were present, because most men had fled. So what happened was that when the soldiers made a follow-up, at exactly ten o'clock, they applauded the community, warning them that if they had not done so they would have been killed.

But now, this youth, Jotham Ngwenya – the one who was the first to be caught, and called a curfew-breaker; the one whom they had taken to each homestead where there was a youth – they had forgotten to kill him. They had been torturing him in a different room, and they forgot him. When they remembered, one soldier had freed him, and so they made a follow-up to his homestead. They found he was with his parents, and they told them, 'No, it was by mistake that he was freed. He was supposed to die with the others. And so we have come to kill him.' The relatives told them that they would give them all their cattle in order to save him, as he had survived by mistake. But the soldiers wouldn't budge. They said they would rather kill everybody. They said he should come out of the homestead and stand by the gate and bid his relatives farewell. When he hesitated, they started assaulting him, and he gave in. He went and stood by the gate, bid all his relatives farewell and they shot him dead.

They then went to a Sibanda family where one boy, who was just a pulp of broken bones, had survived the shooting, though he was badly shot himself. They went there and asked the relatives to take him out. They said he was supposed to die and he should die. Then the relatives couldn't do this; but really, they were threatened until they took him out. They were told to put him by the gate and they were told to bid him farewell and he was shot dead.

They went on to this guy who lost his arm, but his arm was still dangling and they wanted to finish him up. His father was fluent in Shona. Then he spoke to them in Shona and told them that his first son was killed by the Smith regime; the second son was involved in an accident when their car was blown up by a landmine and he had lost a foot. And now the last boy has lost an arm – so he feels, as an old man, that his family is already no more. Wouldn't they kill them before they kill the son? Or wouldn't they just spare him so that at least they can still remain with one son. He convinced them, as he spoke in Shona. As a result, his son survived.

My sister also survived. Now, when she relates it, she says that they assaulted them to nothing, to threads, and when they were assaulting her, alongside her husband and the aunt, she called out, 'Maiwee', which is the Shona way of crying for help when one is in pain. Then they spoke to her in Shona and she responded fluently – she had stayed in Shurugwi, at my auntie's place, throughout the war. So they asked her where she learnt the Shona language, because, they said, their target was the Ndebele-speaking person not a Shona-speaking person. She spoke to them in

Shona and said, 'I grew up with the Mandebvu family and I am their *mainini*.' They forgave her, and this is how she survived, though she lost her husband in the process.

Little did we know then that one of the commanders was a Mandebvu son, David Mandebvu. I only realised this when I interviewed one of the Fifth Brigade cadres, that is Chitekuteku, of Masvingo. When I found this out, I discussed it with my uncles and they were worried about his behaviour. They had noticed that whenever he is with them, he hardly settles. He is not comfortable. Up to now. He would rather be with the kids than with the elders.

•••

Then, I felt I couldn't take it. My best friend, Titus Moyo, had been killed and I didn't know how we had survived; and I didn't know for how long. I decided the only thing to do was to walk to our family homestead in Binga. When I reached there … there was a chicken that I had nursed, after it had been taken by a hawk; one of its wings had been broken and its gizzard torn. I used the wound powders to make it heal. I liked this chicken so much that it used to remain within the kitchen. It used to lay about twelve eggs and hatch out all of them … So when I arrived, I was relating our ordeal – the Fifth Brigade hadn't yet gone up to Binga – and I told my mother that now I would like to kill this chicken as a sacrifice. I said, 'Let's eat it, and these eggs, and then after that let's move away. We might be killed.'

My mother killed the chicken and when my father came, we made a decision that leaving was the best option. We called the neighbourhood – there were about five homesteads around – and we all agreed. We went about ten kilometres away from our homestead and remained in the bush. We ferried water in scotch-carts. A lot of people, badly beaten, came from Lupane; many of them were nursed under our care. Then we would take a scotch-cart overnight and ferry them to Binga where there were buses: the whole of Lupane was without buses because of the curfew.

My aunt, who had tormented me when I resumed school in 1980, also fled after they had killed Naka Mellie's first-born son, a teacher at Nono Primary School; and another teacher was also killed and buried next to the school by the villagers. Some teachers were badly beaten. So my aunt decided to flee to town, but there were no buses, so instead she came to us in Binga, saying: 'We are here. We would like to join your young brother in Bulawayo, but we don't know whether he managed to make it there.' Then my father said, 'What do you want to do with your aunt?' And I and my brother (you would say 'cousin'), Costern, yoked the oxen and took her to Binga, and this is how she survived.

We remained in the forest for three months and then we returned to school. A lot of students came out to greet me. Initially, some of them wouldn't come close to me. They 'knew' I was dead, and they wondered where I was coming from. Later on they came to hear about the ordeal, so they were very happy to realise that I was alive.

So, I continued at school but there was hardly any schooling. Most of the teachers had fled. We had one teacher, and I was one of those students who were chosen to help teach others. And we just rotated. One was Leo Sibanda, my close friend, he used to teach the upper grades and I would teach the Form 1s. But really there was not much learning going on.

The Fifth Brigade were in the area for a long period – maybe the whole year. In 1984 they were still around, though most had moved away, only a few remained. Every weekend we were ordered to go to the Fifth Brigade camp, Cewale Camp, in Mzola 52. We were taught the ZANLA Shona songs, Mugabe praises, denunciations of [Joshua] Nkomo and a lot of ZAPU cadres. We were also taught the liberation struggle pertaining to the ZANU(PF) side. But whenever I could, I would run away – get my bike and cycle home to Binga.

A lot of girls were abused. Actually, every girl was abused – even very young girls. They would just pick anyone. In the process one of my cousins got pregnant; even now she has a child, whom my uncle and aunt are keeping as a result of that rape case. (To make matters worse, this uncle is mentally ill, but he is looking after this child.)

Some girls ended up being hysteric: during the time that the Fifth Brigade lived beside the community, they were hysteric. It was as if they were possessed, and this worried their parents a lot. But still the soldiers would just pick them. It just went on like that. And, of course, people were assaulted. Some were taken into Cewale Dam, a natural dam, and told to get in and not to look back. You get into the water. When you are this deep – up to the chest – then they shoot you dead. Just like that. And there were a lot of crocodiles in that dam.

A lot of people were killed in Cewale: a lot. They dug a very, very deep hole and in that hole they would throw the killed people and then cover it a little bit – with sand, then continue like that. It was very deep. Some of the people who participated in the digging were killed after they had dug the hole. There is one who survived, Stewart Sibanda, whose young brother, if I'm not mistaken, was taken for a dissident and killed the first day the Fifth Brigade arrived.

One day, during this time, when I was going home, I met a guy who asked me where I was from and where I was going, and I told him. He introduced himself as Mr Ndlovu. He said he was from the army and had run away. He said he was very hungry. I told him that there was a plate of food in my hut, if we could go there. We ate together – actually, he ate most of the food. Then he left, without my parents knowing. I kept that as my secret. The following day, he waited for me again. The school was very far away from my homestead in Binga, and I was often quite late, usually after curfew, though I always managed to get past the Fifth Brigade camp before curfew.

The next day he was waiting for me again, and I took him home and this time we really discussed things, and my father and mother found us together. He was shedding tears, relating his ordeal. He said that what made him leave the army was that he was shot at by one ZANLA soldier as he got into a vehicle. The bullet missed him, but he told us, 'Such incidents happen a lot and it's always the ZIPRAs who are killed.' They always claimed the gun had just discharged on its own.

In his case the soldier who shot at him was arrested and they were told that he was going to be charged in a military court, but in fact he was simply sent to another camp. So, when Mr Ndlovu discovered this, he deserted. He said there'd been five ZIPRAs in that unit of the Zimbabwe National Army. But three had been 'transferred' in unclear conditions; nobody knew where they were. They suspected that they'd been killed. So he felt that he was next, as he was one of only two ZIPRAs remaining in his unit.

He'd run away to Binga. He'd been based in the Midlands, and crossed into Nkayi, and went from there to Lupane, and up to Binga. He was enquiring about the whereabouts of other dissidents. I told him I'd seen some groups. (Later, I heard that one was led by Thambolenyoka; one by Geleza, that is Flowing Water. I don't know their real names.) I gave him the directions to the area [in which] they were frequently seen, deep in Binga, and he went there and met them.

Before he went, he came a third time with three other guys. He was carrying an axe. He didn't even have a gun. He came solely to thank me because he said that he'd feared that I would inform on him. In the morning I was going past the Fifth Brigade camp, in the afternoon I was going past the Fifth Brigade camp, but I never informed them of his whereabouts. So he came to thank me, which was a dangerous thing to do, even though they were in the area. And I was grateful for that. I was a ZAPU supporter myself and I couldn't betray a ZAPU cadre.

I continued with my schooling, but things were quite bad and it was not clear what was happening. At some stage I was told that some youth had indicated that I skipped the pungwes at the Cewale camp and they were going to come for me, so I went deep into Binga, to spend my weekend there. Anyway they didn't come. My homestead was very far away, and they had a lot on their plates because they went around the neighbourhood gathering up everyone who was skipping the pungwes, and they were badly assaulted.

I then went on to the homesteads of Twyman Ncube and the late Msankwe Mguni, security guards for Tsetse Control, whom I had known before. When I arrived, the dissidents were there. They were preparing to burn these people in their homesteads, because the dissidents thought they had weapons, and they wanted them. The guards claimed they didn't have any, but the dissidents wouldn't believe them. They said, 'How come you are guarding the fence without guns?' They were smoking dagga, which they'd found in the hut. The commander had put on a dustcoat and he had a machine gun, which had about five live bullets. The belt was quite empty. The machine gun was positioned just so. They had told the guards that they should cook for them, before the final ordeal. And one guy was holding a chicken.

When I arrived, the commander, Mr Geleza, began interrogating me, saying I was a spy and I was going to inform the Fifth Brigade. Suddenly, I heard somebody from among the dissidents calling, 'Mr Moyo'. The commander then asked, 'Where do you know this person from?' and he said, 'Ah-ha, very safe, sir. This person is a friend of mine.' It was Mr Ndlovu. He said, 'Forget about this one,' and he told them how I assisted him with food and did not inform them of his whereabouts.

Then I explained that I had come to hide because I had not been attending the pungwes. Then they said, 'How can you come and hide with people who are sell-outs?' and I said, 'Uh-uh, as far as I know, these are my brothers. When I am here, I am safe. I come because I know my safety is guaranteed.' Then this guy who was holding a chicken just let it go, and said, 'I stand with what he is saying. Whatever we've been told, I will not buy it. This guy won't tell us lies. If he has come here, when he is running away from Fifth Brigade, these people are not sell-outs.' As a result, the guards survived. You know, we spent the whole day together; they actually had to get another chicken, one that the family chose, and cooked for them. They had taken a lot of clothes, radios, and so on, and they returned them all, except for a few items, and these people said, 'Ah please, you can have them.' At six o'clock the dissidents left.

On Monday when I got to school I was told seven dissidents burnt some people in a house nearby. You see the safety of the dissidents was not guaranteed because they were not armed. Even if they had guns, some were not working. They didn't have bullets. As a result, they had a motive to survive; anyone who appeared to be a threat, as far as their informants were concerned, they would rather get rid of. Also, I felt that some of them were very naughty. They had all this anger that they wanted to vent. They wanted to demonstrate that should their orders not be heeded, they can kill, and to a certain extent they had to demonstrate that. This is how I see it. Some people were killed because the dissidents claimed they were sellouts. To make matters worse, some of them started raping women. A few behaved well, but most behaved badly. Men complained that their women, their wives were being abused. So wherever they went, they didn't mend relations with the community. Also they demanded food, and they always wanted meat, and they always said, 'We are many,' so people would cook lots of food only to find that they were just three or so. They developed this habit of eating wherever they went, because they didn't know where they would get their next meal. And, as a result, they were a nuisance to the communities.[7]

I continued with my schooling at Zenzele School, but I was no longer benefiting. We wrote our exams, of course, and I didn't do well. I passed, but not well. So at the end of 1983 I started looking for a school place in Bulawayo. I was staying with my cousin, Jethro Moyo, who had tried to join ZIPRA during the war, and didn't manage. He said, 'Now is a time for war. They won't catch up with me before I get a gun.' And, he joined the dissidents. We have never heard from him since.

I gave my documents to my uncle, the headmaster. I thought he would be able to find me a place, but he did nothing. He didn't even remember that he had my documents. Really, I was so low when I left him, I could have shed tears. I was pushing my bicycle home. Then Mrs Hlabangane stopped me and asked, 'My son, is there a problem with your bicycle, can we assist you?' I said, 'No.' Then she said, 'But why are you pushing it today?' And I started crying. She consoled me, and I related how I had failed to get a school place in Bulawayo and how I'd hoped that my uncle would assist me, because most of his friends were teaching in town. She said, 'Can you go to Bulawayo? Do you have money?' And I said, 'Yes'. And she said, 'Come tomorrow morning.' So I told my family that I was going to Bulawayo. They were not happy, they said, 'If your uncle can't find you a school place, how can you expect to do so?'

Anyway, this lady wrote a letter to her husband, and I took it to him and he approached the secretary for Sizani Secondary School, and she offered us a provisional place. She said, 'If certain students don't pay, you will find a place. But, if they pay, there will be no vacancy,' because I was applying so late.

When I returned to the school with the headmaster's report and the school results the following Monday, one student had not paid, and I got a vacancy for Form 3. I still didn't have money, so Mr Hlabangane paid for me, and offered to keep me. I stayed with him for the first week, but then one of my uncles couldn't take it, he said, 'I haven't failed anyone in my life. In fact, I have been wishing to keep you because you want schooling so much.' So I went to stay with him. But life was not rosy. My aunt was not impressed. My uncle was having an extra-marital affair – he wanted to be a polygamist. This did not go well with his wife. He started sending messages to that lady, sometimes he would send his own children; sometimes he would send me. I have tried to make amends but my aunt has not forgiven me for being a postman.

Anyhow, I remained with them until I completed my O-level. I passed with four

---

7   Besides the dissidents, who were genuine ex-ZIPRAs, badly behaved or not, there were also dissidents called Super-ZAPU who were insurgents backed by apartheid South Africa; and pseudo-dissidents, hit squads sent in by ZANU-PF, whose guise and behaviour provided an excuse for the Fifth Brigade. See also Breaking the Silence: Building True Peace: A Report on the Disturbances in Matabeleland and the Midlands 1980 to 1988 (Harare: The Catholic Commission for Justice and Peace and The Legal Resources Foundation, 1997).

Bs and a C and started looking for employment as a temporary teacher, and I took a job. In the meantime, I also tried for places at colleges for further education, but I couldn't make it. I tried the health sector, I tried apprenticeships. It was difficult because I was Ndebele. There was a lot of discrimination. As long as you were Ndebele, you were guaranteed not to get a place. There were a few who made it, because they had contacts, but I didn't have any and I failed.

So I remained teaching and looking after my family. They had sold a lot of their cattle while they educated me, and I had to pay them back. So I was looking after three of my young brothers who were at school and I was paying fees. My girlfriend was corresponding[8] and I was paying fees and encouraging her to go to school. From 1986 to 1992, I was teaching at Magama Mission. Twice I was offered the post of deputy head, untrained as I was, and twice I rejected it, because there were qualified teachers at the school, though the headmaster felt they were not responsible enough.

At that school, most of the teachers called me 'Grandfather', even those who were older than me, and I accepted it; others called me 'Uncle' and I accepted that. I found myself in the role of an adviser, a resourceful person with social problems, and I liked it. I liked it so much.

Then, I saw a vacancy for training as a rehabilitation technician and I applied and was accepted. The course started. It was in Marondera. But, in the middle of the second week, I was suddenly told to produce certified photocopies of my O-level certificates, which were in Bulawayo. One accountant told me that I was going to lose my place, 'Because they are trying to make room for some children of big chefs.' He said that should I fail to submit my certificates, I would have to leave. I felt threatened. I skipped classes and went to the education head office in Harare, and demanded my certificates. They referred me to the Salary Services Bureau. I went there and demanded the photocopies of my certificates. I showed them my student card and told them I had left the Ministry of Education, and they gave me the certificates. I went back to school, and produced the papers, certified, as they wanted them. And I survived.

The principal did not take it lightly. We had a lot of confrontations with the administration. Two students didn't even have a reference; three were not even interviewed. The school was not happy, but there is nothing they could do. Children of chefs are always given places. Out of 28 students, only two were Ndebele-speaking. Ironically we were both Moyo: a female and a male, so it was as good as having a sister.

I enjoyed myself. At some stage, a student was arrested for having an affair with a minor, and all hope was lost that he was going to rejoin the class. But, just before he was due to appear in court, I went to have a discussion with the father of the

---

8   Doing a correspondence course.

minor. I asked him whether his daughter was pregnant or not, and he said he didn't know. I said, 'If your daughter is pregnant, she has already dropped out of school,[9] and you are going to have to look after the baby. But if you allow this boy to marry your daughter, despite the fact that she is just doing Grade 7, you will have saved yourself from providing all that support and you will charge him something.' He said he wanted Z$500. (It was still a lot of money in 1992.)

We went to the police to say that we would like to settle the issue out of court, and an agreement had been reached, and the man wanted a payment of Z$500. The police officer asked the man if he was happy. He said, 'I am happy if they pay me.' And they said, 'You haven't been paid?' He said, 'No.' The police said, 'Out you go. This case is going to court.' Then we rushed around. I had something in my account, the boy had nothing. So I paid and the following morning the father said, 'No, no, no. Don't charge this person. We have settled this out of court.' So the boy returned to school. The affair ended. The girl was not pregnant, she continued at school, and the guy continued too; he remained supportive of that family, to a certain extent, and really, everybody respected me for that.

At some stage we trainees were attached to Harare Central at the Children's Rehabilitation Unit. There were a lot of mothers at a workshop, conducted by Knowledge Kodzongere, a psychologist. I ended up assisting him. So, at lunchtime, he called me and asked where I did my counselling. I told him I was just a student. And he said, 'For a long time, I've had students attached to this department. I have never had such assistance. It was tremendous. Where did you do your counselling?' I said, 'No, I haven't done any counselling.' Then he took me to the CONNECT offices in Harare and introduced me to the administrator and sourced some funds for me, a sort of small scholarship. They said, 'Just give us a ring if your principal agrees that you start a counselling course, while you are still doing a rehabilitation course.'

The principal said, 'JJ, I wish you luck. Go for it.' The boy's case and various other student problems, [with] which I had been able to assist had convinced the principal that I should do the CONNECT course. All went well. I passed both courses – counselling and rehabilitation, and I was placed at Ingutsheni Hospital. I went there by coincidence. After graduating, this sister from Matabeleland, Mai Moyo, was placed at Ingutsheni and I was placed at Mpilo [hospital[10]] but Mai Moyo didn't want to go to Ingutsheni. My wife – I was married by then – said, 'You should have a heart for your sister. You're a man. Please swop with her.' So I took heed and I swopped with her.

---

9   Young women, girls, who become pregnant while at school or college, are required to leave.
10 Ingutsheni is a hospital for mentally disturbed patients outside Bulawayo; Mpilo is a general hospital in the city.

When I was at Ingutsheni, I made a name for myself. Doctors would phone me to say, 'We understand you did well on Case A and B. Wouldn't you take this one?' I would do so. But that drew a lot of hate from my colleagues, because they were senior, but not offered this opportunity. Some cases would be snatched from their hands and transferred to me, and this did not go down well, but I had to accommodate them. I was also volunteering and doing counselling in the evenings. I encouraged my colleagues to do the same, counselling [had been] my stepping stone. They didn't do so. Even when there were visitors, I was one of the people to take them around. One day, the superintendent, Dr Dube-Ndebele, called me to her office, she said, 'I just wanted to see who this Moyo is.' I said, 'But why?' She said, 'Ah, you never know.' Later on, she told me, 'You're doing the hospital proud, please keep it up'.

I continued there until 1998. My head of department was Mr Francis, an expatriate, he recommended that I should head an Acute Department, but the person supposed to be my subordinate was my senior. This did not go down well with the rehab techs, so I had to request to be placed under her, but I promised that all the programmes, which I had initiated, would continue. She had already been informed that she was supposed to be my subordinate, so she had an attitude, but I managed to cope. One day she said, 'Mr Moyo, you're great. I never thought [it would be so easy].' And, from then, she would just push all the jobs to me, and I would just perform.

But one day we had a confrontation that I cannot forget. She wanted to pick some maize somewhere, and she took patients to assist her. It was during the time when we were supposed to be having sessions with the clients, and I said her behaviour was an abuse of patients. And, really, we had to go over that and she gave in. So, for some time, we didn't go well with each other, until it all fizzled out. Even today I respect her like my mother-in-law and she respects me like her son-in-law. I enjoyed working at Ingutsheni really, it was tremendous.

I had been there for over three years, I had had one or two job offers but I liked it and wanted to stay. It was then that Shari Eppel approached me and said, 'Uh-uh, JJ, many psychologists are referring me to you. We are starting an organisation dealing with torture survivors [Amani Trust]. Would you be comfortable to join us, if you make the grade?' I said, 'Really, I will be willing. I have always wished to do something for such people.' Finally, she asked me whether I had a Class 4 driver's licence, and I said, 'No, but by Friday I will have a learner's licence.' Then she laughed.

They came down to Bulawayo to interview me, and the first thing that happened was that Tony Reeler offered to make me a cup of tea; I thought, 'Uh-uh, the big boss making a cup of tea for such a minor. Let me accept in case I do not pass this interview. At least let me come out with a cup of tea made by the boss.' I got both the tea and the job! I just took leave and joined them right away. I resigned whilst I was on leave, but Ingutsheni Hospital rejected the resignation letter and demanded that I resume work. So I said, I had better be punished. What I am doing is what I like most. I am dealing with torture survivors and I am one myself. As a result, I just accepted the penalties[11] and I remained with Amani. I liked working for Amani, and I still like it and I still wish I could do something for it, but unfortunately it has closed its doors.[12] But, in any case, I enjoyed myself a lot.

I joined in 1998. And by 1999 we began to look at people suffering from this current violence: it was not easy, because we also became targets. By then, I was the programme manager and one of the targets of the CIOs.[13] There were times when I would even risk my life to go and take photographs of burnt houses and so on. Once, in 2000, when I had just returned to Bulawayo, I saw people fleeing. I realised the MDC offices were burning.[14] I went back to my car and I took my camera and went to take some photos. I did this very fast and then left. Then one young man came running and said, 'Sir, you are from which stable?' I said, 'Be specific'. He said, 'Are you from the Chronicle, the Daily? What are you?' And I said, 'Uhuh, I am not any of those, I am just myself.' He said, 'What is your interest, then?' And he produced his ID card. Oh! A constable! Ah … I had a hard time. We went to the CID department, at Magnet House. Oh! I went through grilling! Then, I was taken to the Central Police Station. Oh! I had a hard time! They interrogated me but they never laid a hand on me. They threatened me with electric shocks. They said that as I was taking pictures of the MDC office burning, I must be the one who was sub-contracted to take the pictures of Cain Nkala[15] when he was murdered. They said, 'We won't let you go until you show us the pictures or the video of the

---

11 If you don't serve the statutory notice period, there is a financial penalty

12 In August 2002, Dr Frances Lovemore, medical director of Amani Trust, was arrested on the grounds that the Trust was guilty under POSA (the Public Order and Security Act) and the offices were raided by the police. In November 2002, the Minister of Justice, Legal and Parliamentary Affairs published a list of NGOs which he claimed were a threat to peace and security in Zimbabwe. Amani Trust appeared under this list. In January 2003, Amani Trust received threats that their offices would be petrol bombed.

13 16th November, 2001. 'The police … stood by as the 100-strong mob threw petrol bombs into the building housing the MDC offices, and prevented fire-fighters putting out the blaze' (*Guardian*, 17 November 2001).

14 Cain Nkala was a war veteran allegedly responsible for the abduction and murder of Patrick Nabanyama, an MDC election agent. It was rumoured that when he was brought to trial, he had threatened to expose those at a senior level who had ordered Patrick Nabanyama's disappearance. On 6th November, 2001, Nkala himself was abducted, and subsequently found dead. Many MDC activists were then charged with his murder (see p. 30, n. 8, and p. 31, n. 10).

15 Infiltration by the police is very damaging. Not only does it further endanger victims of violence as we see, for example, from both Sithandiwe Musi's and Sidumiso Moyo's stories, but it creates suspicion and anxiety among colleagues who are working together.

death of Cain Nkala.' I said 'No ways.' They really interrogated me, telling me that I would be treated by my colleagues after they had tortured me. The order was that they should lock me up. They took away the camera. Finally someone said, 'Let's let this man go. He won't run away. Let him come back tomorrow.' The next day, my director organised for a lawyer and one trustee, Archbishop Pius Ncube, to come with me to the police station, and this angered the police. They told Pius off. They told the lawyer off. When the lawyer asked what law they were charging me under and whether taking photographs had become a crime in Zimbabwe, they told him, 'There is no law. The only law that is working at the present moment is the POSA,' and that they could charge him under POSA because he was interfering with police investigations. They started insulting Pius and scolding the lawyer. Eventually, I said, 'Really, I wish you to go and leave me alone. I will see how things go.'

What followed was some slight interrogation, and then they said they wanted to see the pictures. I saw an expatriate coming from the cells, saying, 'We didn't know it was a crime to take pictures in Zimbabwe. We have been taking photographs in Victoria Falls, and when we came to Bulawayo we did the same.' And they said, 'Who told you the MDC offices were going to be burnt? How come you are there on time?' They took us to the Photo Inn where the film was processed and they destroyed the pictures that contained the MDC offices burning. I had photographed some houses that had been burnt here, in Bulawayo, but this Sergeant Nsingo left them alone, and only destroyed the pictures of the offices burning. After that, I was warned that they were monitoring me and if I was found near anything [provocative], I would be in for it.

Over the following week, they kept phoning me on my cellphone pretending to be clients. So I would say, 'I am in my rural home, Gwanda. I am on leave.' Finally this Nsingo came to my house in Bulawayo and demanded to see me. Luckily, I had just gone to look for sugar and mealiemeal. So they told my wife that they would get in touch with me on Monday. So I phoned my director and said, 'Things are bad. I would like to go off for three days. I think they want to detain me.' I went to my rural home, and remained there until Wednesday. Then I met my colleagues and I told them how I was feeling. I said, 'Maybe the only thing to do is to meet this Nsingo – not at the police station but in a public place and I would like to have some of you with me.' My colleagues could not agree because then they could be identified, but they said they would keep a vigilant eye, so that should I be abducted, they would straightaway phone others. So I agreed to meet this CIO at the Wimpy bar. He started discussing all the Amani Trust activities, which they'd heard about from Harare and enquired what we were doing in Bulawayo. I said, 'We do counselling across the spectrum: marriage problems, the lot.' Then came the unexpected he said, 'There's a feeling that you are a good guy and we would like to offer you employment.' I said, 'What employment?' He said, 'We would like you to get into the MDC and ZANU(PF) and help spy for us.' He was trying to appear as if the CIO was neutral and that all he was concerned about was issues of violence. But, of course, he was trying to use me to get into Amani. I replied that for me to attend any political meeting is a non-starter. I told him that clients, whom I have counselled, might come from either camp and, if they see me attending the opposition's meetings, they will think, 'Uh-uh, he's a liar. He's not neutral.' We talked at length and then he let me go, still saying, 'Think about it.' Strangely, that very afternoon, a phone call came in. It was a police officer. He said his boss wanted to meet me at eight o'clock the following morning, and he gave me a name and the number of an office. I replied, 'I am only inches away from your office. Let me come now.' (I thought it would be best to catch them before they were prepared.) They said, 'No, no, no.' I said, 'Uh-uh, I'm coming.' They said, 'OK, come.'

I went to the Central Police Station. I searched for the office. There was confusion. Some people told me that there was no one there. Someone else said that person knocks off at twelve. His juniors told me that the office was not functional. They wanted to know who phoned me. They said, 'No, we don't have a police cadre by that name.' So, I scrolled down the numbers on my cellphone, and asked, 'Where is this phone number coming from then?' It was a land-line; it belonged to their boss! So they phoned him, and he asked them to come up, and they cooked a story. They said that one of my colleagues had given them my cell number because they wanted to contact Mr Sibanda, a colleague, over a theft case. I said, 'A theft case! You're joking!' I thought, 'Maybe they've detained Sibanda already, and this was their way of telling me.' Then, just three minutes after I'd left the station, I received another phone call. It was this CIO, Nsingo, who said, 'There is something fishy happening. I was told that I'm in charge of looking into Amani Trust, but now, without consulting me, they contact you people.'

I went straight to Dumi Sibanda's house. He was not there. I left a message for him to contact me. I wanted to caution him that he was now also in trouble. The following day, the CIO phoned Amani to say, 'We want Dumi Sibanda.' They interrogated him heavily and they threatened him with torture. They accused him of helping MDC cadres, of being in charge of safe houses. He was devastated. He was badly affected. He was told that if he doesn't want to die, he should report on us by a certain date, that they wanted certain files. They also offered him a role as a spy. He was shaken. He was white with fear. Then we took him to South Africa and life went on.[16]

---

16 Infiltration by the police is very damaging. Not only does it further endanger victims of violence as we see, for example, from both Sithandiwe Musi's and Sidumiso Moyo's stories, but it creates suspicion and anxiety among colleagues who are working together.

***

I had numerous phone calls, but I managed because I never turned up. At times I would agree that I was coming, and I wouldn't turn up. I would turn off my cellphone, sometimes for a week, and I wouldn't sleep at home, and so on. Unfortunately, at this time, with Amani officially closed, I am not able to say very much. However Amani's brief was, and is, to provide health services to the victims of political torture – beatings with barbed wire, sticks, gun butts, whips, and those who have had electrical shocks to the genitals, tongue, rape by war vets and youth militia, destruction of homes and property. You should know that Amani was established in 1994. Its aim was to provide counselling to people who had been tortured in the liberation war and during Gukurahundi, those who had not recovered, but we have been taken over by this current wave of violence.

I had a lot of encounters, where it felt threatening. In 1999, for example, when we were doing exhumations [to uncover the remains of people killed during Gukurahundi], the CIOs arrived and stopped us. We argued with them and they wanted to take our director to Gwanda. In the end, both of us went. As we left, they said, 'Your colleagues can continue.' One policeman said, 'Ah! Man, the bones are exposed, already. Let them continue.' So whilst we were in Gwanda, the exhumations were taking place. On the following day, when they said we must stop, the bones were already exposed.

The following day I returned to the police with the IDs of the Argentinians.[17] Everything was recorded. I had a meeting with the Police Commissioner, who was very supportive of the programme and wanted it to continue. Then we made another appointment, when I brought in our director, Shari Eppel. We had tea. The commissioner said he had written two reports about our exhumations and how the police force is benefiting because a lot of people had reported that they had discovered bones – the remains of those who were killed in 1983, '84, by the Fifth Brigade, but the police hadn't known what to do. Now they had a solution. However, the Minister of Home Affairs, and the Registry department, would not budge; the CIOs would not budge. They did not want us to do these exhumations. So we had all those problems and they were an eye-opener to me.

***

The war in the seventies meant that armed men were pitted against each other, each fighting for a particular cause, so the people in the middle were bound to split. Some would support one side, some the other. When the army pounced on people, they said, for example, 'Your son has crossed into Zambia for military training, and you did not report it. Now we have got the information for ourselves and we are burning

---

17 Exhumation experts.

your homesteads down.' But, in most cases, they wouldn't assault the whole village. They would deal with the family, and in most cases the Rhodesian forces would take the head of the family away to prison, or whatever.

On the other hand, when somebody was said to have 'sold out', when a family was said to have been liaising with the Rhodesians, or supportive of the Rhodesian Front, those guerrillas, who were waging the liberation war, would pounce on that family. They wouldn't touch the kids. They would only deal with one or two people, or burn the whole homestead down, but they would spare other lives. But when it came to the Fifth Brigade, after independence, that was savage. That was beyond human thinking. It was really savage. Even an unborn child, one within its mother's womb, would be labelled a dissident and would be wanted dead. And the rape that took place was something else. Gukurahundi remains the worst of all the violence in Zimbabwe. The number of deaths, of rapes, of tortured victims, the denial of rights, all this was imposed on these [Ndebele] communities. Most dissidents were not armed and their number, vis-à-vis the state, was very, very few.[18] Some dissidents took advantage and might have terrorised people using fake guns and so on – because that was that situation. It killed the spirit in people. The repression crossed all sectors: education, natural resources, health, all state resources. Matabeleland was denied and is still denied full access to these resources, right up to today.

Now, I see a trend, it's as if the tactics of Fifth Brigade have persisted. If the state forces target an area, they don't mind if you are on the wanted list or not. They react in a ruthless manner. They focus on the area rather than on the individual. They target a whole village. I feel the very same perpetrators are building up to something that is similar to the eighties – now, today, because Amani has been recording incidents of violence, which is why the government wants us closed down.

∗∗∗

What we are seeing now is the issue of MDC. It doesn't even have a military wing, but it's being targeted in the same way as they targeted ZAPU, and ZAPU had a military wing. Of course, they were disarmed by then, and even the ZIPRA leadership denounced the dissidents. Nkomo was saying, 'No way can a black person fight a black person. The war has been won. The whites have been defeated. A system was fought, and it has been overthrown. Now, no brother can fight another brother. We are all brothers now that we have attained independence; we cannot fight each other.' People were offering themselves in Nkomo's house, wanting to go and fight, but he said 'No'. Dissidents, and there were few, were not supported by ZAPU.

So, if you look at the activities of the dissidents, there was no coordination; not even amongst themselves. Nobody knew where each group was. Only a few groups

---

18 When the Unity Accord was declared in 1987, and an amnesty was arranged for dissidents, there were only 122 who came forward.

met during their operations. The people in the middle, unarmed people, were vulnerable, and they suffered the most. Even the dissidents did not suffer like the people suffered. No. No. Dissidents would come into an area, and barely an hour or two later, the soldiers would be there, claiming that people cooked for the dissidents, knowing the number of dissidents, even knowing the names of the people who served the dissidents, and they would pounce on them. So, to my mind, there were genuine dissidents, and there were others. We saw the state dramatising events, and the very same thing is happening today. Then the dissidents were the alleged enemy, and became the means by which the state could target ZAPU, former ZIPRAs and, by extension, the Ndebele people. Today, the MDC is the 'enemy' and by extension anyone who appears not to support the ZANU(PF) government. From my point of view, these people – war vets, youth militia – find benefit in doing these things. They are given a lot of incentives for doing what they're doing and they are competing to do their worst. To fail means a certain withdrawal of privileges.

On the other hand, there is this component of unity, nationwide, that the MDC has achieved.[19] And [ZANU] are desperate to make sure that this unity does not hold, so they preach their own unity, which is non-existent. We have a regime that is playing with ideas and twisting things to confuse people, and they will do so as long as they're alive. And that means the suffering continues. And that is really the dead end of this road.

I have met a lot of victims, who now say that they would like to inflict equal pain on the perpetrators. Some are crying to be trained militarily. However, military training was not and is not possible, and this is to ZANU's advantage. The government controls everything.

To make matters worse, since we closed our offices and ceased operation, I have gone through a lot of problems, personally. You know, people present themselves to me; they want assistance, and there is very little that I can do because, in the first place, I have to prove to them that we are, in fact, closed. Second, there are my colleagues, who would like to know that everybody is playing it in the way we have agreed. So that makes it very difficult even to see a torture survivor and say, 'You can get assistance this way,' because your own colleagues will say, 'How did you give that person this information?' and if you say, 'I put it across this way,' some might still say, 'No, no, no, you are betraying us.' So this is the state of indecision and the fear that we live with now that we are no longer operational. Just to be seen anywhere near torture survivors, might have problems. To give an example, I approached a client who wanted to testify during a church service for torture survivors: Prayers for Peace. This girl – a militia girl – agreed to testify, and she did. She named the abusers, those people who used to rape them whilst they were at a ZANU(PF) militia camp

---

19 The MDC embraces Shona, Ndebele, black, white, Coloured, and across classes, ages and cultures.

in Jairos Jiri, Burnside. After that, of course, we had to hide her – the CIOs were all over.

But my colleagues – I still feel perplexed about their attitude and at the time I was very emotional, very upset – claimed that I shouldn't have agreed to that girl testifying. But she wanted to. But they still say I shouldn't have agreed because it's so dangerous, and is putting everybody in danger. But we've been doing dangerous work for years, why should being closed make a difference? They also claimed that she'd already gone through a lot and that testifying has disturbed her rehabilitation. They say I didn't inform them that she was going to testify, but she only agreed to do so a few hours before the service.

You know, there were a lot of people who wanted to testify, but we had to cut it to a few people and we had to prioritise, we had to say, 'This is a healing process.' The service was an eye-opener to a lot of people who didn't know what was happening. Of course, the government doesn't want these things to be known; and now my colleagues also don't want this torture known. I am in a dilemma. My own colleagues are afraid, and they are making their fears a reality by demanding that I should do my work as they feel I should, and not as the circumstances demand. Really, I find myself in dilemma and powerless. Yes, I am disempowered. I would like to say it, you know.

The main problem is that all these people that I have met still have a lot of deep-seated anger. This can be misdirected, because the perpetrator cannot be faced. They still feel that some day they have to meet the perpetrator, or they have to be compensated by the perpetrator, and right now they don't have a voice to face the perpetrators. You know, should the perpetrator move from this monstrous position to a level where questions can be asked and answers obtained, or a certain justice done, a lot of people will get satisfaction and relief, a reasonable healing will take place. That's how I see it. And, personally, as a torture victim, that's how I feel.

11

Mehlomakhulu Dox[1]

I was born in Gwanda in 1969, in Wenlonk Nqameni Tribal Trust Land, *Inqama elophondo*, which means a 'ram with horns', within an area called Sitezi not far from the primary school of the same name. I grew up there, with my family: my father, my mother, my grandma, my grandfather; and they were all God-fearing people. Unfortunately all of them are late now. My grandfather was a pastor and my grandmother supported him very much. They were members of the Brethren in Christ Church (BIC) and were leading the Church. As a result my siblings and me attended the same church and grew up observing Christian values.

Our family is a very big family, my siblings were all raised in that one family, that is: my cousins, my nieces and nephews. We were about fifteen children in all. Just one large family and my mother took care of us all.

Just like any other traditional set up, whereby the father is the breadwinner so it was my father who was fending for the family; he was a teacher by profession. My mother lived with my grandfather and grandmother since my father was away at work, and my aunties were also working elsewhere.

It was a happy family because my mother was a master farmer, so she spent most of her time in the fields with my grandfather assisting her. She grew maize, sorghum *(amabele)*, sweet potatoes, groundnuts, round nuts *(indlubu)* a lot of melons and pumpkins, and beans *(indumba)*. We used to harvest a lot of those. We would cook the *indumba* leaves and dry them to make dried vegetables *(umfushwa)*, which largely contributed to our relish. A good relish is often problematic in rural areas but we always enjoyed one made from *indumba* beans.

We also kept a lot of goats because they thrive in Region 5, and the vegetation is just so good for goat production because of the *isinga /umlaladwayi*, a thorn tree mostly found in the dry regions. Goats enjoy those leaves as well as those of

---

1 The author has chosen to remain anonymous.

umtshatshatsha, typical trees often found in the dry areas of Matabeleland South. Goats often give birth to twins or triplets, so you find that people in my area have a lot of goats. It used to be a great task to separate the kids from the mother goat. They never wanted to leave their mother, but we had to separate them because of the hyenas. When they went to feed in the bush, the hyenas and jackals could easily prey on the young kids.

Things became difficult during the war in the seventies. I was young by then (*sighs*), but you know, the war disturbed everything, because, when it started, I was doing Grade 3, and the schools in our home area had to close down. Since my father was a teacher, he came and took us away, together with my younger siblings, to continue with our education at Filabusi District, where he was heading one of the schools there. My older brothers went to school in Bulawayo.

Things were not rosy during that era, because when we were in class we would hear gunshots, and would sometimes see a troop of soldiers in big trucks driving into the school, and they would ask us when we last saw their opponents. I remember one day when we were in the playground, the guerrillas and soldiers clashed just near the school. I saw fire flashing in the air. I guess those were bullets. The teachers ordered us to lie down, we did so, and this continued for about an hour, eventually it calmed down and we ran to our classrooms. Fortunately no one was hurt. On that day we dismissed early fearing for our lives. Eventually the school closed in around 1979.

A couple of schools in Filabusi were functional during that period because the guerillas would use the teachers to source clothes for them in the form of jean trousers and shirts. The fact that we were staying in the teachers' cottage would see them giving my father a list of items to bring them on pay day from Bulawayo. I am not sure whether they were giving him cash to buy or not, but he used to go to Bulawayo to buy their staff.

One could safely say it was their money because those orders were very huge. Also the guerillas could step into any shop and demand cash. Sometimes they would loot a shop and leave it just empty. Gwatemba store on the Masvingo highway was looted and eventually they burnt down the store. It was one of the biggest shops in Filabusi that served the community. The guerrillas collected the cash from the till and they asked the community to loot everything from the store. Then they burnt down the store. No one was killed, since they were ordered to vacate the store prior to the looting. The remains of that store still stand up today: a very sad story.

When independence came people were very excited for the happy Zimbabwe, happy to gain their freedom at last. Little did they know that there was going to be a second phase of their suffering in the 'dissident era'. Freedom meant that things were going to normalise since most of the stores were closed during the war. Community survived through barter trade, since there were no shops. Only those families whose children were working in the city of Bulawayo or Gwanda had access to those essential commodities such as cooking oil, sugar, soap, etc. and the community would do barter trade to access such items. The spirit of sharing kept the community surviving until independence in 1980. At my home place stores were not burnt but were shut down and often vandalised by hooligans. In every society hooligans will always be there, so we cannot rule them out.

When the schools reopened I proceeded to Grade 4 and I went up to Grade 7. Then I went to Mtshabezi High School, a boarding school situated about 40 km away from Gwanda town. This was in 1984. The school is run by Brethren in Christ Church and has two institutions nearby, Ekuphileni Bible Institute and Mtshabezi Hospital.

I started Form 1 at Mtshabezi, in 1984. We were really enjoying school – just being a boarder was exceptionally good and exciting. If your parents send you to a boarding school, you say, 'Ha, they have done me a great favour'.

You know the rural set up, if you are at home, as a girl child, you don't have time to concentrate on school books, you have to herd cattle, gather firewood, fetch water, that's the order of the day, when you come from school, there are a lot of house chores. These are not avoidable; they are part and parcel of growing up in the rural areas. Also, there is no electricity, not even solar – it wasn't there during our times. So, when you are sent to a boarding school, that's when you have that feel of a town life. Because there is electricity, there is tap water, there is just everything at your fingertips. So going to a boarding school was really a pleasure. We enjoyed that.

Parents would only send you to a boarding school if they knew you are intelligent, because such schools are expensive. If you don't work hard and prove to them that you have got brains, you don't go to boarding school, instead they send you to an 'Upper Top', day schools offering secondary education. Going to an upper top wasn't good, because learning was compromised when compared to a boarding school. Of course, some students would pass, but not many, maybe in Form 4 classes, you will find five or six children passing – so even the level of education wasn't that good. Often the teachers that were sent to those upper tops were not trained. Most of them were just temporary teachers, and most were not secondary school teachers, they were primary-trained schoolteachers. Government would just retrieve teachers from primary schools, and deploy them to secondary school. So the pass rate in those upper tops wasn't good. As a result parents would struggle to send their children to boarding schools, to run away from those upper tops.

In 1984 while I was doing my Form 1, I had a taste of Gukurahundi. We used to have our supper at quarter to five in the boarding school, and before that we would go for a bath after the day's activities; then we could go to the dining room for supper. As we were bathing, we heard men shouting in big voices and those were the soldiers in red berets – the *gukurahundi* soldiers. I was just from the bathroom, half dressed. In a boarding school, you know, it is just girls in their own dormitories and boys in theirs, the separation is very pronounced. So in our dormitories we could be very free because we were just girls: running half naked from one dormitory to the other was very common. Our bathrooms were within our dormitory separated by a long passage, with a main entrance of a glass door that was mostly left open.

So when I just peeped down the passage, those soldiers were standing in front of the main entrance of the dormitory. We could see them in the corridor while we were running to our beds to get dressed.

The soldiers were shouting, ordering all of us to get out of the dormitory. It was chaotic, because it was a sudden command. Frightened, we quickly ran out and they ordered us to the girls dining hall, which was a stone's throw away from the dormitory.

At the same time, other soldiers were doing the same thing in the boys' dormitories and ordering the boys to their dining room. When we got to our dining room, they had a list of names; I don't know where they got that list from. They called up all the big girls and they just took them away. If you tried to resist, they would clap you. They were very fierce.

Since most of the students at the school were locals, I guess they got the list from the community. The community fearing for their lives would say anything since Gukurahundi soldiers were very aggressive. Remember, the community had just lived through the war era when some people were labelled sell-outs. I'm sure this was what was happening in giving the names to the Gukurahundi soldiers. Also, sending children to a boarding school was envied by many and this caused some jealousy. So whenever the community saw soldiers, they would just say anything, anything, just to protect themselves.

So, they, the Gukurahundi had this list of names. They did not get it from the school or from the school head. Then those soldiers, they took those girls and boys away from the school. There were about eight girls; and the soldiers didn't even care if they were being disturbed in their learning. They didn't give a damn.

Those boys and girls came back after some three to four days. Prior to resuming their lessons they were sent to Mtshabezi Hospital where they were examined and received some counseling. I suspect the girls were raped. Dr Boyd was in charge of the hospital, so he took care of them. Then, after some time, they came back to school, but they never shared anything with us. I don't know whether they shared something with the matron, but (*sighs*)… I was only in Form 1, and those girls were doing Form 4.

As for the boys, ah, I think they disappeared for a week, I don't know what really happened, but they came back. They came back, but some said they were beaten. The soldiers, they needed information from them, because the soldiers said that there were dissidents in the community. The soldiers were saying that our parents were harbouring dissidents, so they wanted information about them; they wanted information about where the dissidents had put those AK-47s. They were looking for those guns. The Gukurahundi soldiers would employ any strategy to get information from any one. Probably those big girls suffered because they suspected that they were in love with the dissidents, they said that those dissidents would have been getting food from their homes. They saw the boys as king informants, *imjibha*.

But, ah, we never saw them, the so-called dissidents. Gukurahundi soldiers were looking for those dissidents from our community, our mothers were beaten up because they were said to be feeding those dissidents who were said to be doing a lot of havoc. So the soldiers were saying the whole of our district was populated with dissidents, so they wanted to eliminate all of them and retrieve all the guns that they had escaped with. So Gukurahundi was very brutal.

The incident of taking those boys and girls away from school traumatised us. We were much disturbed, and wondered who was next. This did not end there. A series of rallies were conducted whereby they would address the community at business centres and they imposed a curfew from 6 p.m. to 6 a.m. One day, they ordered the whole school to a rally at Wabayi business centre. They used their big trucks to ferry us there. There was no food, no water, nothing. We spent the whole day chanting slogans, '*phansi lababulali*', literally meaning 'down with the killers'. They were saying the dissidents are dragging down the peace and tranquility that they, the red berets, had fought for.

On that particular day, no one was harassed, but they were addressing us on and on. We were made to listen to them saying a lot of things about the so-called dissidents; then we were made to sing, and after that they took us back in their trucks to school. And this was not the only rally; they took us again to Wabayi, to Mtshazo to Sitezi, to Vumbachigwe – often places that were far from the school.

The most disturbing thing at that time was the curfew, 6 to 6, so if they found you outside those times, you would be in very big trouble, 6 to 6, no movement. The most horrifying thing … I don't want to think about this … they came to our homestead to find my mother; she was in a big house, so when my family saw them coming, my grandfather and my grandmother instructed my mother to stay inside. So, my grandmother came out and approached them with my grandfather, and they [the red berets] the Gukurahundi asked them about the dissidents. My grandmother said they didn't know anything. They then said why have you locked the rooms. Who is inside? Then my grandmother told them, my daughter-in-law. Then the soldier said, 'Take her out'. My grandmother refused. She just laid down on the ground and said to them, if you want kill me go ahead but don't touch my family. Don't take my daughter-in-law. They shouted at my grandmother and told her that they were going to teach her a lesson, They started hitting her with big logs, they thoroughly beat her; then they took their long knife and cut her from the neck down her back. It was a terrible wound, and she was bleeding. My grandmother was very old by then. I think when they left her, they thought maybe she was dead, but she didn't die.

This is very hard to talk about … Then, during that evening, they took my grandfather and a lot of males from around the area, they beat them hard, very hard, and they took them to a place called Esikalini a long way from our home, near the dip tank. Then they told the men to dig a pit. Then they killed most men there. They shot them, and just put them in that pit. So my grandfather, they beat him hard, and when they saw that he was helpless, they also shoved him into that pit. Now, what my grandfather says is that when they were beginning to put back the soil on top of the bodies, and my grandfather – he was being put in that pit alive – so while he was in that pit and they were busy filling it up with sand, the army commander just came to him and said: Do you have children close by in Gwanda? My grandfather answered, 'Yes'.

So they just removed him from that pit. I don't know what saved him, maybe it was his God – he was a God-fearing man – but he just told us that one of them had mercy on him, and removed him. He said, 'You're an old man, you don't deserve to die here'. So he was put back in the same truck that had collected the majority of them – all men. They took him to Mtshabezi Hospital where he was treated by Dr Boyd, a white man who saved a lot of souls during that time.

Some people disappeared for ever we never saw them again.

***

Back at our homestead, my mother rescued my grandmother. She managed to get a scotch cart to take my grandmother to Mtshabezi hospital, and she was treated there. The wound on her back took a long time to heal and it remained a permanent scar, but we all know and we say, 'Hah, *gogo* was a hero'. She survived *gukurahundi*. But, her injuries were permanent. She was never as strong as she used to be, because of that beating and the cutting. She used to be very strong, a hard worker, she would work and fend for the family, but after that incident, her power was reduced. But she survived.

So our experience of *gukurahundi* was one month, yes, one month in 1984. I was fortunate. The soldiers never touched me. I was very young – they wanted the big girls and the big boys.

The soldiers they never came back. Even at home at Sitezi, it was hectic during that period, 1984, but after that they never came back. Up to now we have never heard anything more about those red beret soldiers.

I managed to complete my secondary education, proceeded to high school, and eventually enrolled at tertiary institutions. What was very disturbing in those tertiary days was that my college mates from the Shona-speaking side would refer to us as dissidents. They would call us all sorts of names. Division between Shona speaking and Ndebele speaking people will never die because of these experiences. Especially when they mention Gukurahundi because it did so much harm and no good.

People still bleed when Gukurahundi is mentioned. I remember in 2019 just before COVID, we were attending a funeral for Umfundisi Rev. Mabhena. The late Mabhena was very influential in trying to find reconciliation between the Ndebele and the Shona people because of this hatred that was perpetrated by Gukurahundi. He went to the extent of inviting the former President of Zimbabwe to Matabeleland to address the issue, and to at least apologise to the people of Matabeleland; that's when our former president made that statement that *gukurahundi* 'was a moment of madness'.

I was in that funeral, mourning our dearest Mfundisi Rev. Mabhena where a number of politicians graced the funeral and speaker after speaker was talking about Rev. Mabhena, and his boldness in seeking reconciliation but when the Governor of Matabeleland South, Angeline Masuku, took to the floor and told the mourners that Gukurahundi's intention was misinterpreted by the people of Matabeleland. She said that the Fifth Brigade was sent to restore peace and tranquility, since the dissidents were dragging down development in Matabeleland. This did not go well with the mourners. All the comrades told the govenor to sit down and shut up; that we were in a church and at a funeral.

The situation was very chaotic. The governor just turned the service into a political rally within the wink of an eye. Fortunately, the former President of the Mennonites, the Rev. D. Ndlovu, calmed the situation down. If he had not done that, there would have been a riot.

But, if you mention anything concerning *gukurahundi* in Matabeleland, people will react because it was a very very painful period. The people of Matabeleland are still bitter. If you want to touch their souls, talk about *gukurahundi* because, there are people who died and up to now, we don't know where they are buried or how they were buried. They disappeared. Their bones were never retrieved for proper burial. Money can't buy peace, it can't heal the wounded hearts. The loss of our beloved ones leaves a scar. Since then life has never been the same. People who were injured like my grandfather and grandmother, they never recovered properly.

Bibliography

Acemoglu, D., D. Ticchi, and A. Vindigni (2010). 'A Theory of Military Dictatorships', *American Economic Journal: Macroeconomics*, 2(1), pp. 1-42.

Adams, T.E., C. Ellis and S.H. Jones (2017). 'Autoethnography', in *The International Encyclopedia of Communication Research Methods*. Hoboken, NJ: John Wiley & Sons.

Alexander, J. (1998). 'Dissident Perspectives on Zimbabwe's Post-Independence War', *Africa: Journal of the International African Institute*, 68(2), pp. 151-182.

——— (2021). 'The Noisy Silence of Gukurahundi: Truth, Recognition and Belonging', *Journal of Southern African Studies*, 47(5), pp. 763-785.

——— and J. McGregor (2013). 'Introduction: Politics, Patronage and Violence in Zimbabwe', *Journal of Southern African Studies*, 39(4), pp. 749-763.

——— and J. McGregor (2017). 'African Soldiers in the USSR: Oral Histories of ZAPU Intelligence Cadres' Soviet Training, 1964–1979', *Journal of Southern African Studies*, 43(1), pp. 49-66.

——— and B.M. Tendi (2008). 'A tale of two elections: Zimbabwe at the polls in 2008', *ACAS Bulletin: Special Issue on the Zimbabwe Crisis*, 80, pp. 5-17.

———, J. McGregor and T. Ranger (2000). *Violence and Memory: One Hundred Years in the 'Dark Forests' of Matabeleland*. Oxford: James Currey.

Althusser, L. (1971). *Lenin and Philosophy and Other Essays*. London: New Left Books.

Amadiume, I. and A. An-Na'im (2000). *The Politics of Memory: Truth, Healing and Social Justice*. New York: Zed Books.

Amnesty International (2002). *Zimbabwe: Toll of Impunity*. London: Amnesty International.

Anderlini, S.N. (2011). 'World Development Report Gender Background Paper.' Washington, DC: World Bank.

Anderson, B. (2006). *Imagined Communities: Reflections on the Origin and Spread of Nationalism*. London: Verso Books.

Ansre, G. (1977). 'Four Rationalisations for Maintaining the European Languages in Education in Africa', *Kiswahili*, 47(2), pp. 55–61.

Antze, P. and M. Lambek (eds) (1996). *Tense Past: Cultural Essays in Trauma and Memory*. London: Routledge.

Arthur, P. (2009). 'How "transitions" reshaped human rights: a conceptual history of transitional justice', *Human Rights Quarterly*, 31(2), pp. 321-367.

Asakhe Films (2020). *I Want My Virginity Back: A Story of Rape during Gukurahundi*. A documentary film by Zenzele Ndebele.

Assmann, A. (2007). 'Europe: A community of memory?', *Bulletin of the GHI Washington*, 40, pp. 11-25.

Asuelime, L.E. (2018). 'A Coup or not a Coup: That is the Question in Zimbabwe', *Journal of African Foreign Affairs*, 5(1), pp. 5-24.

Auret, D. (1992). *Reaching for Justice: The Catholic Commission for Justice and Peace, 1972-1992*. Gweru: Mambo Press.

Bakker, C. (2005). 'A Full Stop to Amnesty in Argentina: The Simón Case', *Journal of International Criminal Justice*, 3(5), pp. 1106-1120.

Barahona de Brito, A., C. Gonzaléz-Enríquez and P. Aguilar (2001). *The Politics of Memory: Transitional Justice in Democratizing Societies*. Oxford: Oxford University Press.

Bassiouni, M.C. (2008). *International Criminal Law, Volume 1: Sources, Subjects and Contents*. Leiden: Brill Nijhoff.

Bell, C. (2000). *Peace Agreements and Human Rights*. Oxford: Oxford University Press.

Bellamy, A.J. (2010). 'The Institutionalisation of Peacebuilding: What Role for the UN Peacebuilding Commission?', in O. Richmond (ed.), *Palgrave Advances in Peacebuilding*. London: Palgrave Macmillan.

Berkeley, B. and E. Schrage (1986). *Zimbabwe, Wages of War: A Report On Human Rights*. New York: Lawyers Committee for Human Rights.

Berman, E.G. (2001). 'The International Commission of Inquiry (Rwanda): Lessons and Observations from the Field', *American Behavioral Scientist*, 45(4), pp. 616-625.

Bhattacharyya, G. (2008). *Dangerous Brown Men: Exploiting Sex, Violence and Feminism in the 'War on Terror'*. London: Zed Books.

Bhebe, N. and T. Ranger (eds) (1995). *Soldiers (vol 1) and Society (vol 2) in Zimbabwe's Liberation War*. University of Zimbabwe Publications.

Bilali, R., Y. Iqbal and S. Freel (2020). 'Understanding and Counteracting Genocide Denial', in L.S. Newman (ed.), *Confronting Humanity at its Worst: Social Psychological Perspectives on Genocide*. Oxford: Oxford University Press.

Blair, D. (2002). *Degrees in Violence: Robert Mugabe and the struggle for power in Zimbabwe*. London: Continuum.

Boesten, J. (2014). *Sexual Violence During War and Peace: Gender, Power and Post-Conflict Justice in Peru*. New York: Palgrave Macmillan.

Boot, M. (2002), 'Nullum crimen sine lege and the subject matter jurisdiction of the International Criminal Court: genocide, crimes against humanity, war crimes'. Doctoral thesis, Tilburg University.

Boraine, A.L. (2006). 'Transitional Justice: A Holistic Interpretation', *Journal of*

International Affairs, 60(1), pp. 17-27.

―――, J. Levy and D. Tutu (1997). *Dealing with the Past: Truth and Reconciliation in South Africa*. Cape Town: IDASA Publications.

Bourdieu, P. (1991). *Language and Symbolic Power*. Cambridge: Polity Press.

Bowring, B. (2014). 'The Russian Language in Ukraine: Complicit in Genocide, or Victim of State-Building?', in L. Ryazanova-Clarke (ed.), *The Russian Language outside the Nation*. Edinburgh: Edinburgh University Press.

Bratton, M. and E. Masunungure, (2008). 'Zimbabwe's Long Agony', *Journal of Democracy*, 19(4), pp. 41-55.

Brounéus, K. (2008). 'Analyzing reconciliation: A structured method for measuring national reconciliation initiatives', *Peace and Conflict: Journal of Peace Psychology*, 14(3), pp. 291-31.

Caldas-Coulthard, C.R. (2003). 'Cross-cultural representation of "otherness" in media discourse', in G. Weiss and R. Wodak, *Critical discourse analysis*. London: Palgrave Macmillan.

Cameron, H. (2018). 'The Matabeleland massacres: Britain's wilful blindness', *The International History Review*, 40(1), pp. 1-19.

Carroll, E.C. (2013). 'Hybrid Tribunals are the Most Effective Structure for Adjudicating International Crimes Occurring Within a Domestic State', *Law School Student Scholarship*, 90.

Carver, R. (1989). *Zimbabwe a Break with the Past: Human Rights and Political Unity: An Africa Watch Report October 1989*. New York: Human Rights Watch.

――― (1993). 'Zimbabwe: Drawing a Line Through the Past', *Journal of African Law*, 37(1), pp. 69-81.

Cassese, A. (2003). *International Criminal Law*. Oxford: Oxford University Press.

Catholic Commission for Justice and Peace in Zimbabwe (CCJPZ) and Legal Resources Foundation (LRF) (1997) *Breaking the Silence, Building True Peace: A Report on the Disturbances in Matabeleland and the Midlands, 1980 to 1988*. Harare: CCJPZ and LRF.

Chappell, L. (2003). 'Women, Gender and International Institutions: Exploring New Opportunities at the International Criminal Court', *Policy and Society*, 22(1), pp. 3-25.

Chaumba, J., I. Scoones and W. Wolmer (2003). 'From Jambanja to Planning: the Reassertion of Technocracy in Land Reform in Southeastern Zimbabwe?' Brighton: Institute of Development Studies.

Chikwava, B. (2018). 'An interview with Novuyo Rosa Tshuma', *Wasafiri*, 33(2), pp. 46-49.

Chimhundu, H. (ed.) (1992). *Duramazwi reChiShona*. Harare: College Press.

Chiwome, E.M. (1996). *A Social History of the Shona Novel*. Gweru: Mambo Press.

Christiansen, L.B. (2005). 'Yvonne Vera: Rewriting discourses of history and identity in Zimbabwe', in R. Muponde and R. Primorac (eds), *Versions of Zimbabwe: New approaches to literature and culture*. Harare: Weaver Press.

Chung, F. (2006). *Re-living the Second Chimurenga. Memories from the Liberation Struggle in Zimbabwe*. Uppsala: Nordic Africa Institute.

Clandinin, D.J. and J. Rosiek (2007). 'Mapping a Landscape of Narrative Inquiry: Borderland Spaces and Tensions', in D.J. Clandinin (ed.), *Handbook of Narrative Inquiry: Mapping a Methodology*. Thousand Oaks: Sage Publications.

Clark, J.N. (2008). 'The three Rs: Retributive Justice, Restorative Justice, and Reconciliation', *Contemporary Justice Review*, 11(4), pp. 331-350.

Clark, P. (2009). 'Establishing a Conceptual Framework: Six Key Transitional Justice Themes', in P. Clark and Z.D. Kaufman (eds), *After Genocide: Transitional Justice, Post-Conflict Reconstruction & Reconciliation in Rwanda and Beyond*. New York: Columbia University Press.

Cole, M. (2014). 'The Language of Genocide and Human Rights: Naming, Judging, Acting'. The Kenan Institute for Ethics. Durham, NC: Duke University.

Coltart, D. (2016). *The Struggle Continues: 50 Years of Tyranny in Zimbabwe*. Auckland Park: Jacana Media.

——— (2018). 'After Mugabe: Mnangagwa's Choice', *Journal of Public Policy and Ideas*, 34(1), pp. 51-58.

Confino, A. (1997). 'Collective Memory and Cultural History: Problems of Method', *American Historical Review*, 102(5), pp. 1386-1403.

Corey, A. and S.F. Joireman (2004). 'Retributive Justice: The Gacaca Process in Rwanda', *African Affairs*, 103, pp. 73-89.

Crisis in Zimbabwe Coalition (CiZC) (2011). *The military factor in Zimbabwe's political and electoral affairs*. Harare: CiZC.

Curran, J. (1992). *Mass Media and Democracy Revisited*. London: Edward Arnold.

——— (1996). 'The New Revisionism in Mass Communication Research', in J. Curran, D. Morley and V. Walkerdine (eds), *Cultural Studies and Communication*. London: Edward Arnold.

——— and M. Gurevitch (1977). *Mass Media and Society*. London: Edward Arnold.

Dallaire, R. (2004). *Shake Hands with the Devil: The Failure of Humanity in Rwanda*. Toronto: Vintage Canada.

Delic, A. and E. Avdibegovic (2015). 'Shame and Silence in the Aftermath of War

Rape in Bosnia and Herzegovina: 22 Years Later', in H. Glaesmer and S. Lee (eds), *Interdisciplinary Perspectives on Children Born of War – from World War II to Current Conflict Settings*. Hannover: Conference Center of Schloss Herrenhausen.

Derrida, J. (1993). *Specters of Marx: The State of the Debt, the Work of Mourning and the New International*. New York: Routledge.

Devonish, H. (2010). 'The Language Heritage of the Caribbean: Linguistic Genocide and Resistance', *Glossa*, 5(1), pp. 2-3.

Diamond, L. (2008). 'Democracy in Retreat', *Real Clear Politics*, 17 March.

DioGuardi, S.C. (2016). 'Breaking the Protracted Silence about Genocidal Rape in Kosovo', in J. DiGeorgio-Lutz and D. Gosbee (eds), *Women and Genocide: Gendered Experiences of Violence, Survival, and Resistance*. Toronto: Women's Press.

Domingo, P., R. Holmes, A.R. Menochal and N. Jones (2013). 'Assessment of the Evidence of Links between Gender Equality, Peacebuilding and State building: Literature Review'. London: ODI.

Donohue, W.A. (2012). 'The Identity Trap: The Language of Genocide', *Journal of Language and Social Psychology*, 31(1), pp. 13-29.

Doran, S. (2017). *Kingdom, Power and Glory: Mugabe, ZANU, and the Quest for Supremacy, 1960-1987*. Midrand: Sithatha Media.

Dorman, S.R. (2016). *Understanding Zimbabwe: From Liberation to Authoritarianism*. London: Hurst.

Downing, J.D., A. Mohammadi and A. Sreberny (1995). *Questioning the Media – A Critical Introduction*. London: Sage.

Dube, A.B. (2015). 'Universal jurisdiction in respect of international crimes: Theory and practice in Africa'. PhD thesis, University of the Western Cape.

Dube, T. (2021). 'Gukurahundi Remembered: The Police, Opacity and the Gukurahundi Genocide in Bulilimamangwe District, 1982-1988', *Journal of Asian and African Studies*, 56(8), pp. 1848-1860.

Duggan, C. and R. Jacobson (2009). 'Reparation of Sexual and Reproductive Violence: Moving from Codification to Implementation', in R. Rubio-Marin (ed.) *The Gender of Reparations: Unsettling Sexual Hierarchies while Redressing Human Rights Violations*. Cambridge: Cambridge University Press.

Dzimiri, P., T. Runhare, C.T. Dzimiri and W. Mazorodze (2014). 'Naming, Identity, Politics and Violence in Zimbabwe', *Studies of Tribes and Tribals*, 12(2), pp. 227-238.

Einarsen, T. (2012). *The Concept of Universal Crimes in International Law*. Oslo: Torkel Opsahl Academic EPublisher.

Ellis, C., T.E. Adams and A.P. Bochner (2011). 'Autoethnography: An Overview', *Historical Social Research*, 36(4), pp. 273-290.

Ellis, R.W.J. (2006). *Without Honour*. Seattle: CreateSpace.

Elster, J. (2004). *Closing the Books: Transitional Justice in Historical Perspective*. Cambridge: Cambridge University Press.

Entman, R.M. (1993). 'Framing: Toward Clarification of a Fractured Paradigm', *Journal of Communication*, 43, pp. 51-58.

Eppel, S. (2004). '"Gukurahundi": The need for truth and reparation', in B. Raftopoulos and T. Savage (eds), *Zimbabwe: Injustice and Political Reconciliation*. Cape Town: Institute for Justice and Reconciliation.

――― (2008). 'Matabeleland: Its Struggle for National Legitimacy, and the Relevance of this in the 2008 Election', *Perspectives*, 2(8), pp.1-7.

――― (2013). 'Repairing a Fractured Nation: Challenges and Opportunities in Post-GPA Zimbabwe', in B. Raftopoulos (ed.), *The Hard Road to Reform: The Politics of Zimbabwe's Global Political Agreement*. Harare: Weaver Press.

――― (2014). '"Bones in the Forest" in Matabeleland, Zimbabwe: Exhumations as a Tool for Transformation', *International Journal of Transitional Justice*, 8(3), pp. 404-425.

――― and B. Raftopoulos (2009). *Developing a Transformation Agenda for Zimbabwe*. Cape Town: Idasa.

Fairclough, N. (1993). 'Critical Discourse Analysis and the Marketization of Public Discourse: The Universities', *Discourse & Society*, 4(2), pp. 133-168.

Fernandez, L. (1999). 'Reparations Policy in South Africa for the Victims of Apartheid', *Law, Democracy & Development*, 3(2), pp. 209-222.

Fischer, M. (2011). 'Transitional Justice and Reconciliation: Theory and Practice', in B. Austen, M. Fischer and H.J. Giessmann (eds), *Advancing Conflict Transformation. The Berghof Handbook II*. Opladen/Framington Hills: Barbara Budrich Publishers.

Fiske, J. (1987). *Television Culture*. London: Routledge.

Fontein, J. (2010). 'Between tortured bodies and resurfacing bones: The politics of the dead in Zimbabwe.' *Journal of Material Culture*, 15(4), pp. 423-448.

Fowler, R. (1991). *Language in the News: Discourses and Ideology in the Press*. London: Routledge.

Gavron, J. (2002). 'Amnesties in the Light of Developments in International Law and the Establishment of the International Criminal Court', *International and Comparative Law Quarterly*, 51(1), pp. 91-117.

Giblin, J. (2017). 'The Performance of International Diplomacy at Kigali Memorial Centre, Rwanda', *Journal of African Cultural Heritage Studies*, 1(1), pp. 49-67.

Giliomee, H. (2013). *The Last Afrikaner Leaders: A Supreme Test of Power*. Charlottesville, VA: University of Virginia Press.

Gomery, J.H. (2005). 'The Pros and Cons of Commissions of Inquiry', *McGill Law Journal*, (51), pp. 783-790.

Gottschall, J. (2004). 'Explaining Wartime Rape', *Journal of Sex Research*, 41(2), pp. 129-136.

Gramsci, A. (1971). *Selections from the Prison Notebooks of Antonio Gramsci*. Translated by Q. Hoare and G. Nowell-Smith. New York: International Publishers.

Graybill, L.S. (1999). 'South Africa's Truth and Reconciliation Commission: Ethical and Theological Perspectives', *Ethics & International Affairs*, (12), pp. 43-62.

Guduza, M. (n.d.). *Makhathini Bhekisizwe Guduza an autobiography*. Unpublished.

Gusha, I. (2019). 'Memories of Gukurahundi Massacre and the Challenge of Reconciliation', *Studia Historiae Ecclesiasticae*, 45(1), pp. 2-14.

Gwekwerere, T. and D. Mpondi (2018). 'Memory, identity and power in contemporary Zimbabwe: Movement for Democratic Change electoral narratives and Zimbabwe African National Union-Patriotic Front counter-discourses', *Africology: The Journal of Pan African Studies*, 12(3), pp. 3-23.

Hadebe, S. (2001). 'The songs of Lovemore Majayivana and Ndebele oral literature', in R.H. Kaschula (ed.), *African Oral Literature: Functions in Contemporary Contexts*. Cape Town: New Africa Books.

Halbwachs, M. (1992). *On Collective Memory*. Chicago and London: University of Chicago Press.

Hall, S. (1977, 1982) The Rediscovery of "ideology": Return of the Repressed in Media Studies', in M. Gurevitch, T. Bennett, J. Curran and J. Woollacott (eds), *Culture, Society and the Media*. London: Routledge.

―――― 'Race, Culture, and Communications: Looking Backward and Forward at Cultural Studies', *Rethinking Marxism*, 5(1), pp. 10-18.

Hansen, T.O. (2011). 'Transitional Justice: Toward a Differentiated Theory', *Oregon Review of International Law*, 13(1), pp. 1-46.

Harber, C. (1985). 'Weapon of War: Political Education in Zimbabwe', *Journal of Curriculum Studies*, 17(2), pp. 163-174.

Hardy, J. (2014). *Critical Political Economy of the Media: An Introduction*. New York: Routledge.

Harris, L.T. and S.T. Fiske (2009). 'Social Neuroscience Evidence for Dehumanised Perception', *European Review of Social Psychology*, 20(1), pp.192-231.

Hayner, P. (1994). 'Fifteen Truth Commissions – 1974-1994: A Comparative Study', *Human Rights Quarterly*, 16(4), pp. 597-655.

―――― (2001). *Unspeakable Truths: Confronting State Terror and Atrocity*. New York, London: Routledge.

Heller, K.J. (2017). 'What is an International Crime? (A Revisionist History)', *Harvard International Law Journal*, 58(2), pp. 353-420.

Helliker, K. and T. Murisa (2020). 'Zimbabwe: continuities and changes', *Journal of Contemporary African Studies*, 38(1), pp. 5-17.

Herman, E.S. and N. Chomsky (1988). *Manufacturing Consent: The Political Economy of the Mass Media*. New York: Pantheon Books.

Hirsch, M. (1992). 'Family Pictures: Maus, Mourning, and Post-Memory', *Discourse*, 15(2), pp. 3-29.

Hleza, E.S.K. (1991). *Uyangisinda Lumhlaba*. Gweru: Mambo Press.

Hodzi, O. (2012). 'Sexual Violence as a Political Strategy in Zimbabwe: Transitional Justice Blind Spot?' Oxford Transitional Justice Working Paper Series: Debates.

Human Rights Watch (1996). 'Shattered Lives: Sexual Violence During the Rwandan Genocide and its Aftermath'. New York: Human Rights Watch.

Huyse, L. (2003). 'Zimbabwe: Why Reconciliation Failed', in D. Bloomfield, T. Barnes and L. Huyse (eds), *Reconciliation After Violent Conflict: A Handbook*. Stockholm: International IDEA Publications.

International Criminal Court (ICC) (2011). *Elements of Crimes*. The Hague: ICC.

International Law Commission (ILC) (1996). *Commentary to Article 7 of the Draft Code of Crimes Against the Peace and Security of Mankind*.

——— (2017). *Chapter VII: Immunity of State Officials from foreign criminal jurisdiction*.

Janks, H. (1997). 'Critical Discourse Analysis as a Research Tool', *Discourse: Studies in the Cultural Politics of Education*, 18(3), pp. 329-342.

Jastromb, E. (2011). 'Facing History: Memory and Recovery in the Aftermath of Atrocity', *Penn State Journal of International Affairs*, 1(1), pp. 15-24.

Jessee, E. (2017). 'The danger of a single story: Iconic stories in the aftermath of the 1994 Rwandan genocide', *Memory Studies*, 10(2), pp. 144-163.

Jones, N., J. Cooper, E. Presler-Marshall and D. Walker (2014). 'The Fallout of Rape as a Weapon of War: The Life-long and Intergenerational Impacts of Sexual Violence in Conflict.' London: ODI.

Kalley, J.A., E. Schoeman and L.E. Andoret (1999). *Southern African Political History: A Chronology of Key Political Events from Independence to Mid-1997*. London: Greenwood.

Kasapas, G. (2008). 'An Introduction to the Concept of Transitional Justice: Western Balkans and EU Conditionality', UNISCI Discussion Papers No. 18.

Katz, I. (1991). 'Gordon Allport's "The Nature of Prejudice"', *Political Psychology*, 12(1), pp. 125-157.

Kayitana, E. (2017). 'Immunity Ratione Materiae of Foreign State Officials before Rwandan Courts', *Nnamdi Azikiwe University Journal of International Law and Jurisprudence*, 8(2), pp.161-173.

Khumalo, N.B. (2017). 'A Look at the Reasons Behind the Establishment of Movements Aimed at Resuscitating the Ndebele/ Mthwakazi Kingdom in Post-Colonial Zimbabwe', *Oral History Journal of South Africa*, 5(1), pp. 103-113.

────── (2018). 'Silenced genocide voices in Zimbabwe's archives: Drawing lessons from Rwanda's post-genocide archives and documentation initiatives', *Information Development*, 35(5), pp. 705-805.

Killander, M. and M. Nyathi (2015). 'Accountability for the Gukurahundi atrocities in Zimbabwe thirty years on: Prospects and Challenges', *The Comparative and International Law Journal of Southern Africa*, 48(3), pp. 463-487.

King, E. (2010). 'Memory Controversies in Post-Genocide Rwanda: Implications for Peacebuilding', *Genocide Studies and Prevention*, 5(3), pp. 293-309.

Kirby, S. and K. McKenna (1989). *Experience, Research, Social Change: Methods from the Margins*. Toronto: Garamond Press.

Kosicki, P.H. (2007). 'Sites of aggressor-victim memory: The Rwandan genocide, theory and practice', *International Journal of Sociology*, 37(1), pp. 10-29.

Kössler, R. (2007). 'Facing a Fragmented Past: Memory, Culture and Politics in Namibia', *Journal of Southern African Studies*, 33(2), pp. 361-382.

Kriger, N. (2003). *Guerrilla Veterans in Post-war Zimbabwe: Symbolic and Violent Politics, 1980-1987*. Cambridge: Cambridge University Press.

Kritz, N.J. (1995). *Transitional Justice: How Emerging Democracies Reckon with Former Regimes*. Washington, DC: USIP.

Lang, B. (2020). *Writing and the Moral Self*. London: Routledge.

Lederach, J.P. (1999). *The Journey Towards Reconciliation*. Scottdale, PA: Herald Press.

Leatherman, J.L. (2011). *Sexual Violence and Armed Conflict*. Cambridge: Polity Press.

Leebaw, B.A. (2008). 'The irreconcilable goals of transitional justice', *Human Rights Quarterly*, 30(1), pp. 95-118.

Lemkin, R. (1947). 'Genocide as a Crime under International Law', *The American Journal of International Law*, 41(1), pp. 145-151.

────── (1953). 'Nature of Genocide: Confusion with Discrimination against Individuals Seen'. *The New York Times*, 14 June.

Lin, A.M.Y. (2000). 'Bilingualism or Linguistic Segregation? Symbolic Domination, Resistance and Code Switching in Hong Kong Schools', in: D.S.C. Li, A.M.Y, Lin and W.K. Tsang (eds), *Language and Education in Postcolonial Hong Kong*. Hong Kong: Linguistic Society.

Lindgren, B. (2002). 'The Politics of Ndebele Ethnicity: Origins, Nationality and Gender in Southern Africa'. PhD thesis, Uppsala University.

——— (2005). 'Memories of Violence: Recreation of Ethnicity in Post-Colonial Zimbabwe', in: P. Richards (ed.), *No Peace No War: An Anthropology of Contemporary Armed Conflicts.* Oxford: James Currey.

Lyrefelt, J. (2020). 'Echoes of the past: The legacy of the Herero-Nama genocide in Namibia'. Master's thesis, Stockholm University.

Maciejczak, J. (2013). 'Sexual Violence as a Weapon of War'. Thesis, King's College London.

Maedl, A. (2011). 'Rape as a Weapon of War in the Eastern DRC? The Victims' Perspective', *Human Rights Quarterly,* 33(1), pp. 128-147.

Maedza, P. (2019). '"Gukurahundi – A moment of madness": Memory rhetorics and remembering in the postcolony', *African Identities*, 17(3-4), pp. 175-190.

Mafeza, F. (2013). 'Restoring Relationship between Former Genocide Perpetrators and Survivors of Genocide against Tutsi in Rwanda through Reconciliation Villages', *International Journal of Development and Sustainability*, 2(2), pp. 787-798.

Magagula, D.M. (1991). *Sasisemeveni.* Harare: Longman.

Malunga, S. (2021). 'The Killing fields of Matabeleland: An examination of the Gukurahundi genocide in Zimbabwe', *African Yearbook on International Humanitarian Law*, pp. 1-45.

——— (2022) 'Unpacking Gukurahundi Atrocities Against the Ndebeles of Zimbabwe: What Are the Possibilities for Individual Criminal Responsibility of the Perpetrators Under International Criminal Law?', in E.C. Lubaale and N. Dyani-Mhango (eds), *National Accountability for International Crimes in Africa.* London: Palgrave Macmillan.

Mamdani, M. (1996). *Citizen and Subject: Contemporary Africa and the Legacy of Late Colonialism.* Princeton, NJ: Princeton University Press.

——— (2001). *When Victims become Killlers: Colonialism, Nativism, and Genocide in Rwanda.* Princeton, NJ: Princeton University Press.

Mangena, T. (2019). *Contested Criminalities in Zimbabwean Fiction.* New York: Routledge.

Mani, R. (2002). *Beyond retribution: Seeking justice in the Shadows of War.* Cambridge: Polity Press.

Maringira, G. (2021). 'The Military Post-Mugabe', *Journal of Asian and African Studies*, 56(2), pp. 176-188.

——— (2017). 'Politicization and Resistance in the Zimbabwean National Army', *African Affairs,* 116(462), pp. 18-38.

Martin, D. and P. Johnson (1981). *The Struggle for Zimbabwe.* Harare: Zimbabwe

Publishing House.

Maseko, B. and P. Matunge (2020). 'Language Ideologies and Language Practices in Health Services: Patients' Experiences in Post-Colonial Zimbabwe', *Alternation - Interdisciplinary Journal for the Study of the Arts and Humanities in Southern Africa*, Special Edition, 36, pp. 335-358.

Mashingaidze, S. (2021). 'Robert Mugabe's Will to Power', *The Africa Governance Papers*, 1(1).

Mashingaidze, T.M. (2005). 'The 1987 Zimbabwe National Unity Accord and its Aftermath: A case of peace without reconciliation?', in C. Hendricks and L. Lushaba, *From National Liberation to Democratic Renaissance in Southern Africa*. Dakar: Codesria.

—— (2010). 'Zimbabwe's Illusive National Healing and Reconciliation Processes: From Independence to the Inclusive Government 1980–2009', *Conflict Trends*, 1, pp. 19-27.

Masunungure, E.V. (2011). 'Zimbabwe's Militarised Electoral Authoritarianism', *Journal of International Affairs*, 65(1), pp. 47-64.

Mazarire, G.C. (2017). 'ZANU's External Networks 1963-1969: An Appraisal', *Journal of Southern African Studies*, 43(1), pp. 83-106.

McAdams, A.J. (ed.) (1997). *Transitional Justice and the Rule of Law in New Democracies*. Notre Dame, IN: Notre Dame Press.

Meernik, J. (2005). 'Justice and Peace? How the International Criminal Tribunal affects Societal Peace in Bosnia', *Journal of Peace Research*, 43(3), pp. 271-287.

Meier, C. (2010). Das Gebot zu vergessen und die Unabweisbarkeit des Erinnerns: Vom öffentlichen Umgang mit schlimmer Vergangenheit. Munich: Siedler Verlag.

Meisenberg, S.M. (2004). 'Legality of amnesties in international humanitarian law: The Lomé Amnesty Decision of the Special Court for Sierra Leone', *Revue internationale de la Croix-Rouge/International Review of the Red Cross*, 856, pp. 837-851.

Meredith, M. (2002). *Mugabe: Power and Plunder in Zimbabwe*. Oxford: Public Affairs.

Mills, G. and G. Wilson (2007). 'Who dares loses? Assessing Rhodesia's Counter-Insurgency Experience', *The RUSI Journal*, 152(6), pp. 22–31.

Minow, M. (1998). *Between Vengeance and Forgiveness: Facing History after Genocide and Mass Violence*. Boston: Beacon Press.

Mlalazi, C. (2012). *Running with Mother*. Harare: Weaver Press.

Mhlanga, B. (2013). 'Ethnicity or tribalism? The discursive construction of Zimbabwean national identity', *African Identities*, 11(1), pp.47-60.

Mombeshora, S. (1990). 'The Salience of Ethnicity in Political Development: The Case of Zimbabwe', *International Sociology*, 5(4), pp. 427-444.

Moorcraft, P. (2012). *Mugabe's War Machine: Saving or Savaging Zimbabwe*. Johannesburg: Jonathan Ball Publishers.

Moore, D. (2018). 'A very Zimbabwean coup: November 13-24, 2017', *Transformation: Critical Perspectives on Southern Africa*, 97(1), pp. 1-29.

Moore, L. (2009). '(Re)covering the Past, Remembering Trauma: The Politics of Commemoration at Sites of Atrocity.' *Journal of Public and International Affairs*, 20, pp. 47-64.

Moser, C.O.N. and F.C. Clark (eds) (2001). *Victims, Perpetrators or Actors: Gender, Armed Conflict and Political Violence*. London: Zed Books.

Moyo, G. (2014). 'Understanding the Executive-Military Relations in Zimbabwe,' *Journal of African Union Studies*, 3(2/3), pp. 69-86.

Moyo, T., F. Sibanda and M. Mazuru (2013). 'Angles of Telling and Angles of Reality: Representations of the Gukurahundi Period in Selected Zimbabwean Fiction in Shona, Ndebele, and English', *Matatu*, 41(1), pp. 35-50.

Mpofu, M. and C. Moyo (2017). 'Theatre as alternative media in Zimbabwe: Selected case studies from Matabeleland', *Journal of African Media Studies*, 9(3), pp.507-520.

Mpofu, S. (2015). 'When the Subaltern Speaks: Citizen Journalism and Genocide 'Victims" Voices Online', *African Journalism Studies*, 36(4), pp. 82-101.

────── (2019). 'Art as Journalism in Zimbabwe: The case of Owen Maseko's banned Zimbabwean genocide exhibition', *Journalism Studies*, 20(1), pp. 60-78.

Mpofu, W.J. (2021). 'Gukurahundi in Zimbabwe: An Epistemicide and Genocide', *Journal of Literary Studies*, 37(2), pp. 40-55.

Mugari, I. (2020). 'The dark side of social media in Zimbabwe: Unpacking the legal framework conundrum', *Cogent Social Sciences*, 6(1), pp. 1-15.

Mukonori, F. SJ (2017). *A Memoir: Man in the Middle*. Harare: House of Books.

Mungoshi, C. (1983). *Kunyarara Hakusi Kutaura?* Harare: Zimbabwe Publishing House.

Murambadoro, R. (2015). '"We cannot reconcile until the past has been acknowledged": Perspectives on Gukurahundi from Matabeleland, Zimbabwe', *African Journal on Conflict Resolution*, 15(1), pp. 33-57.

Musiyiwa, M. (2008). 'The mobilization of popular music in the promotion of national unity in Zimbabwe', *Muziki*, 5(1), pp. 11-29.

Muwati, I., G. Mheta and Z. Gambahaya (2010). 'Contesting "patriotic history": Zimbabwe's liberation war history and the democratization agenda', *South African Journal of African Languages*, 30(2), pp.170-179.

Muzondidya, J. (2009). 'From Buoyancy to Crisis, 1980-1997', in B. Raftopoulos and A. Mlambo (eds), *Becoming Zimbabwe: A History from the Pre-Colonial Period to 2008*. Harare: Weaver Press.

Myers, D.G., S.B. Wojcicki and B.S. Aardema (1977). 'Attitude comparison: Is there ever a bandwagon effect?', *Journal of Applied Social Psychology*, 7(4), pp. 341-347.

National Language Policy Advisory Panel (NLPAP) (1998). *Report on the Formulation of a National Language Policy*. Unpublished.

National Transitional Justice Working Group (NTJWG). (2021). 'Statement in Response to Commissioner Obert Gutu's Utterances about Gukurahundi'. Harare: NTJWG.

Ncube, B.J. (2017). 'Diasporic Online Radio and the Mediation of Zimbabwean Conflict/Crisis', in O. Ogunyemi (ed.), *Media, Diaspora and Conflict*. Cham, Switzerland: Palgrave Macmillan.

Ncube, G. (2018). 'Of dirt, disinfection and purgation: Discursive construction of state violence in selected contemporary Zimbabwean literature', *Tydskrif vir Letterkunde*, 55(1), pp. 41-53.

────── (2022). 'Gukurahundi Revisited in the "Second Republic"', in O. Nyambi, T. Mangena and G. Ncube (eds), *Cultures of Change in Contemporary Zimbabwe: Socio-Political Transition from Mugabe to Mnangagwa*. London: Routledge.

────── and G. Siziba (2017a). 'Compelled to Perform in the "Oppressor's" language? Ndebele Performing Artists and Zimbabwe's Shona-centric *Habitus*', *Journal of Southern African Studies*, 43(4), pp. 825-836.

────── (2017b). '(Re)membering the Nation's "Forgotten" Past: Portrayals of *Gukurahundi* in Zimbabwean Literature', *The Journal of Commonwealth Literature*, 52(2), pp. 231-247.

Ndawana, E. (2020). 'The military and democratisation in post-Mugabe Zimbabwe', *South African Journal of International Affairs*, 27(2), pp. 193-217.

Ndhlovu, F. (2006). 'Gramsci, Doke and the Marginalisation of the Ndebele Language in Zimbabwe', *Journal of Multilingual and Multicultural Development*, 27(4), pp. 305-318.

────── (2008a). 'The Conundrums of Language Policy and Politics in South Africa and Zimbabwe', *Australian Journal of Linguistics*, 28(1), pp. 59-80.

────── (2008b). 'The Politics of Language and Nationality in Zimbabwe: Nation Building or Empire Building?', *South African Journal of African Languages*, 28(1), pp. 1-10.

────── (2009). *The Politics of Language and Nation Building in Zimbabwe*. Bern: Peter Lang.

Ndlovu, I. and B. Dube (2013). 'Response to Maurice T. Vambe's "Zimbabwe genocide: voices and perceptions from ordinary people in Matabeleland and the Midlands provinces, 30 years on"', *African Identities*, 11(4), pp.353-366.

Ndlovu, M. (2017). 'Facing history in the aftermath of Gukurahundi atrocities: New media, memory and the discourses on forgiveness on selected Zimbabwean news websites', *Peace and Conflict Studies*, 24(2), pp. 1-20.

―――― (2018). 'Gukurahundi, New Media and the "Discourses of Silence": The Reproduction of the Hegemonic Narratives of the Matabeleland Post-Colonial Violence on Selected Zimbabwean News Websites', *African Identities*, 16(3), pp. 275-289.

―――― (2018a). 'Speaking for the dead: testimonies, witnesses and the representations of Gukurahundi atrocities in new media', *Journal of African Cultural Studies*, 30(3), pp. 293-306.

―――― and LA.. Tshuma (2021). 'Bleeding from one generation to the next: The media and the constructions of Gukurahundi postmemories by university students in Zimbabwe', *African Studies*, 80(3-4), pp. 376-396.

Ndlovu, N. (2019). 'The Gukurahundi "genocide": Memory and justice in independent Zimbabwe'. Faculty of Humanities, UCT Department of Historical Studies.

Ndlovu, T.M. (2001) *Ukuhluzwa Kwamanoveli EsiNdebele Aka1956 Kusiyafika ku1971*. Harare: University of Zimbabwe Publications.

Ndlovu-Gatsheni, S. (2003). 'The Post-Colonial State and Civil-Military Relations in Matabeleland: Regional Perceptions', in G. Cawthra and R. Williams (eds), *Ourselves to Know: Civil-Military Relations and Defence Transformation in Southern Africa*. Pretoria: Institute of Security Studies.

―――― (2006). 'Nationalist-Military Alliance and the Fate of Democracy in Zimbabwe,' *African Journal of Conflict Resolution*, 6(1), pp. 49-80.

―――― (2008). 'Nation Building in Zimbabwe and the Challenges of Ndebele Particularism', *African Journal on Conflict Resolution*, 8(3), pp. 27-56.

―――― (2011). 'The changing politics of Matabeleland since 1980'. Solidarity Peace Trust.

―――― (2012a). 'The death of the Subject with a capital 'S' and the perils of belonging: a study of the construction of ethnocracy in Zimbabwe', *Critical Arts*, 26(4), pp. 525-546.

―――― (2012b). 'Rethinking 'Chimurenga' and 'Gukurahundi' in Zimbabwe: A Critique of Partisan National History', *African Studies Review*, 55(3), pp. 1-26.

Nettelfield, L.J. (2006). 'Courting Democracy in Bosnia and Herzegovina: The Hague Tribunal's Impact in a Postwar State'. PhD thesis, Columbia University.

Ng, L.C., N. Ahishakiye, D.E. Miller and B.E. Meyerowitz (2015). 'Narrative characteristics of genocide testimonies predict posttraumatic stress disorder symptoms years later', *Psychol Trauma*, 7(3), pp. 303-311.

Ngara, E.A. (1982.) *Bilingualism, Language Contact, and Language Planning: Proposals for*

Language Use and Language Teaching in Zimbabwe. Gwelo: Mambo Press.

Ngwenya, D. (2018). *Healing the Wounds of Gukurahundi in Zimbabwe: A Participatory Action Research Project*. Cham, Switzerland: Springer.

Nhengu, D. and S. Murairwa (2020). 'The Efficacy of Governments of National Unity in Zimbabwe and Lesotho', *Conflict Trends*, (1), pp. 7-15.

Ni Aolain, F. (2013). 'What Does Postconflict Security Mean for Women?', in A.M. Tripp, M.M. Ferree and C. Ewig (eds), *Gender, Violence, and Human Security: Critical Feminist Perspectives*. New York: New York University Press.

Niezen, R. (2018). 'Speaking for the dead: The memorial politics of genocide in Namibia and Germany', *International Journal of Heritage Studies*, 24(5), pp. 547-567.

Nhongo-Simbanegavi, J. (2000). *For better or worse? Women and ZANLA in Zimbabwe's liberation struggle*. Harare: Weaver Press.

Njoroge, F.M. (2016). 'Evolution of Rape as a War Crime and a Crime against Humanity'. SSRN Electronic Journal.

Nkomo, D. and B. Maseko (2017). 'Sixteen Officially Recognised Languages: Milestones and Challenges for Linguistic Democracy in Zimbabwe', in M.K. Ralarala, K. Barris, E. Ivala and S. Siyepu (eds), *African Languages and Language Practice Research in the 21st Century: Interdisciplinary Themes and Perspectives*. Cape Town: CASAS.

Nkomo, J.M. (1984). *The Story of My Life*. London: Methuen.

Nouwen, S.M.H. (2006). 'Hybrid Courts: The Hybrid Category of a New Type of International Crimes Courts', *Utrecht Law Review*, 2, pp. 190-214.

Nowrojee, B. (2012). 'Making the Invisible War Crime Visible: Post-conflict Justice for Sierra Leone's Rape Victims', *Harvard Human Rights Journal*, 18, pp. 85-106.

Nyambi, O. (2014). 'Silenced voices, resuscitated memory, and the problematization of state historiography in Yvonne Vera's novel *The Stone Virgins*', *Sage Open*, 4(2), pp. 21-58.

Nyamfukudza, S. (2005). 'To skin a skunk: Some observations on Zimbabwe's intellectual development', in M. Palmberg and R. Primorac (eds), *Skinning the Skunk: Facing Zimbabwean Futures*. Uppsala: Nordic Africa Institute.

Ohorchak, O. (2011). 'Role of Memory Policy in Constructing National Identity. Case Study: Ukraine'. Master's thesis, University of Göttingen.

Olusoga, D. and C.W. Erichsen (2010). *The Kaiser's Holocaust: Germany's forgotten genocide and the colonial roots of Nazism*. London: Faber and Faber.

Orentlicher, D. (1991). 'Settling Accounts: The Duty to Prosecute Human Rights Violations of a Prior Regime', *Yale Law Journal*, 100(8), pp. 2537-2615.

——— (2008). *Shrinking the Space for Denial: The Impact of the ICTY in Serbia*. New York: Open Society Institute.

Organ for National Peace, Reconciliation, and Integration (ONHRI) (2014). *Strengthening the National Peace and Reconciliation Infrastructure in Zimbabwe: Key Milestones of the ONHRI (2009-2014)*.

Pankhurst, D. (1999). 'Issues of Justice and Reconciliation in Complex Political Emergencies: Conceptualising Reconciliation, Justice and Peace', *Third World Quarterly*, 20(1), pp. 239-256.

Park, J. (2007). 'Sexual Violence as a Weapon of War in International Humanitarian War', *International Public Policy Review*, 3(1), pp. 13-19.

Paulet, V. (2019). 'Universal Jurisdiction Annual Review 2019: Evidentiary challenges in UJ cases'. Paris: International Federation for Human Rights.

Perriello, T. and M. Wierda (2006). *The Special Court for Sierra Leone under scrutiny*. New York: International Center for Transitional Justice.

Phillipson, R. (1992). *Linguistic Imperialism*. Oxford: Oxford University Press.

Phimister, I. (2009). '"Zimbabwe is Mine": Mugabe, Murder, and Matabeleland', *Safundi*, 10(4), pp. 471-478.

―――― (2012). 'Narratives of progress: Zimbabwean historiography and the end of history', *Journal of Contemporary African Studies*, 30(1), pp. 27-34.

Porter, E. (2007). 'Women's Truth Narratives: The Power of Compassionate Listening', *Critical Half: Bi-Annual Journal of Women for Women International*, 5(2), pp. 20-25.

Potts, D. (2006). '"Restoring order"? Operation Murambatsvina and the Urban Crisis in Zimbabwe', *Journal of Southern African Studies*, 32(2), pp. 273-291.

Public Library of Science (PLoS) Medicine Editors. (2009). 'Rape in War is Common, Devastating and Too Often Ignored', *The Public Library of Science Medicine Editors*, 6(1), pp. 1-3.

Radio France Internationale (RFI) (2019). 'Ghosts of Gukurahundi still haunt survivors', 12 March.

Raftopoulos, B. (2019). 'Zimbabwe: Regional Politics and Dynamics', in W.R. Thompson (ed.), *Oxford Research Encyclopedias: Politics*. Oxford: Oxford University Press.

―――― and A. Mlambo (eds) (2009). *Becoming Zimbabwe – A History from the Pre-colonial Period to 2008*. Harare: Weaver Press.

Raisov, B. and A. Simsek (2018). 'The Role of Media in Peaceful Resolution of Civil Wars: The Case of Tajikistan from the Perspective of Peace Communication', *Online Journal of Communication and Media Technologies*, 8(3), pp. 215-236.

Ranger, T.O. (1995). *Are we not also men?: The Samkange Family and African Politics in Zimbabwe, 1920-64*. London: James Currey.

―――― (2004). 'Nationalist Historiography, Patriotic History and the History of the Nation: The Struggle over the past in Zimbabwe', *Journal of Southern African Studies*',

30(2), pp. 215-234.

Reiger, C. and M. Wierda (2006). 'The serious Crimes Process in Timor-Leste: In Retrospect'. International Center for Transitional Justice.

Reyntjens, F. (2004). 'Rwanda, Ten Years On: From Genocide to Dictatorship', *African Affairs*, 103(411), pp. 117-210.

——— (2013). *Political Governance in Post-genocide Rwanda*. Cambridge: Cambridge University Press.

Rigby, A. (2001). *Justice and Reconciliation After the Violence*. London: Lynne Rienner Publications.

Roht-Arriaza, N. (1990). 'State Responsibility to Investigate and Prosecute Grave Human Rights Violations in International Law', *California Law Review*, 78(2), pp. 449-513.

——— (2006). 'The New Landscape of Transitional Justice', in N. Roht-Arriaza and J. Mariezcurrena (eds), *Transitional Justice in the Twenty-First Century: Beyond Truth versus Justice*. Cambridge: Cambridge University Press.

Rose, G. (1997). 'Situating Knowledges: Positionality, Reflexivities and Other Tactics', *Progress in Human Geography*, 21(3), pp. 305-320.

Rose, S. (2015). 'Sexual Violence in Conflict Zones: A History of the Neglected War Crime'. Zürich: European Network for Conflict Studies.

Rubio-Marín, R. and P. de Greiff (2007). 'Women and Reparations', *International Journal of Transitional Justice*, 1(3), pp. 318-337.

Ruhanya, P. and B. Gumbo. (2022). 'The Securocratic State: Conceptualising the Transition Problem in Zimbabwe', *Third World Thematics: A TWQ Journal*.

Rwafa, U. (2012). 'Representations of Matabeleland and Midlands Disturbances through the Documentary Film *Gukurahundi: A Moment of Madness* (2007)', *African Identities*, 10(3), pp. 313-327.

Ryngaert, C. (2008). *Jurisdiction in International Law*. Oxford: Oxford University Press.

Sachikonye, L.M. (2002). 'Whither Zimbabwe? Crisis & Democratisation', *Review of African Political Economy*, 29(91), pp. 13-20.

——— (2011). *When a State turns on its Citizens: 60 Years of Institutionalised Violence and Political Culture*. Harare: Weaver Press.

Saunders, R. (1999). *Dancing out of Tune: A History of the Media in Zimbabwe*. Harare: Edwina Spicer Productions.

Scarnecchia, T. (2011). 'Rationalizing *Gukurahundi*: Cold War and South African Foreign Relations with Zimbabwe, 1981-1983', *Kronos*, 37(1), pp. 87-103.

Schlesinger, P. (1993). 'Wishful Thinking: Cultural Politics, Media, and Collective Identities in Europe', *Journal of Communication*, 43(2), pp. 6-17.

Sibanda, B. (2021). 'The Language of the Gukurahundi Genocide in Zimbabwe: 1980-1987', *Journal of Literary Studies*, 37(2), pp. 129-145.

Sibanda, N. (2020). '"Gukurahundi in Retrospect": Theatre Performance as a Cultural Public Sphere', *Ephemera: Journal of Theatre and Performance Studies*, 3(6), pp. 22-40.

Simic, O. (2018). *Silenced Victims of Wartime Sexual Violence*. New York: Routledge.

Sithole, M. (1985). 'The Salience of Ethnicity in African Politics', *Journal of Asian and African Studies*, 20(3-4), pp. 181-192.

——— (1995). 'Ethnicity and Democratisation in Zimbabwe: From Confrontation to Accommodation', in H. Glickman (ed.), *Ethnic Conflict and Democratization in Africa*. Atlanta: African Studies Association Press.

——— and J. Makumbe (1997). 'Elections in Zimbabwe: The ZANU (PF) Hegemony and its Incipient Decline', *African Journal of Political Science*, 2(1), pp. 122-139.

Siziba, G. (2017). '"Ode to the nameless", Poems by Gugulethu Siziba 1979-2017'. www.gugulethusiziba.org.

——— and G. Ncube (2015). 'Mugabe's fall from grace: satire and fictional narratives as silent forms of resistance in/on Zimbabwe.' *Social Dynamics: A Journal of African Studies*, 41(3), pp. 516-539.

Skutnabb-Kangas, T. and R. Dunbar (2010). *Indigenous Children's Education as Linguistic Genocide and a Crime against Humanity? A Global View*. Guovdageaidnu-Kautokeino, Norway: Galdu-Resource Centre for the Rights of Indigenous Peoples.

Slyomovics, S. (2009). 'Reparations in Morocco: The Symbolic Dirham', in B.R. Johnston and S. Slyomovics (eds), *Waging War, Making Peace: Reparations and Human Rights*. New York: Routledge.

Small, A. (2007). 'The Duty of Memory: A Solidarity of Voices after the Rwandan Genocide', *Paragraph*, 30(1), pp. 85-100.

Smith, A.D. (1991). *National Identity*. London: Penguin Books.

Sriram, C.L. (2007). 'Justice as Peace? Liberal Peacebuilding and Strategies of Transitional Justice', *Global Society*, 21(4), pp. 579-591.

Stahn, C. (2019). *A Critical Introduction to International Criminal Law*. Cambridge: Cambridge University Press.

Stauffer, C.S. (2009). 'Acting out the myths: The power of narrative discourse in shaping the Zimbabwe conflict of Matabeleland, 1980-1987'. PhD thesis, University of KwaZulu Natal.

Steininger, S. (2018). 'The Kosovo Specialist Chambers – A New Chapter for International Criminal Justice in the Balkans', *Völkerrechtsblog*.

Steinmetz, G. and J. Hell (2006). 'The Visual Archive of Colonialism: Germany and Namibia', *Public Culture*, 18(1), pp. 147-184.

Stone, B., A. Colman, A.D. Brown, J. Koppel and W. Hirst (2012). 'Towards a Science of Silence: The Consequences of Leaving a Memory Unsaid', *Perspectives on Psychological Science*, 7(1), pp. 39-53

Tannenbaum, M. (2012). 'Family Language Policy as a Form of Coping or Defence Mechanism', *Journal of Multilingual and Multicultural Development*, 33(1), pp. 57-66.

Taussig, M. (1999). *Defacement: Public Secrecy and the Labor of the Negative*. Redwood City, CA: Stanford University Press.

Tendi, B.M. (2013). 'Ideology, Civilian Authority and the Zimbabwean Military', *Journal of Southern African Studies*, 39(4), pp. 829-843.

―――― (2020). *The Army and Politics in Zimbabwe: Mujuru, the Liberation Fighter and Kingmaker*. Cambridge: Cambridge University Press.

Todd, J. (2007). *Through the Darkness: A Life in Zimbabwe*. Cape Town: Zebra Press.

Toivanen, R. (2007). 'Linguistic Diversity and the Paradox of Rights Discourse', in D. Castiglione and C. Longman (eds), *The Language Question in Europe and Diverse Societies: Political, Legal and Social Perspectives*. Oxford: Hart Publishing.

Tombs, D. (2014). 'Silent No More: Sexual Violence in Conflict as a Challenge to the Worldwide Church', *Acta Theologica*, 34(2), pp. 147-165.

Tompkins, T.L. (1995). 'Prosecuting Rape as a War Crime: Speaking the Unspeakable', *Notre Dame Law Review*, 70, pp. 845-890.

Truth and Reconciliation Commission (TRC) (1998). *Truth and Reconciliation Commission of South Africa Report*. Cape Town: Juta.

Tshuma, L.A. and M. Ndlovu (2020). 'Immortalizing "Buried Memories": Photographs of the Gukurahundi Online', *Journal of Genocide Research*, 24(3), pp. 380-401.

Tshuma, N.R. (2018a). 'Old faces, new masks: Zimbabwe one year after the "coup"', *The Elephant*.

―――― (2018b). *House of Stone*. London: Atlantic Books.

Tuchman, G. (1978). *Making News: A Study in the Construction of Reality*. New York: The Free Press.

Tutu, D. (1998). 'Without Forgiveness, There Is No Future', *Exploring Forgiveness*, (1), pp. 351-375.

United Nations (2021). 'Conflict Related Sexual Violence: Report of the United Nations Secretary-General'. New York: United Nations.

United Nations Development Programme (UNDP) (2014). 'Support to Peace Building and Increased Access to Sustainable Livelihoods: Midterm Evaluation of the UNDP Zimbabwe Integrated Peace Building Programme'. Harare: UNDP.

United Nations Peacekeeping (n.d.). 'Conflict-Related Sexual Violence'. New York:

United Nations.

United States Institute of Peace (USIP) (2008). *Transitional Justice: Information Handbook*. Washington, DC: USIP.

Uvin, P. (2002). 'The Development/Peacebuilding Nexus: a Typology and History of Changing Paradigms', *Journal of Peacebuilding & Development*, 1(1), pp. 5-24.

Van Schaack, B. (2008). 'Crimen Sine Lege: Judicial Law making at the Intersection of Law and Morals', Georgetown Law Journal, 97.

Vera, Y. (2002). *The Stone Virgins*. Harare: Weaver Press.

Waldahl, R. (2004). *Politics and Persuasion: Media Coverage of Zimbabwe's 2000 Election*. Harare: Weaver Press.

Waldorf, L. (2009) 'Revisiting Hotel Rwanda: Genocide Ideology, Reconciliation, and Rescuers', *Journal of Genocide Research*, 11(1), pp. 101-125.

Werbner, R. (1991). *Tears of the Dead: The Social Biography of an African Family*. Harare, Baobab Books.

———(1995). 'In Memory: A Heritage of War in Southwestern Zimbabwe', in N. Bhebhe and T. Ranger (eds), *Society in Zimbabwe's Liberation War, Vol. Two*, Harare: University of Zimbabwe Publications..

——— (1998). 'Beyond Oblivion: Confronting Memory Crisis', in *Memory and the Postcolony: African Anthropology and the Critique of Power*. London: Bloomsbury.

Vambe, M.T. (2012). 'Zimbabwe Genocide: Voices and Perceptions from Ordinary People in Matabeleland and the Midlands Provinces, 30 Years On', *African Identities*, 10(3), pp. 281-300.

van Dijk, T.A. (1988). *News Analysis. Case Studies of International and National News in the Press*. New York: Routledge.

——— (1993). 'Principles of Critical Discourse Analysis', *Discourse & Society*, 4(2), pp. 249-283.

Verheul, S. (2017). '"Government is a Legal Fiction": Performing Political Power in Zimbabwe's Magistrates' Courts after 2000'. DPhil thesis, University of Oxford.

Wetherell, I. (1997). 'The Matabeleland report: A lot to hide.' *Southern African Report*, 12(3), pp. 21-30.

World Health Organization (WHO) (2012). 'Understanding and Addressing Violence against Women: Sexual Violence'. Information note. Geneva: WHO.

Yap, K. (2001). 'Uprooting the weeds: Power, ethnicity and violence in the Matabeleland conflict'. PhD thesis, University of Amsterdam.

Zappalà, S. (2001). 'Do Heads of State in Office Enjoy Immunity from Juridiction for International Crimes? The *Ghaddafi* Case Before the French *Cour de Cassation*',

European Journal of International Law, 12(3), pp. 595-612.

Zerubavel, E. (2006). *The Elephant in the Room: Silence and Denial in Everyday Life*. Oxford: Oxford University Press.

Zimbabwe Democracy Institute (ZDI) (2017). 'Zimbabwe transition in a muddy terrain: Political economy under military capture'. Harare: ZDI.

Zimbabwe Women Writers. (ZWW) (2000). *Women of resilience: The voices of women ex-combatants*. Harare: Zimbabwe Women Writers.

Zondo, J. (2018). 'We Bhalagwe'. Poem performed at Ibhetshu likazulu commemoration of Ndebele genocide, Bhalagwe, Matobo District, 21 February.